D1450480

reTURN on imagination

Realizing the Power of Ideas

Tom Wujec | Sandra Muscat

FINANCIAL TIMES
Prentice Hall

A Pearson Company

London • New York • San Francisco • Toronto • Sydney • Tokyo • Singapore
Hong Kong • Cape Town • Madrid • Paris • Milan • Munich • Amsterdam

Canadian Cataloguing in Publication Data

Wujec, Tom
    Return on imagination : realizing the power of ideas

Second syllable of the word, return, in the title, printed upside down.

ISBN 0-13-062285-0

1. Creative ability in business. I. Muscat, Sandra II. Title.

HD35.W84 2001   650.1   C2001-901234-9

ISBN 0-13-062285-0

Art Direction: Mary Opper
Cover Concept: Sputnik Art and Design
Interior Design: David Cheung Design Inc.
Page Layout: David Cheung Design Inc.

1 2 3 4 5 FR   06 05 04 03 02

Printed and bound in Canada.

ATTENTION: CORPORATIONS
Books are available at quantity discounts with bulk purchase for educational, business, or sales promotional use. For information, please email or write to: Pearson PTR Canada, Special Sales, PTR Division, 26 Prince Andrew Place, Don Mills, Ontario, M3C 2T8. Email ss.corp@pearsoned.com. Please supply: title of book, ISBN, quantity, how the book will be used, date needed.

Visit the Prentice Hall Canada Web site! Send us your comments, browse our catalogues, and more. **www.pearsonptr.ca**

A Pearson Company

To **Elliott** and **Mikayla**
for their permission
and ability to see the potential

Contents

Acknowledgments

Without the vision, support, and openness of others, this work could not have been possible. Thanks are due to the editorial and design staff at Viking Canada for sharing the vision, and to Westwood Creative Artists for making the connection. To John Sweet for doing so much in such a small amount of time when the rest of the world was making merry. To the support and participation of numerous colleagues and friends (and their 42 cents worth), including Beatrice Lamontagne, David Weinstein, Jean Marie Bowcott, Roger Morier, Mark Carter, Bill Buxton, Erina Kelly, Kevin Tate, and Severin Wille. And a special thanks goes to the participants who invested their time in the Imagination Survey.

We owe a debt of gratitude to all those as far back as Aristotle who have done so much thinking, writing and talking about this subject before us; as well as to those in the marketplace courageously creating imaginative businesses and living imaginatively rich lives. Their work and ideas have been invaluable resources and wells of inspiration.

There were numerous brave souls willing to share their thoughts and experiences about imagination so openly with us. The heart and spirit of their ideas helped form the heart of this work. They are (in alphabetical order):

Claude Bernier	Beverly Malcolm
Rick Blickstead	Dave Martin
Tom Campbell	Kristi McKinnon
Piero Carceranno	Charlie Menendez
Marg Clarkson	Ray Niley
Bill Dresselhaus	Bruce Nussbaum
Scott Ellison	Maureen O'Donnell
Luigi Ferrara	Frank Pearson
Bran Ferren	Warren Pratt
Margot Franssen	Sabaa Quao
Carolyn Gallagher	Jim Rait
Peter Goldie	Robert Ramsey
Gary Hawton	Daniel Richard
R.J. Hickson	Tom Razmilovic
Doug Hector	Bill Shaw
Danny Hillis	Norm Simon
Gray Holland	Bob Steinburgler
Bruce Jenson	Kerry Stirton
Mark Johnson	Mark Sylvester
Seth Weaver Kahan	William Thorsell
Steve Kaneko	Laurens van den Acker
Alan Kay	Doug Walker
Doug Keeley	David Wexler
Tom Kelley	Ted Woerner
John Kennedy	Richard Saul Wurman
Jaron Lanier	Joyce Wycoff
Al Lopez	Moses Znaimer

Preface

Take a look at the last two decades. We've done it all. We inverted organizational pyramids, flattened our management structures, downsized our workforce, re-engineered our systems, brainstormed, consulted, and focus-grouped ourselves into a spin. We created micro-niches and boutiques, mass market designer goods, and customized product lines. We've branded and re-branded our organizations and ourselves so that even individuals have their own unique selling proposition. We identified our core competencies. The lightning-flash success of the dot-coms has come and gone.

Now we are buying, selling, and trading anything we can think of—literally. Innovative thinkers are calculating the financial worth of their company's ability to generate ideas, so they can prove that their greatest assets include the collective brainpower of the individuals who power the machine. And in the process they are increasing their asset value on paper by millions.

Imagination is the workshop of your mind, capable of turning mind energy into accomplishment and wealth.

Napoleon Hill

For more than twenty years we've had the opportunity to work with an incredible range of people from all walks of business and creative life. Our experience spans numerous disciplines and segments, including sales, marketing, product development, design, training, publishing, technology, 3-D computer animation, interactive multimedia, information visualization systems, retail, manufacturing, and distribution. In other words, the view has been very broad.

Our personal interests and desire for richer lives have continually driven us to seek imaginative and alternative approaches. Over the years the frustration people feel in their work has been a constant theme—frustration arising from limitations, restrictions, stress, and boredom. This has been expressed to us by people at all levels of the organizational pyramid, from entrepreneurs in dot-com start-ups to CEOs in enormous, globally focused organizations. We have also experienced these frustrations ourselves, first-hand. The world of commercial head-butting spares no one.

Our fast-paced, economically driven culture, particularly during times of slowdown and pressure, has come to ignore and undervalue the role of imagination, treating it as marginal or recreational. As a result, the potential growth of business is limited. Business often views imagination as a resource or a problem-solving tool. Imagination is reserved exclusively for certain parts of the product development process or marketing cycle. It is a mode that some people tap into temporarily to provide themselves with a competitive edge. More often than not, business offers lip service to imagination, entertaining it but giving it less credence when the time for decision making is at hand.

The idea for *Return on Imagination* was born of our belief that a different path, a more positive experience, is possible. Our argument is simple: business and imagination are equally important, and it is time to intertwine them in a more significant way than ever before.

Businesses drive economies and generate markets, giving us the currency and opportunities to bring certain dreams into reality. They provide employment and necessary products and services to help sustain our worlds. And they also afford us a forum to be productive, make a contribution, express ourselves, and be of service to our communities.

Imagination is the unseen world, which speaks in poetry and metaphor. It is the source river of our inner worlds where we experience the meaning in our lives. Imagination gives us a core sense of ourselves. And since all things begin with a thought, and all of us are capable of imaginative thought, it is a great equalizer in the realm of possibility. Imagination is the place of genesis.

Take only
your imagination seriously.

Leigh Hunt

Businesses that fail to embrace the richness and possibilities that imagination holds limit their scope and potential, their people, their customers' experience, and their markets. What would computing be like today if Andy Grove, Steve Jobs, Bill Gates, and countless others didn't act on their sense of possibility? Imagination without purpose, structure, or application is essentially invisible. What purpose would Jeff Bezos' thought to create an on-line bookstore named after the world's largest river have served had it remained only in his head? We extract the best from imagination and business when they are interconnected. The benefits of doing so have a profound momentum that sweeps beyond the conventional world, coming back with broader scope, ever expanding the world of possibility.

The development of *Return on Imagination* included interviewing dozens of business leaders, professionals, and artists, from independent, self-employed micro-business owners to senior-level corporate executives in Canada, the United States, Europe, and Asia. Though their opinions were diverse, strong trends clearly emerged from our discussions with them. We also conducted the Imagination Survey via the Net, posted at **www.ideakit.com**. We received ideas and input from people in all industries and from many backgrounds, living in North America, South America, Europe, Asia, and Australia. Our intent was not to produce a formal survey but to gather ideas from as many different points of view as we could reach. We put out the idea and, true to the power of the Web, the idea propagated around the planet. You will be able to access more updates, information, and resources at the **ideakit.com** site.

In addition to conversations too numerous to tally, we sourced information from newspapers, news broadcasts, countless books, periodicals, and magazines, videos, and of course the World Wide Web. Our sources are indexed at the back of the book.

The first two chapters of *Return on Imagination* explore the role of imagination in business, the effect of escalating market pressures and relentless change, and the opportunities these present. In chapter 3 we look closely at the four elements of imagination and how each applies to business. Chapter 4 explores the value of ideas and metrics for the Imagination Economy. Chapter 5 focuses on how to foster personal imagination. Encouraging team imagination is discussed in chapter 6, and chapter 7 explains how to link the world of the imagination with the tangible world of reality through the creative prototyping process. Chapter 8 is filled with case studies of imaginatively run businesses, and the final chapter invites you to look at the deeper role of imagination and business in light of aspiration.

Following chapters 3 through 7 are mental play breaks, which are designed to give your rational mind a break and let your imagination soar.

The experience of creating this work has been incredibly expanding. We feel sincerely privileged to have shared the truly rousing and imaginative thoughts of others and to have observed a great number of inspired businesses. Although there is abundant cynicism out there, as we face some tremendous challenges in our markets and overwhelmingly complex problems in our world, there are many stories that testify to the genius of the human imagination. We found a great and growing desire in most people to apply the power of imagination to make our lives, experiences, and world more fulfilling and inspiring.

We hope you find *Return on Imagination* rich and full, that it sparks and inspires your imagination, and that it contributes positively to your personal and professional worlds.

The Big Idea

We live in a time of exponential growth. Everything about our world is changing faster than ever and in every conceivable direction. We are connected to every corner of the world. Competition is intense. We have real individual power. We have more freedom than ever before. More people have more freedom than ever before. There's more of it, it's different from what it used to be, and it's fierce. We are flooded by data all the time, everywhere, and it's growing. Our lives are lived on the exponential growth curves of change.

The human brain
has not evolved significantly
in the past 20,000 years.
The cerebral cortex still has
about 9 billion neurons.

Our capacity to learn
hasn't really changed much.
Our ability to process information
is about the same.
The conscious human mind holds
about seven things at once.

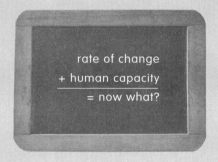

rate of change
+ human capacity
—————————
= now what?

The Options:
Keep innovating the way we always have. Just try harder.
Make it "new and improved."
Make it a different color. Make it cheaper.
Make it faster.
Knock off the other guys.
Try something completely different.

Not Different, but **Different**

Tap into another world.

A world that's deeper, more profound.

A world that has alternative ways of measuring success.

A world that inspires, informs, and clarifies.

A world that simplifies and flows.

A world of breakthroughs.

We could bring a lot more to the table than just incremental change.

Like **what?**
We could invest in the power of ideas.
Not just better, faster, cheaper ideas, but ideas that make a real difference.
Ideas are the new currency.
They entertain and engage.
They circulate and dissolve barriers.
They inspire us to fulfill our higher potential.
They unleash astonishing amounts of energy.
They enrich lives.
Our future depends on the possibilities we define,
the decisions we make,
and the ways we bring our vision into reality.
Real power is the capacity to originate and
implement the ideas that create lasting and positive change.
We could trust in the power of imagination to
discover and invent something new.

But how?

?

?

?

?

?

?

?

Just imagine ...
Turn on your entire brain.
Be your whole self.
All of it. Every last little bit.
Let go of the world's relentless rush to formulate,
solve, and implement.
Stay loose and let little ideas evolve into good ones.
Nurture the ideas that are important.
Give them time.

Give them s p a c e .

Let them breathe.

Play with them like Lego pieces.
Not everything of value comes from logic and rational explanation.
Create environments where ideas flow freely.
Build skills for bringing inspiration to reality.
Use tools to stimulate imagination.
Design so the spirit of inspiration
continues to circulate.
Believe in beauty.
Seek truth.

Dream .

Think about your place in the world.

Welcome
to the world
of possibility.

Imagination is what makes all things possible.

Enter the
Imagination
Economy

1

We live in a time
where creativity,
innovation, and
imagination
drive the world.

As big ideas go, this notion doesn't seem particularly new or revolutionary. In fact this story has been retold so many times that it has become something of a cliché: the new rules of the game require speed, flexibility, and radical innovation. Germinal companies are selling to global markets almost from their incorporation. Established firms must reinvent their operations—even their business models—to stay competitive in the new landscape. They are trying to lead their own revolutions by creatively destroying old hierarchical organizations to encourage new, more responsive, and stronger structures to emerge.

What is new is that the appetite for ideas has reached a tipping point. Success, in our sharply competitive and chaotic world of rapid change and endless choice, depends more than ever on the flow of imaginative ideas—ideas that stimulate and expand the interconnections between individuals and business.

This is more than cliché. Companies as diverse as Unilever and Nike, ItalDesign and The Body Shop, and a growing legion of others, are putting imagination at the center of their business. Koziol, a German-based global brand of home and office products, takes mundane objects—vegetable scrubbers, umbrellas, and toothbrushes—and transforms them into cute, colorful, and functional critters. Their motto: *Ideas for friends*. Their idea: to produce fun, useful products. Their trend: setting the trend. Their vision: bringing a smile to everyday routines. Working within these simple parameters they have created a thriving business and a community of hundreds of designers.

Jones Soda is a Seattle premium soda manufacturer that produces dozens of fun-flavored drinks—WhoopAss, BadaBing, and D'Peach Mode, to name a few. Part of its international success stems from an innovative labeling strategy that incorporates ever-changing photos, many of which are submitted by its consumers through the Jones Soda Web site. Everything from frogs to families, pets to sporting events and sunsets—in fact, anything that's fit to print—appears on the bottles, fostering a strong customer following and an inspired brand character. This has also led to fourteen consecutive quarters of growth.

Marionnaud, a perfume store on the north side of the Champs-Élysées, offers an extraordinary retail experience. Though it sells products that can be found in most other department stores, translucent Plexiglas walls that reach from floor to ceiling and glow with slowly changing and vividly iridescent colors accompanied by an ethereal soundscape distinguish Marionnaud. Within moments the environment whisks walk-in customers from the rushed and bustling street to a relaxed and flowing state of mind, one conducive to appreciating the world of fragrance and beauty.

Philips Design produces a remarkable collection of innovative products. Everything that Philips' five hundred designers produce—kettles, video projectors, sophisticated medical devices—is driven by a splendid vision: to create harmonious relationships between people, objects, and the environment, both natural and man-made. Their results are impressive. Philips regularly wins international design awards, their business continues to grow, and all the while they maintain a balance between humanity and commerce, using design to promote personal growth, for consumers and partners as well as employees. Philips walks the talk. What sets them apart from the rest is that they make much of their R & D efforts public. Their on-line galleries are designed as "simulations of people's imaginations in the form of objects, images, environments and sounds, [to help] them to imagine new lifestyles, enhanced by the intelligent combination of design and technology."[1] The feedback from their visualizations goes into the development of next-gen products.

Ideas are the factors that lift civilization. They create revolutions. There is more dynamite in an idea than in many bombs.

John H. Vincent

Putting imagination at the center of business can lead to remarkable transformations. It has enabled the World Bank to achieve the unthinkable, advancing technology that could bring clean drinking water to the 600 million people in the world who live without it, by converting discarded plastic pop bottles into solar-powered water purifiers. Imagination led The Body Shop to create a business model that encourages fair trade and genuine self-esteem while actively leading in the care of our planet, its people, and its long-term health. Imagination enabled the city of Bilbao, Spain, with a depressed economy and no art collection to speak of, to build an outrageous art gallery with no straight walls that has turned the entire region into a cultural hub. Imagination gave a young Canadian entrepreneur the courage to create Phattycakes, a hip line of full-size clothing for teenagers in a world that tries to hide anything that's not skinny. It provided Patagonia with the vision to set as its priority the building of a very long-term, sustainable business, where quarterly profit is not the final metric. And imagination furnished AIDS on-line and Cancer on-line with much-needed computer processing time for the development of cancer and AIDS drugs by accessing idle computer cycles from hundreds of thousands of volunteer computers through peer-to-peer networking.

Businesses that have invested in imagination have seen the power of ideas to create opportunities and solve problems. Imaginative ideas dissolve barriers and enhance lives. They engage and entertain. They open in us a sense of the possible. Imagination connects us through shared ideas, values, and priorities. We know intuitively that our future—personal, corporate, and social—ultimately depends on the ideas we envision, the possibilities we define, the decisions we make, and the ways we bring our vision into reality. Power resides in the capacity to originate and implement ideas that create lasting and positive change. Ideas are the currency of the future.

Knowing this, it's perplexing just how little time and how few resources most businesses invest in fostering the collective imagination of their workforce. There's no question that most businesses understand the urgent need to generate new product ideas, develop better processes, and invent faster and cheaper ways to get to market. *Better*, *faster*, *cheaper*, and *more profitable* will always be driving concepts in the world of commerce. But few businesses implement strategies to sustain innovation, and fewer still realize the potential of investing in the full richness of imagination.

Focusing on quarterly results and yielding to urgency keeps them caught in an endless loop of delaying what they intuitively know to be important. As Arie de Geus, economic visionary and former head of corporate planning at Royal Dutch/Shell, states, "A company's success no longer primarily depends on its ability to raise investment capital, but on the ability of its people to learn together and to produce new ideas."[2]

Imagination + Business = Magic

The goal of investing in imagination is to create a flow of new ideas. "Innovation has moved from a good idea to an imperative," affirms Paul Saffo, director of the Institute for the Future think-tank in Menlo Park, California.[3] But there are different depths to imagination and innovation.

True innovation is driven by a profound imagination. It incorporates a different way of thinking, a sea change in business processes, even a shift in structure. Innovation is not only about designing new products; it's about creating or delivering things to customers they may not ever have thought of, that would improve or enhance their lives.

Major innovations that cause fundamental change bear the hallmark of being true and simple. Duke Energy Corporation not only sells oil but, through mining its databases, also sells ways for its customers to reduce energy costs. The Big Idea is one that connects easily with the essential by cutting through complex and unnecessary details and detours. Consider the Razor scooter. This little contraption is really just a skateboard with a stick. It seems so obvious, so simple—so brilliant.

On the grandest scale, imagination has the very real potential to change the world. However, this can happen only in a culture that is open to the possibilities of the imagination. "An individual innovation has value, but it doesn't make or break the company any more," says Tom Kelley, general manager of IDEO Product Development, the design consultancy that helped create such breakthrough products as the Palm Pilot. "That's why you need the culture of innovation."[4]

Tim Brown, CEO of IDEO, supports the principle that recurring flows of ideas sustain continuous innovation: "Innovation is our lifeblood. Without it, we wouldn't exist. For us, innovation is as fundamental as, say, accounting. We need to know how much money we've made; we also need new ideas. More important, we have to be able to implement those new ideas elegantly and beautifully."[5]

Imagination operates at different levels, just as the force of gravity can cause waterfalls to flow as well as galaxies to organize themselves into spirals. At a personal level, imagination is the intimate conversation one has with ideas. At a group level, imagination operates through the sharing of ideas and the creation of a common vision and understanding. And at a market level, imagination flows by a number of means, from word of mouth and the Web to the actual experience of using a product or service.

Though the personal, group, and market layers of imagination operate in different domains, they are connected. Many factors that stimulate personal imagination—permission, playfulness, and openness, to name a few—are equally effective in helping ideas to percolate through groups of people. The representation of an idea, through its context and mode of expression, determines how people hold it in their imagination and what they do with it. Imagination has the power to redefine business and our role in it.

What Is Imagination Anyway?

Despite the word's familiarity, the true meaning of *imagination* is nebulous, relating to concepts as diverse as fantasy, illusion, innovation, and artistic achievement. Defining *imagination* precisely is about as easy as catching a wisp of smoke with your fingers.

We know that imagination is a quality of mind and spirit that is alive and vibrant. We associate imagination with a powerful inner spark, with verve and passion, and we recognize it in all kinds of different things, from our children's finger paintings to a Kandinsky, from a BMW concept car to a Bang & Olufsen stereo system, from a new way to package vegetables to the experience of looking up at clouds and seeing eggplants and countries on a map.

It's tough to define *imagination* because "it" is not a single thing, an entity in the brain that we can point to and say, "There it is." Imagination is an emergent **property** of consciousness, the result of a rich orchestration of different mental activities, blending memory, reasoning, anticipation, questioning, comparison, analysis, and other forms of thought into a unified internal experience.

The Imagination Survey

I think imagination is pretty much the center of existence. *Imagination is seeing with the mind.* **The ability to conceive things that haven't been seen yet.** *That which gives us art, enjoyment, delight.* **It fires the development of things ... but more importantly, of emotions and ideas and whole philosophies/approaches to life and living.** The chance to expand your horizons—without necessarily having to pay for it. A great gift that goes to the very definition of my character and self-image. Using it enables me to excel, and to differentiate myself from the pack. **Imagination is the ability to dream, create, and take yourself to another dimension within yourself.** *To be able to see or imagine things that are or are not a reflection of reality but that we can see with our inner mind.* Imagination is childlike wonder. *The ability to develop an idea or concept, either by hand or thought.* **To imagine is to dream. It is the vivid colors in your thought that transport you from the present—a sometimes monotonous struggle of life into a realm created by you and for you.** *It is the freedom to just be!* **What gives color to a black and white world.** *A creative force that makes the impossible possible.* **Believe that your mind, body, and soul can lead a whisper of an idea to a prize forever in the life of all who understand.** *Everything you think.* **Endless as a child, limited as an adult.** *The thoughts, the ideas, the dreams, and the hopes of a creative process that is individualistic with no bounds or rules of constraint.* **Envisioning what isn't yet, but what you'd like to be.** The ability to challenge myself to question everything, and creatively develop new solutions. **Imagination is simply the power to conceive of something, anything—a product, a process, a poem, a unifying principle—that isn't immediately in front of you.** *Imagination is my mental resourcefulness.*

I support Shelley's view that poets are the "unacknowledged legislators of the world"—Imagination rules! In his massive autobiographical poem, "The Prelude," Wordsworth recounts vivid meditative moments. These, "recollected in tranquility," become what Wordsworth calls "Spots of time," full of "the spontaneous overflow of powerful emotions," in which he learns something of moral value and his agitated spirit is soothed. My own experience confirms that the ignited imagination soothes the agitated spirit. And then there's Sylvia Plath's view—10% inspiration and 90% perspiration ... **The ability to escape from reality with no negative repercussions on your present life situation.**

A creative force that makes the impossible possible. Seeing past established process to potential. Imagination comes from the soul. **Imagination is what adds an infinite amount of colors between black and white.** *One's interpretation of reality and possibility both require imagination. The totality of thought, whimsy, feeling, all the electrical impulses in the brain.* **The ability to create new ideas from old data or information.** *A capacity to mix and match two or more elements of reality or fantasy to produce a desired result.* Very difficult for me. I'm sure I have one, but I have a hard time using it or expressing it. This is great .... I'm stumped at your first question. *The ability to conceive things that haven't been seen yet.* **The ability to, if only for a short time, lose touch with reality ... producing the ideas that shall soon become reality.**

Imagination to me is conceptualizing pictures, words, ideas and putting them together to form something of worth. Could be a daydream, invention, motivation, and many other things. I also use it to break out of norm types of thinking. Abstract thought. Break out of my box. To go anywhere in the universe. To accomplish things mentally before doing them physically. **It's wonderland, no limitations.** *The most honest expression of myself.* **Imagination is everything in my life—without it I don't know what I would do!!! I'm still a kid so I rely on it for about everything. I try to understand what management wants and then I reduce it to its Zen essence. Then I let my imagination express that essence in a creative way.** It's a worldview thing. People love to be turned on by bigger and better visions of the way things could be. Combined with effort—and brazenness—so much more can be accomplished. **Personally, imagination is a necessary part of my day. I have two small children and I try to come up with activities for them to develop imaginations of their own. For me, imagination is a form of stress relief—it allows me to feel good, feel stimulated, productive, and creative. It is very rewarding when you dream up something and then put it into action. I think it is a gift.** *Seeds for reality are planted in the imagination.* **Life would not be worth living for me. I live a great part of my spare time imagining.** *Imagination helps me to change things on a dime. Without imagination, life becomes a real routine. Although I figure that imagination is a gift, developing and improving our imagination is a challenge.* **Imagination is the dreams I have every waking moment. It allows me to see in my mind's eye what I want something or someplace or even someone to be. It can hurt as well as enlighten. It seems to work best for me in my personal life and somewhat for my business life.** *Imagination allows you to set goals. Imagination is what keeps me from joining the boys on the park bench; I can see the promise of the future.* **It's what supports my life, it's the energy of my dreams.** *My personal life and my business life have to be the same or I don't live with integrity.* **It is what makes a day interesting.** *Professionally: Without it I wouldn't be able to work. Personally: I would be dead.* **Without imagination, I would not be able to recast old questions in new contexts so that there comes a way to answer the questions in the first place.** *I use my imagination to keep my work as a writer fresh and to keep me vital and alive as a person.* **In publishing, imagination is the difference between circulation and condensation.** *It's something that puts your reality into perspective.* **Imagination from a business perspective is vital for it allows me to see opportunities where it might not always be the obvious. It also allows me to tap into a customer's needs and hopefully a chance to fill that requirement. Personally, my thoughts are that without imagination we would all be like government drones. Now that is scary. Just imagine!** *I'm a writer, which means I harvest my imagination, put it into words for popular consumption, then sell the product. My e-mail account is my imagination export highway.*

Imagination and Creativity

For many people, imagination is synonymous with creativity. But there is an important difference between the two. Imagination is the vital impulse that lives in every person from their first glimmering of awareness. It's the magic in the mind, the genie in the bottle, the *élan vital*. Imagination is spontaneous. When the mind sees, feels, and senses something it has never encountered before, the experience satisfies a fundamental urge to discover, learn, and grow. Everyone has imagination. Well formed or vague, imagination provides the pulse and is the organizing element of consciousness.

Imagination is the spark. Creativity is the engine.

Creativity, in contrast, is the *expression* of imagination. Creativity is what a person does to develop the imaginative impulse and manifest it in reality. Creativity is the way a person brings ideas into the tangible world so that others can share and feel them. Creativity involves talent, training, and skill that can be learned and developed; imagination simply flows on its own.

Though business views ideas as being a dime a dozen, all business begins with ideas and all business survives through the exchange of value. The results of imaginative work fill our lives. If you look at the objects populating the room you are now sitting in, you can imagine the journey each took from being a concept in someone's mind to assuming tangible form. Every object—from the highest-tech gadget to the simplest lamp or window frame—is the result of someone's imagination and its subsequent creative expression.

Though some objects are more inventive or useful than others, each began as an idea, carrying potential to be an amazing product. Each went through a process where the idea was sketched, drawn, prototyped, patented, milled, machined, sold, and shipped to the place it now occupies. Imagination is simply the very human capacity to experience, construct, and manipulate mental imagery: the ability to see, hear, and feel things that are not physically present. This simple definition helps us understand the elements of the Imagination Economy.

What you **imagine** steers what you see, feel, think, and experience.

Imagination Is Pervasive

In this sense, we cannot *not* use our imagination. Every person experiences a constant stream of images and words that create a personal sense of the world. We imagine all day and all night—why our loved one is late for dinner, how to triumph in tomorrow's presentation, what route we'll take to the grocery store, where to keep money safe in a chaotic market. We actively use our imagination to make sense of our lives, employing a variety of sophisticated mental processes to create context and meaning. This is true for us both as employees and as consumers.

Imagination Is Contagious

Ideas, by their nature, flow, releasing a cascade of possibilities. See a new product—a Razor scooter, a next-gen phone, a fair-trade investment—and your mind starts to roll, creating scenarios of how you might use it. Start talking with a friend, and the two of you roll faster and further. Products that excite the imagination capture the market's attention and make people want to talk about them. Seth Godin understands the transmittable nature of ideas very well. In *Unleashing the Idea Virus* he writes:

> The notion that an idea can become contagious, in precisely the same way that a virus does, is at once commonsensical and deeply counterintuitive. It is commonsensical because all of us have seen it happen: all of us have had a hit song lodged in our heads, or run out to buy a book, or become infected with a particular idea without really knowing why. It is counterintuitive, though, because it doesn't fit with the marketer's traditional vision of the world. The future belongs to marketers who establish a foundation and process where interested people can market to *each other*. Ignite consumer networks and then get out of the way and let them talk.[6]

Ideas—good or bad—spread quickly if they stimulate the imagination.

Imagination Creates a Sense of Reality

How else do we create our sense of reality but with our imagination? This is not to suggest that the world does not exist beyond our imagination. It does say that how we define our world—how we believe it works, the way we feel about it, what we consider possible and impossible—is hemmed in by the flow of imagination.

There was a time when Web sites were regarded as weak marketing vehicles for computer nerds with no real business application. Not too long ago, wireless communication was considered a fad. What are the ideas we now consider to be minor fads or fringe technology that may emerge as major market forces?

Every era is defined by the shared reality of the people living in it. The Renaissance, the Reformation, the industrial age, and the information age each carried its own sense of what was possible. Not too long ago, business was being conducted in an atmosphere of irrational exuberance; all things seemed achievable. The dot-com era came and went.

Business, like every cultural endeavor, evolves as new tools emerge and social conditions change. The tools people use to work and the range of human activity possible in the culture define each major economic era. *New Economy* became part of the business vocabulary in the mid-1990s, when economists determined that the combination of digital technology and intellectual capital had become more valuable than bricks and mortar. Many of the richest and most powerful people in the world no longer own factories or real estate holdings. Instead, they wield intellectual capital—ideas in all forms, from software to movies.

The U.S.-based Progressive Policy Institute described the New Economy as "a knowledge and idea-based economy where the keys to job creation and higher standards of living are innovative ideas and technology embedded in services and manufactured products. It is an economy where risk, uncertainty, and constant change are the rule, rather than the exception."[7]

The New Economy has affected every industry and business sector. Among large-cap companies we have seen Microsoft's market capitalization grow to be at the same level as General Electric's. At the other end of the spectrum, a farmer living in Nebraska can now use satellite imaging to plan and monitor his crop from an on-line service. The Imagination Economy is a natural outgrowth of the New Economy.

The quality of the imagination is to flow and not to **freeze**.

Ralph Waldo Emerson

Now, in the current economic downturn, we're living in a world of pessimism, focused on cost cutting and layoffs and a return to the safety of tried-and-true. The collective imagination will shift again with the next economic upswing, but meanwhile, in tough times, it's more important than ever to converse with the imagination.

Imagination Motivates Behavior

We can't escape our mental images and ideas any more than we can avoid our feelings and desires. Imagination presents us with a world of options. It informs us of what's possible and what's not.

For consumers, imagination directs and even determines purchasing decisions in the way it supports desires, enhances fears, or underscores aspirations. Success requires that we become experts at divining our customers' desired experiences and creating products that address those desired experiences succinctly.

The Flow of Ideas

The concept of idea flow is central to success in the Imagination Economy. Investing in imagination requires opening valves at the personal level so that we can reach in and tap into the imaginative energy that flows through each of us; it needs an environment where people feel safe to put their ideas forward; and it means designing products and services that stimulate the imagination of customers, encouraging them to interact in ways that fill their experiential desires. Common to all of these goals is developing a culture where the sharing and exploration of possibilities is an ongoing activity.

IDEAFLOW

Germ Idea Concept Prototype Development Launch Interaction Community

As well as strategies to foster the imagination, we need ways to stop the busyness that prevents the deeper imagination from flowing. Investing in imagination means creating an environment that allows the imagination to flourish, and developing the tools to bring imaginative ideas to the world.

Whether you are discussing the concept literally or figuratively, imagination is a form of energy. To invest in this intangible energy is to treat business as an ecosystem that operates through the exchange of ideas and experiences. Think of how Amazon.com is a machine that stimulates the imagination of the customers it serves. This approach is a radical departure from a focus on the tangible aspects of business: inventory and human contact. The new mindset provides the flexibility and freedom to see the spaces and gaps in business, to perceive the possibilities, and to focus on the human experience. We can't stimulate the imagination directly, but we can create environments where imagination flows. And by doing that, we expand our traditional definition of the elements of business. What has made Amazon.com so captivating is that it successfully created a new model rather than simply putting a retail store on-line, as so many others have done.

Investing
in Imagination

So, what does investing in imagination really mean? The answer is simple. First, slow down, and find or create an environment where the imagination can decouple itself from the shared reality of business. Then let it do what it is so good at: picturing what could be, what you and your team think would be amazing and inspiring. Focus on the inner experience of the customer—how the customer will see, feel, connect with, represent, internalize, and share the spirit and value of your idea. Whether the idea that emerges is a Web site, a reworking of the value of your current business, or a new way to distribute fuel, the connecting thread is imagination. Now work together to bring that vision to reality.

Imagination
rules the world.

Napoleon Bonaparte

It sounds far too simple and idealistic, doesn't it? The truth is, there is no single prescriptive list of techniques that will bring repeated success or permanent harmonious change. The real work of imagination is never a quick fix. As long as our activities are dynamic, so too will our solutions be.

Believe in Possibility

Personally and professionally, imagination begins with permission—to dream, to desire, to wonder, to expand, to feel safe, to make sense, to speculate, to make a difference, to know, to reach as far as possible. Without connecting to this desire for free thought, nothing is possible. The change involves seeing business as a pattern of fluid energy rather than as a fixed entity. Believing in possibility means creating and defining our future for ourselves. And as the future is not a fixed point, we must be flexible and malleable as we go.

Man's mind stretched to a new idea **never** goes back to its original dimensions.

Oliver Wendell Holmes, Jr.

The Segway Human Transporter™—the latest brainchild of inventor Dean Kamen—is a quintessential result of imagination drawing from the world of possibility. The Segway is a transporter designed to accelerate personal mobility without isolating its operator from other pedestrian traffic. It has two wheels and a handle, is battery-powered, and moves by responding to body prompting. In other words, it's a way to zoom along, almost as you would on foot, with the aid of technology. This human transporter inspires countless new ideas about commuting and workflow. It confronts urban issues of overcrowding and maintaining cleaner environments. It invites great advancement in the realm of engineering. And its quantum-leap innovation makes us realize that anything is in our grasp, if we are open to it.

Understand the Force of Imagination

Imagination is a real force that connects a designer's inspiration to a customer's experience, from the moment of purchase through continued interaction with the product. The designer's insight and understanding of the product application, and the consumer's experience with the product, bring energy and value to its use. The manifestation of great imagination is what makes us look at Philippe Starck's design and say, "Now *that's* a lemon press!"

The force of imagination is particularly powerful when it connects to shared values. Sustainability, integrity, boldness, empowerment, innovation—whatever the values an organization aspires to, they create a magnetic pull that attracts like-minded people. It's no small coincidence that investment companies offering socially responsible portfolios represent one of today's fastest-growing financial markets.

Focus on the Human Experience

Though we have been speaking of imagination and business as if they were independent entities existing outside us, nothing could be further from the truth. Businesses are communities of people who work together in productive activities that provide something of value to the people they serve while sustaining themselves economically. Businesses do not exist *outside* communities; they exist *because of* them. Thus, investing in imagination means investing in the human experience at all levels, from the people creating to the people serving to the people buying. Focusing imagination in this way moves the spotlight from the *process* of creating things to the *experience* of things. In the Imagination Economy new value is created in what people experience, think, and feel in their interaction with a product or service. A twelve-year-old girl picks up a pop bottle and sees photos of a dog just like her own, and the pop connects to her reality; she talks about it with her friends and they want to see a bottle like that one. A visitor to Paris walks into a store with glowing walls and somehow the perfume smells better. You don't just purchase a cup of coffee at Starbucks; you have the entire latte experience, deeply submerged in the world of java.

Customers are no longer satisfied with incremental improvements. What's the point of another packaging of chewing gum, another feature added to a coffee maker, or another way to lace up a running shoe? These lackluster enhancements are easily duplicated and provide the slimmest of competitive advantage. The consumer also knows there's no real innovation involved.

Imagination represents the complexity of human experience and is as much about feeling as it is about thinking. It is organic and unpredictable. Investing in imagination therefore calls for more than simply investing in people; it is a celebration of humanity.

Imagination cannot be treated as a commodity because it is so deeply personal. Employees and consumers need to feel they have control over their own lives. This occurs when they are free to think, create, and pursue what appeals to them from an array of real choices. As simple a thought as this may be, it can push the panic button. If we let people do whatever they want, how will we ever get anything done? How will we ever capture customer loyalty?

Tapping into the power of imagination means making room for all the quirks, craziness, friction, and foibles that come with being human. If we want people to be at their best, we must allow them free expression of their complexity. If what you want is human genius, realize that all the other stuff is part of the package.

Finding Your Authentic Voice

Our businesses are complex, interconnected webs of activity that reflect who we are and what we value. As we increasingly derive our sense of ourselves from the work we do, our work becomes a forum for self-expression. It is essential to feel that our contribution is a true reflection of who we are.

Connecting to the power of imagination—your own imagination, your business's imagination—is about digging down to the ideas that emerge from your core. They bubble up because you have made the room that allows them to. From the point of view of business, this is what gives you a competitive advantage. From a personal point of view, it's about finding your authentic voice, the one that speaks with substance and integrity.

People have a desire to realize their potential, enjoy a wide range of experiences, live full, balanced lives, and make meaningful contributions. The business world seems a natural environment for self-expression and imaginative thought. That is why people experience extreme frustration when opportunities for imaginative expression are restricted at work, as is so often the case. The workplace needs to offer opportunities for self-expression and to facilitate the achievement of a balanced life for its employees. We experience satisfaction when our personal values are aligned with those of our employer, and when we can see and feel the results of our personal contribution resonating through the company's success.

Be **true** to the impulse of imagination. Don't become sidetracked by minutiae.

Everyone has a range of identities. For example, you may be someone's parent, someone's child, a volunteer, an inventor, a graphic artist, and a musician. When you are creating design work, and are therefore focusing your energy on your "graphic artist" persona, you do not stop being any of those other things simply because they are not currently at the forefront. Authenticity involves bringing *all* parts of yourself into your work. This requires integration. When we approach things with all aspects of our personality, we have much broader experience, a greater diversity of viewpoints, and a more wide-ranging wisdom to bring to the table. One personal motto for Carolyn Gallagher, organizational development consultant for the World Bank, is "Bring your whole self to work."[8] That might not just include everything you are today, but everything you have been and all those things you will become.

If you seek to engage the full power of imagination, you need to know that it's not just about getting ideas on a particular product line or process. When you open the tap to imagination, you must be prepared to take whatever comes out: that means truth, fears, impossibilities, and wild fancies, as well as great ideas.

Develop Skills to Bring Imagination to Reality

Of course, from the point of view of business, good ideas are just part of the story—and at times just a small part. It's the ability to transform those ideas into tangible products, real services, and revenue that forwards the goals of the business. The challenge is to get the good idea all the way to the customer.

To do this requires developing the personal and corporate skills to transform the imaginative impulse into reality. That's the roll-up-your-sleeves and get-your-hands-dirty work of pitching the idea, testing it, playing with it, knowing what to change and what to keep. It's figuring out what your customer wants and needs, getting people fired up about the idea, building a prototype of it, and bringing it to market.

Imagination is not a magic solution, a formula that will solve all business problems and guarantee a better return on your investment. It is an investment designed to yield the best possible solution, the most authentic solution, the one with vision, the one that fulfills the potential of a business and its people.

The **best idea** in the world is worth precisely **dick** if it doesn't make it through the gauntlet of capers, lawyers, clients, and the **dark side** of bean-counters.

Richard Seymour

Redefining Success

The big news is that success is no longer measured exclusively by financial gain. In this diverse and complex world overloaded with activity, information, and conflict, to define success strictly by the bottom line is to miss the bigger picture.

Margot Franssen, president of The Body Shop in Canada, acknowledges that the financial part of a business is essential to organizational health and longevity. But she also states that the money coming into a business is like the groceries coming into the home: food is necessary for maintaining a healthy family, but it is not the essence of the family. Your family is defined by its relationships, experiences, and collective wisdom. Continuously maintaining a narrow focus on one aspect—even one as important as finance—means neglecting the richness of all the other pieces that go to create the whole.[9]

Levi Strauss & Co. is one of the world's largest brand-name apparel marketers, with annual sales exceeding $4.6 billion in more than eighty countries, and it holds one of the world's most recognized trademarks, registered in more than 160 countries. The company has made a commitment to ethical business practices and social responsibility through employee community involvement and scholarship programs, an ethical code for manufacturing, and the creation of the Levi Strauss Foundation. The Foundation's giving programs are designed to provide support for communities where Levi Strauss has a business presence. The priorities for grant making are AIDS prevention and care, economic empowerment, social justice, and youth empowerment. The Foundation made $16 million in grants in forty countries in 2001.

Imagine a world in which the business of business is to make a worthwhile contribution to life on earth.

Seth Weaver Kahan

Seth Weaver Kahan, independent storyteller and senior information officer for the World Bank, states that suggesting your business is strictly about finance is like saying your being is strictly about breathing. Never before has it been more necessary to stretch ourselves beyond the basic metrics of for-profit thinking. The world increasingly demands that, along with our desire for financial success, we believe in and pursue a greater good; that as businesses we are of some value to the people and communities we serve; and that we do this with absolute authenticity.[10] This means taking a holistic approach by thinking, acting, and working from our core values. Authenticity is critical to quality and longevity in this New Economy. We understand this when we understand humanity's great need to hold on to something solid, something of true worth in today's relentlessly changing world.

The Journey of Imagination

Imagination is a doorway to freedom, the ultimate exercise of personal choice. We think of freedom as the ability to define alternatives and choose between them. But the imaginative mind transcends this by being able to define itself and its own reality, creating entirely new sets of alternatives.

The history of business is highlighted by examples of this kind of redefinition, by revolutionary new technologies and business models, by novel ways of identifying value and exchanging commerce. These acts of creative imagination make up the leading edge of freedom that defines the world and ourselves.

Because it is a radical expression of freedom, the imaginative act is a heroic process that requires strength of character. Imaginative people are not "good" or "bad," "happy" or "fulfilled." More often we hear words like *courageous*, *persistent*, *committed*, and *free*. These qualities become important when one's challenges involve self-discovery, unremitting inquiry, and personal expression.

To free your imagination is to embark on an unpredictable journey. You must put yourself on the line. The pursuit of imaginative freedom delivers both pleasure and pain. Imaginative work offers the deep satisfaction of coming up with an idea and bringing it to market, of seeing your work make a difference; the fulfillment of being immersed in your medium or of doing something that brings good to a large number of

The most **imaginative** people I know have **hope** for the future. For without that, what's the point?

J. Rick Blickstead

people. There is also the philosophical pleasure of bringing fresh ideas and connections into the light, and the sheer joy and thrill of creation. But the fruits of imagination are not always pleasant. There are too many examples of tragic vision, of genius in the service of deception, greed, even violence, for us to maintain unrealistically romantic ideas about the creative act. And although insight can come naturally and easily, bringing an idea to the world takes effort. Sometimes, it must be said, that effort is not very pleasurable.

Indeed, imagination can be dangerous and frightening. We cannot open our businesses or ourselves to new ideas and fresh insight without risking the security of our assumptions and the solidity of our previously imagined reality. We can't generate ideas and put them forward without chancing rejection and disapproval. Imagination is the boldest initiative of the mind, an adventure that takes its hero to the New World of knowledge. The pleasure lies not in the safe harbor but in the sail.

Enter the Imagination Economy

21

2 The Pressures on Imagination

The relentless pace of economic,
technological, and social change
is simultaneously constricting
and expanding
the flow of imagination.

Constant change is deeply embedded in our culture; it is intertwined with every aspect of our lives. Most of us now face a situation where vast amounts of data are piling up on our brain's front door. Though we've increased and sped up the generation and delivery of information, we haven't discovered how to make sense of it all. Our brains can process ideas only so fast. But if you were hoping for a return to business as usual, forget it. The incredible period of experimentation we have seen in the past few years has changed the business environment irrevocably.

The **pressures** keep our imaginations busy, crowded, and engaged, so that we have little room to let the **deeper** ideas emerge.

The rate of economic, technological, and social transformation places a critical amount of pressure on the imagination: pressure to produce and deliver; pressure to use technological tools so as not to be left behind; pressure to understand and make sense of the information storm that surrounds us. The very concept of change is now inbred in our business/technological society, and has become such a core part of our collective way of thinking that we take it for granted.

The effects of these economic and social pressures are insidious. They keep our imaginations so busy with what's urgent and immediately before us that we neglect what's truly important and what could be. Ironically, the same pressures that keep us distracted from the big picture, tied to ever-faster innovation, could enable us to see beyond the tidal wave of change.

The hectic pace adds stress to every aspect of our lives. Because we have to focus on a broader range of issues all the time, and spend less time on any one bit of information, we become increasingly superficial. We make time only for what appears to be the most urgent part of the problem confronting us.

Continually reacting to current developments keeps a company stuck behind the eight ball and leads inevitably to crisis. The need to slow down is crucial; to undergo a period of self-examination, reconsider the boundaries that define business, and clarify what success really means. If we take the time to do some scenario planning, consider the big picture, and look at other industries to spot trends and anticipate changes, then the relentless market pressures represent an opportunity rather than a threat, a catalyst for rethinking the role and vision of business.

So here's the paradox: the need to generate a sense of possibility has never been more urgent, but the urgency itself diminishes the perception of possibility by the imagination. We need to take our foot off the accelerator to be able to assess our situation clearly and see where our opportunities lie. What you can create depends entirely on what you can envision.

Smart Technology is a global developer of interactive whiteboards and multimedia furniture, with an annual growth rate of 50 percent maintained over five years. It has garnered innovation and business awards internationally, and captured attention and market share in industries as diverse as automotive, education, government, and military. Founder, chairman, and CEO Dave Martin built the company from the ground up and emphasizes the imagination's capacity to make connections:

I've often described business as the most interesting game that you can play, like playing chess in three dimensions in real time. And I think business gives us who are interested in solving problems and puzzles a really interesting framework for solving some really interesting and complex problems. It requires a huge amount of imagination and creativity. The whole point of innovation, which I define as creating new products for new markets, means that you need lots of different tools.[1]

Martin believes that to be successful, skills need to be honed to the point where they're not just at a surface level, a mile wide and an inch deep. He and his partners spend their professional lives learning the many diverse areas involved in growing a company—like law, marketing, and product development—in enough detail to ask good questions. He summarizes:

An entrepreneur is regularly taking hats off - taking the legal hat off and putting on engineering, and continuously doing that. That's why I talk about it like a chess game. You're in a speeded-up environment and you don't have all the time in the world, but you have to have enough of a background to address each problem in turn. Like a chess game, you have to be able to imagine what the chess game is like today, this minute, and then what it's going to look like after you make your move and after the next person makes their move. And perhaps play three, four moves ahead to see how the board may play itself out.[2]

Smart Technology has been playing the field, creating agreements with major players like Intel and Xerox, by anticipating markets years in advance. Both foresight and the willingness to say no to demands that rise from changing market pressures enable Smart Technology to be in control as the business grows.

The overall business landscape, the never-ending spread of technology, and the turbulent and divergent social transformations of recent years are three broad areas in which our world is changing with startling rapidity. Success in this radically altered economy not only depends on anticipating the effects of growth and transformation in each of these areas, but in perceiving how the interrelationships between them create new trends and drive change.

Markets and Business Processes

Business has steadily shifted from making *things* to making, moving, and protecting *intangibles*. This new way of creating value is global, ever more pervasive, and ushering in an environment of persistent instability.

1. Switch from Making to Moving

Whereas the manufacturing economy perfected the mass production of goods, today's economy focuses on flexibility and customization. Only 20 percent of the U.S. workforce now spends its time actually making things; the other 80 percent moves those things, makes them better, processes or generates information, or provides services to people.

As a result, the measure of value has shifted from the tangible to the intangible. The economic output of the U.S. economy—the value of what is *produced*—is roughly the same today as it was a century ago, yet its real economic value is twenty times greater. The difference is accounted for by intangibles. Anti-lock brakes, a product of a generation of R & D, are loaded with electronics. They don't weigh any more than conventional brakes, but they provide a great deal more value to drivers. A Starbucks latte may not taste that much better than any other, but ambience makes it a more enjoyable experience.

Number of computer programmers in North America
1960: **5000**
2001: **1.3 million**

Managers, lawyers, bankers, sales reps, accountants, insurance managers, teachers, and many public sector employees also drive the information economy. The handling and managing of information, rather than breakthrough knowledge generation, are the keys to success for these workers.

2. Value of Intangibles

As business output shifts from the tangible to the intangible, governments have set up a global legal infrastructure to protect the value of intellectual property. Copyrights, patents, trademarks, and other legal instruments enable the creator of an idea to bring it to market and own the process, thus retaining a competitive advantage.

Idea husbandry—the art and science of generating and protecting intellectual property—is now a $2.2-trillion global business, according to U.K. author John Howkins. Incorporating fifteen sectors, from advertising to design, publishing to R & D, it is the fastest-growing component of the global economy, with growth of 5 percent compared with 2 percent in the economy overall.[3]

All kinds of innovators, in myriad businesses, are looking for the NEXT BIG THING. But the problem with home-run ideas is that they infect other businesses. The Razor scooter is a brilliant and simple idea—and easily copied. Razor USA, the holder of the patent, sued successfully fifteen times in its first year of business. No wonder the growth of patents has skyrocketed.

Owning Knowledge

Worldwide patent applications filed, millions

Source: World Intellectual Property Organization

3. Increase in Global Trade

The dramatic expansion of global trade has created a fiercely competitive landscape around the world. Forty years ago the world economy was a series of local industries locked in closed national economies. You competed with the businesses across town and across the country. Today's economy is a mesh of integrated global markets managed by international players. You are competing with businesses on the other side of the world, some larger, some smaller, and many more competitive. Many factors are driving this change: global capital markets; fewer economic and trade barriers; and technological innovation.

In 1995 the portion of world trade that is called global (that is, the product or service crossed a country's border) was one-seventh of the world's output. By 2000 that portion had grown to about one-half. Today you can also buy and sell stocks just as easily in Johannesburg or Jakarta as in London, New York, or Toronto.

With the creation of three enormous trading blocs—the Americas, Europe, and Asia—globalization is really just beginning. The worldwide markets of finance, marketing, communications, manufacturing, and transportation will continue to grow. The promoters say that this growth will boost trade, productivity, and standards of living throughout the world. The detractors say the cost of globalization will be even greater inequities in wealth, environmental standards, working conditions, and health.

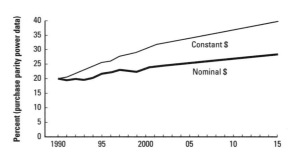

World Trade as a Percentage of World GDP: 1990–2015

Note: The constant dollar curve departs from the nominal curve largely because of the fall in price of IT-related traded goods in the 1990s and their expected price decline in the future.

Source: CLA's Long-Term Growth Model

4. Market Sensitivity

An economic environment in which millions of investors, all with the same basic objectives, simultaneously share the same information has created a market ultra-sensitive to change. The effect on the investor: stock valuations that ride on a tripwire; on the company: the need to make quarterly, not annual, budgets.

The machinery of the global markets creates a structure that physicists recognize as a chaotic system, one whose underlying principles of persistent instability and emergent patterns are definable but not predictable. Like magnetic desk toys that swing haphazardly, the markets oscillate by the push and pull of many pressures.

A company's valuation—its stock or worth—is measured by the market's anticipation of future earnings, itself an act of collective imagination. The rise and fall of dot-com businesses was largely driven by the exuberant belief that consumers would change their buying habits, followed by the realization that they would not. Shared ideas, emotions, rumors, conversations, representations, and analysis create exaggerated swings in stock valuation.

Market sensitivity creates an environment in which companies are less able to insulate workers by keeping them on during a quarterly downturn or by investing in basic research or employee training.

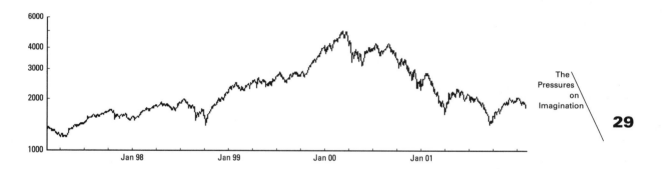

5. Intense Competition

The combination of open marketplaces and new technologies makes it easier for a growing number of companies to enter new markets. The effect: the burning need to bring better products and services to market faster and cheaper.

Forty years ago IBM had 2,500 competitors; today it has 50,000. Fifteen years ago there was one viable digital camera on the market; today you can choose from over two hundred. Product life cycles are shrinking and the desire for the "next new thing" is fiercer than ever. Innovate or die.

But that's just part of the story. Companies are redefining the nature of their business. The growth of digital cameras has dramatically affected Kodak and Polaroid by changing how people take photographs. Michael Bloomberg puts it this way: "What's likely to kill you in the new economy is not somebody doing something better, it's somebody doing something different."[4]

Pursuing incremental improvement while rivals reinvent the industry is like fiddling while Rome burns.[5]
Gary Hamel

6. Co-opetition and Collaboration

At the same time as competition is increasing, so is collaboration among competitors. Management guru Peter Drucker suggests that the dynamic of networks, partnerships, and joint ventures is the main organizing principle in the New Economy.

There is no place to hide.
Walter Wriston

To illustrate the complexity of co-opetition, Boeing presents three scenarios with three companies. In scenario one, each company bids for one contract—they compete. In scenario two, the contract is so large, Company A acts as a supplier to Company B—they collaborate. And in scenario three, Company A and Company B build technology together—they become part of a single larger virtual organization. Managing the relationships and the intellectual property in scenario three is especially challenging.

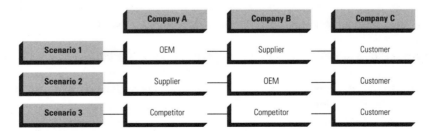

	Company A	Company B	Company C
Scenario 1	OEM	Supplier	Customer
Scenario 2	Supplier	OEM	Customer
Scenario 3	Competitor	Competitor	Customer

Multifaceted Roles Make for Complex Business Interactions

7. Speed of Change

Thirty percent of 3M's revenues are from products less than four years old. Seventy-seven percent of Hewlett Packard's revenues are from products less than two years old. Eighty percent of Macromedia's revenues are from products less than one year old.

Innovation and technology are shortening product development and replacement cycles. In 1990 in the U.S., companies took an average of 35.5 months to bring products to market, but by 1995 companies were introducing new products on average every 23 months. By 2000 that had dropped to eleven months.

Cars that took six years from concept to production in 1990 now take less than two years. Renault has stated that its goal is to produce a complete vehicle—from design to off the assembly line—in nine days. A far-fetched goal, maybe, but you have to admit they have a vision.

The pace of innovation can be so fast that companies have to run just to stay in place. The morphing sequence at the end of Michael Jackson's 1994 *Black or White* video cost several hundred thousand dollars and was produced with custom software. Two years later morphing software was commercially available for US$349. Now it's available freely on the Web.

Innovation is the one business competence need for the future.

Peter Drucker

8. Churning

The idea that "creative destruction" is an inherent part of a healthy economy was introduced by Joseph A. Schumpeter over sixty years ago. Schumpeter suggested that markets are in a perpetual state of dynamic equilibrium. Innovators introduce new products that upset the order in a market, unleashing a "wave of creative destruction" that forces organizations to innovate or die. The process of continual cross-fertilization "revolutionizes the economic structure from within, incessantly destroying the old one, incessantly creating a new one ... Stabilized capitalism is a contradiction in terms."[6]

Even sixty years ago, then, far-seeing economists could predict a constant churning leading to job creation and destruction, an increase in the number of firms that emerge and die every year. This turbulence will continue to unsettle even as it continues to drive innovation and growth. As less innovative and efficient companies die or contract, healthier ones will take their place. It's just going to be more of the same—only faster.

The March
of Technology

Technology has extended the reach and power of imagination. Information technology in particular enables us to create, manipulate, and distribute ideas among a wider range of people faster than ever before.

1. Microchips

In 1965 Intel's co-founder, Gordon Moore, wrote and delivered a now famous paper describing how the processing power of computer chips doubled every eighteen months and would continue to do so into the foreseeable future. Moore's Law, as it is now known, states that every eighteen months computing performance will double and processing power will cost 50 percent less. With a few deviations from this curve, the law has held.

In the early 1970s inventor Danny Hillis gave a talk to a large audience at the Hilton Hotel in New York City, describing this exponential curve and projecting it into the future. One of Hillis's predictions was that sooner or later there would be more microprocessors than people in the United States. The entire audience laughed. In the question-and-answer session one audience member asked, "What are you going to do with all those microprocessors? It's not as if you need one in every doorknob!" But if you go back to the New York City Hilton today (or to any other Hilton for that matter), there is in fact a microprocessor in every doorknob.[7]

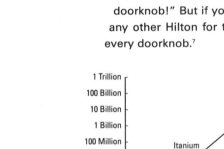

• Number of Transistors

Source: Intel-Corp.

The impact of microchips on our society is staggering. They appear in everything from cars to pens to coffee makers. If the automobile had made as much progress in the past fifty years, a car today would cost a hundredth of a cent and go faster than the speed of light. Really. This out-of-control growth has set the pace for business and consumers and established the mass expectation that things will only get faster and cheaper and that technology will provide a solution for all our ills.

2. The Internet

What can be said about the Internet that hasn't already been said since it hit Main Street? Beginning at UCLA and Stanford University in 1969, ARPANET was an obscure project designed to link universities and research centers, but it has now developed into the fastest-growing communication network in the history of humanity. The Internet connects hundreds of millions of people globally, allowing virtually instant access to any on-line database, group, organization, or individual, anywhere, any time.

Incredibly, we take it for granted now. Business and consumer acceptance of the Internet as a communications tool, an entertainment forum, a publishing technology, and a digital marketplace is unprecedented in its speed and reflects our culture's capacity to embrace change. And the rate of growth continues to be staggering: Internet data traffic is doubling every three to four months. And while high-income countries have forty times as many computers per capita as a country in Africa, the current Internet host growth rate in Africa is almost twice the developed world's average.

Metcalf's Law states that the value of a network is proportional to the square of the number of nodes in the network. Accordingly, the Internet has become the nervous system for business. Databases previously exclusive to certain groups, such as lawyers or doctors, are now a mouse click away. Easy entry to such enormous amounts of data changes the way we access information and requires the development of new research skills.

The really big news about the Internet is the rate at which connection speeds are increasing. The proliferation of high-bandwidth—currently cable and ADSL—and other disruptive technologies on the near horizon will dramatically change the nature of the Web's content and the ways in which we can use it. And combining this with wireless communication will provide yet more ways to connect people.

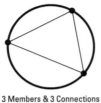

3 Members & 3 Connections

6 Members & 15 Connections

Metcalf's Networking Law

The value of the network rises exponentially with new members.

3. Digitization

Return
on
Imagination

34

Technology can create, capture, and reproduce all forms of data—text, images, videos, sounds, 3-D representations—with such fidelity that we can't tell the difference between the original and a computer-generated or -enhanced version. In fact, a sizable proportion of Hollywood special effects are the ones we don't notice. Industrial Light and Magic derives revenues from the digital removal of such intrusive things as telephone wires and the addition of background buildings because it's cheaper than physically altering the actual location.

Digital tools have revolutionized almost every type of content creation. Writing, editing, and illustrating a book, or designing a car or a cancer-fighting drug, on a laptop is no longer anything out of the ordinary. Digitization usually doesn't speed up creation time, but "undo" and "revert-to-saved" options give creators the freedom to explore directions they might not otherwise. But perhaps the most significant change brought about by digitization is the capacity to make limitless copies of digital data and share them with collaborators and customers. This has had enormous implications, from the legal issues of Napster to the nature of collaboration; and it has transferred value from the media to the digital source—from the cost of a CD to the MP3 file.

Digitization extends the reach of the collective imagination and is one of the key factors enabling ideas to be copied throughout a culture. Major news events are now documented by way of multifarious Web sources. But the wide reach of digitization also has the capacity to mislead. The delightful essay "Floss," a speech supposedly given to a Harvard graduating class by Kurt Vonnegut, was one of the most copied documents on the Internet in 1999. But Vonnegut had never seen it until a friend e-mailed it to him.

4. Disruptive Technologies

A decade ago, few people predicted the extent of the Internet's impact on business, education, and everyday life. The Internet is just one example of a disruptive technology. Whereas evolving technologies make incremental changes to a product, disruptive technologies can entirely redefine a market. For example, digital cameras have disrupted the photographic market, seriously threatening massive and well-established businesses such as Kodak and Polaroid.

History is filled with examples of technologies that disrupted successful businesses. Digital Equipment was one of the most profitable mini-computer manufacturers, whose founder called the personal computer "just a toy." In the space of a few short years, small PC start-ups hit the manufacturer from below and took over its market share. In the 1950s, Kresge's launched a revolutionary business model of lower margins but higher inventory turnover that undermined Woolworth's variety stores.

Clayton M. Christensen, author of *The Inventor's Dilemma*, defines disruptive technologies as "simple, convenient-to-use innovations that initially are used ... at the low end of the market."[8] On the horizon are technologies that will disrupt and change markets perhaps as dramatically as the Net. Wireless technology, for one, has already transformed telecommunications, and future wireless applications will undoubtedly create another set of sea changes.

The Movement in Society

Such far-reaching changes in global business and technology have huge implications for society at large. The net effect is to change how people interact and what their priorities are.

1. Demographics

People are living longer. Life expectancy at birth in North America, Western Europe, Asia, and South and Central America has increased an average of twenty-five years in the last century. This means the population is aging. In twenty-five years those aged 65 and over will outnumber the world's youth population by more than two to one. This means business will need to be flexible enough to serve a market of extreme contrasts.

The shift in demographics and the amount and distribution of wealth creates an ever more complex marketplace. On the one hand, the Baby Boomers are arriving at the later part of life. Now beginning to have grandchildren, they are slowing the pace of their lives, pursuing the kinds of experiences they want to have. They also have more money than ever to do it with. They demand service, convenience, and quality.

On the other hand, the Gen-Yers, the self-proclaimed Fresh generation, are savvy consumers who know they are being marketed to and like it. They want to be impressed, praised, appreciated, and heard. They are massive consumers, demanding newness and freshness in the messages and products being directed to them.

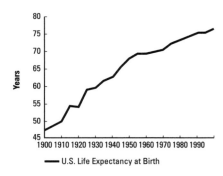
U.S. Life Expectancy at Birth

2. Consumerism

For many demographic groups, consumerism is the fastest-growing religion. Its message: happiness through limitless acquisition of material wealth and physical pleasure. Advertising helps to create this idea, through the fifteen thousand commercials a typical TV viewer sees in a given year.

The pressure on business to meet this insatiable demand is compounded by direct customer access to increased media and market information. In a relatively short period of time, with a minimal amount of effort, customers can easily research your company, its viability, your global competitors, alternative products and services, feedback from other customers, and what the media has to say. Book readers are looking at Web reviews on Amazon.com and BN.com as closely as they read the cover when deciding to buy a book. Purchasers of digital technology look to ZDNET.com to amass product reviews before making a decision to buy.

The result is an increasingly knowledgeable and sophisticated consumer with a growing appetite for ever-newer products and services. Trying to live up to customer demands while serving the needs of the business has become a frantic endeavor.

3. The Changing Workforce

As work takes up a larger portion of our lives, it is replacing the family and friendship network, creating a generation of people who live where they work. Our co-workers become our families, our workplaces become the arena where we live our lives, and many of us seek to define ourselves through the work we do.

This network is neither stable nor fixed. Daniel Pink, writing in *Free Agent Nation*, estimates that 33 million Americans work on their own or as contractors for other organizations. In the United States, 30 percent of all jobs are in flux, either coming into being or dying, expanding or contracting, every year. Even that last bastion of job security, the civil service, has been undergoing restructuring, outsourcing, and downsizing.[9]

For many, working from home removes the conflicting pressures to have an accomplished professional life and live in alignment with personal values. Using technology to our advantage, we can shift between professional and personal activities several times over the course of one day. As a result, it becomes almost impossible to segregate the world of work from the rest of our lives. What we do becomes who we are. Therefore, it is critical that we experience fulfillment by means of self-expression through our businesses.

4. The Rise of the Individual

Technology makes it possible for individuals to have far more influence than ever before in history. People are now their own bankers, brokers, accountants, medical researchers, and disc jockeys. This personal empowerment is having an enormous impact on the business world, as the music industry has already experienced to the tune of half a billion dollars at the hands of Napster and its clone sites. Businesses must be quick to adjust the products and services they deliver in order to survive the rapid changes in customer needs.

The rise in freedom of self-expression and interconnectivity has increased the power of the individual to effect change on a global scale. Amnesty International's fall 2001 ad campaign featured a full-page photo of one thirteen-year-old girl with a caption that reads: *Amanda Bueno vs. Pakistan*. The ad describes how Amanda is feared as she applies pressure on international politicians from her living room.

Of course, the power of one has its dark side too. On September 11, 2001, it took only a handful of men to hijack four U.S. jets and take down the World Trade Center Twin Towers and a chunk of the Pentagon.

5. Access to Data

It's staggering how much information is available from the Internet and other sources. You can easily find out just about anything about anything, including subjects you never even knew existed. And the volume of data is doubling every nine months. That means the information you will have to consider when making a decision two years from now will be eight times greater than the already overwhelming amount available today.

Making sense of this data, boiling it down to a manageable form, will be an ongoing challenge in the Imagination Economy. Deciding what kind of food, detergent, or clothing to buy may not be all that important to one's life, but finding out about new cancer treatments will be.

Although we have easy access to mountains of data, it is neither equally distributed nor of equal quality. As one interviewee for this book complained, "It's easier for me to get information about medieval egg-painting or some obscure band from Sweden than about what's going on in our manufacturing plant next door."

Data is not information. Information is not knowledge. Making sense of it all takes real work and imagination. Being able to sort through vast amounts of data in order to connect with what's relevant and reliable is now an essential skill for just about everyone.

6. Media and Data Overload

Over the last thirty years the amount of information the average person can produce, using word processing technologies, spreadsheets, and graphics packages, has doubled or tripled. According to architect and author Richard Saul Wurman, a weekend edition of the *New York Times* contains more data than the average person living in the sixteenth century was exposed to in a lifetime.[10]

The media is relentless in bombarding us with information. But it's not only the quantity that overwhelms us, it's also the variety, frequency, placement, and complete saturation into our lives. The messages are so insistently in our faces, it is becoming near impossible to visit a public restroom without being confronted by yet more advertising— more noise for the imagination.

We do not live in an information age, but in an age of data noise.

7. The Quest for Experience

In 1998 over 50 percent of consumer spending went on lifestyle and fun. Paul Saffo of the Institute of the Future says there is a hierarchy of consumer desires, and entertainment sits at the top of it.

Over the past decade many retail outlets have undergone transformations that embody the idea of shopping as theater. We no longer just go out to buy a toy; we have an experience traveling through different toylands at FAO Schwarz. We no longer simply buy a pair of running shoes; we stroll through a museum of sports that pays homage to the ideals of competition, endurance, speed, and winning, and marvel at the athletes who embody these qualities.

As the complexity of life increases, we look for more meaning in our material goods. Rolf Jensen, director of the Copenhagen Institute for Future Studies, says, "We need a good story and we are willing to pay for it."[11] Our purchasing decisions become emotional rather than rational.

Converting a product into a story is a key principle of the Imagination Economy. In 1996 a bar at the Copenhagen airport imported chunks of Greenland's ice cap in order to reinvent the common ice cube. When you ordered an ice-age cube, you didn't just get a piece of ice; you got the experience of ultra-pure water with trapped air bubbles that were older than the Sphinx. The story was the product. And the product was the timeless experience of drinking from history.

8. The Values-Based Society

The trend toward values alignment has become serious business. Having witnessed the results of social myths promising that money will make us happy, attractive, and eternally young, consumers don't have the brand loyalty they once did. A growing body of consumers believe that happiness and fulfillment come from self-defined core values and adherence to personal beliefs.

The past decade has seen the widespread adoption of several values: sustainable environmentalism, where keeping the planet healthy is the top priority; the backlash against globalization, focused not so much on trade between nations as on unfair trade, where the profits of a running-shoe manufacturer are made at the expense of people who are paid a hundredth the amount earned by the workers who will buy the shoes; and health and fitness, where some consumers make lifestyle choices designed to improve their vitality and overall well-being.

Businesses that want loyalty need to deliver messages that resonate with their customers. Making decisions based only on financial
objectives may be fatal. Staying in touch with your customers' values
is one way to develop long-term relationships with them.

And just as consumers seek to align themselves with the companies they buy from, so do employees desire value-based relationships
in their work. In order to be sustainable, the workplace must offer more
than a weekly paycheck.

The Opportunity That Is Perpetual Change

Philips Design is a company that understands the power of embracing
change and using it to create a brighter future. Philips's vision, "Let's
make things better," drives it to continually conduct and publish
research on socio-economic and technological trends. This commitment to understanding broad areas of influence allows Philips to identify and respond to emerging trends. With this knowledge in hand, it is
able to design innovative, customer-focused products that anticipate
needs that will be created by future change.

There's no rest in the new economic game. The pressure may be
deadly, but the gap between imagination and possibility has never been
smaller. The Internet provides us with unprecedented access to galaxies
of raw material and opportunities for expression. Technology offers us
extraordinary tools with which to create and communicate. Our social
freedoms have empowered us, and enhanced communication lets us
link up easily and quickly with others who share similar ideas.

Our response to the pressures that change brings is based on a
fundamental choice facing us in the Imagination Economy. We can
choose to continue to innovate in the ways we have done before, using
the same metrics for success: an annual 10 percent growth. We can also
question the pressures themselves. Is newness always good? Is the
constant overturning of our lives, the change that continually seizes us
in its grasp, a good thing? Do we actually need to innovate all the time?

Almost two and a half millennia ago, **Plato** wrote, "All things are in flux," and **Heraclitus** said, "Nothing endures but change."

The sheer complexity of the world we face is increasing astronomically, and the intensity of the pressure has reached a crisis point for many people. A desire for simplicity and clarity is becoming more pronounced. Douglas J. Cardinal, architect and member of the Order of Canada, puts it emphatically: "The knowledge that we have that is defined, I believe, is too limited to solve the problems we face today. I believe we must go beyond the created knowledge we have today and be willing to leap into the unknown, to a land where all possibilities can occur."[12]

Imagination affords us that chance—to look at the big picture, foresee the trends, and uncover the possibilities. Only in this way are we able to turn incessant change into opportunity, rather than folding under its unforgiving pressure.

3

Exploring the Worlds of Imagination

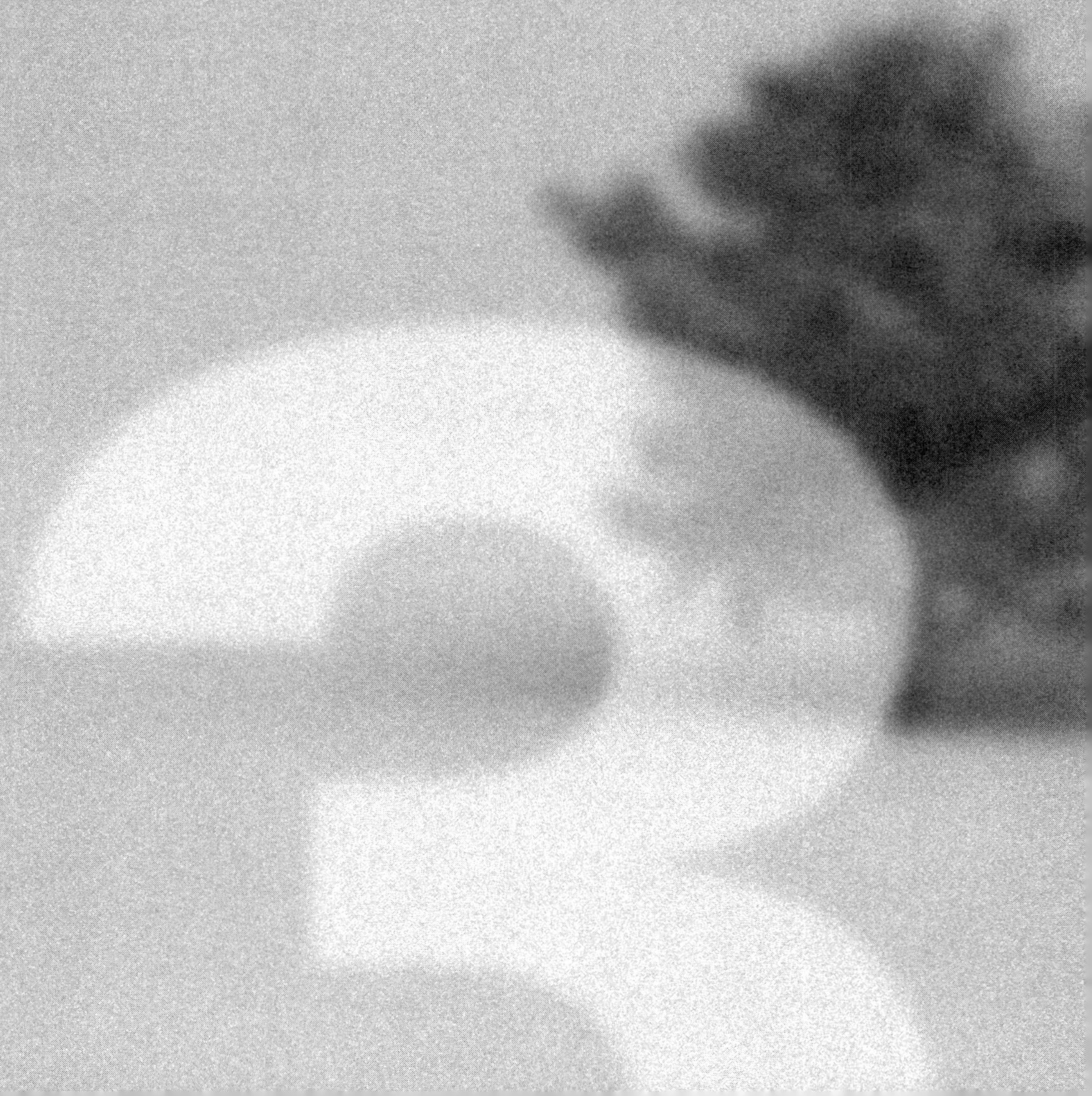

Though imagination is a
remarkably rich and complex
aspect of human consciousness,
the principles by which
it operates are actually
quite simple.

Intangible, Invisible, Indefinable

Though many people claim to have no imagination, what they really mean is that they have lost touch with its creative energy. To have no imagination is impossible; it is our constant companion. Imagination is the fount of who we are, yet we do not have the capacity to devise and control it as we can with creativity. We can cultivate, tend, enjoy, and participate in the things of the imagination, but we can't outwit it or shape it to the designs of the willful ego. It involves our most intangible aspects—what we experience in our inner world. Our ideas and speculations, hopes and fears, aspirations and sensitivities, musings and recollections, plans and strategies are undetectable to anyone but ourselves. In a way it's ironic that these parts of us that others can't see, feel, or touch are what make us most who we are.

We know more about the interior of the stars than the process going on in our heads.

Richard Gregory

Not all the operations of the mind occur at the level of conscious awareness. Cognitive psychologists are revealing the extent to which mental activities take place well beyond the borders of everyday awareness. Moreover, there is increasing evidence to support the folk wisdom of incubation—letting ideas simmer and stew, taking a much less deliberate approach to thinking and problem solving. There are slower ways of operating that have less to do with conscious ways of knowing, and these are equally powerful in the development of understanding and the creation of new ideas. This is the great unwritten story of imagination.

If you work on your mind with your mind, how can you **avoid** immense confusion?

Seng Ts'ang

The formal introduction of creativity as a fundamental business tool is relatively recent. Alex Osborne coined the term *brainstorming* in 1954, and creativity did not emerge as a subject for discussion in business schools until the past two decades. This is curious, since the idea of imagination has been written about for over two and a half thousand years; and while the realms of psychology, philosophy, and mythology have produced a large body of literature on imagination, the world of business has developed relatively little. Perhaps it is because imagination is invisible, immeasurable, and ethereal—not the normal currency of business. In a world where quantifiable results are critical, this presents an obvious dilemma: how do we go about understanding, fostering, and measuring the value of imagination?

Imagination has an unlimited capacity to hold any size of thought or dimension of idea—from an image as simple as a circle to systems as complex as an automobile engine or the molecular structure of a protein molecule. Making the shift from trying to understand imagination in its entirety to focusing on the way it works is instructive. Exploring the four key activities of imagination provides us with guidelines for considering, applying, and measuring imagination in our business.

What is Mind? No Matter. What is Matter? Never Mind.

Though these aspects do not initially appear to speak to the spontaneous character of imagination, they are the fundamental mechanisms that cause the energy of imagination to flow. These four properties together create a self-perpetuating system that automatically and spontaneously generates ideas.

The Four Key Aspects of Imagination

1. Representation: Seeing with the Mind's Eye

The inner representation of a physical object is perhaps the most familiar aspect of imagination, and indicates the tendency of the brain to create mental models. The word *image* is derived from the Latin root *imitare*, which means "to imitate." The word *imagination* originates in the Greek *phantázein*, "to make visible" or "present to the mind."

The capacity to see images, hear sounds, smell, taste,
and feel within your mind is the heart of imagination.
Imagination's ability to represent is not the same thing as perception.
It is a construction of impressions,
emphasizing some aspects of experience over others.

Representation Exercise
Imagine holding a $10 bill in your hand.
Make the image as vivid and clear as you can.

Over the past two decades research has indicated that no single part
of the brain is responsible for the creation of visual and auditory images.
There is no one place that controls or directs the way we see mental
imagery; imagination activates many parts of the brain simultaneously.

If our brains were simple enough to be **understood**, then we would be too simple to **understand** them.

If a person in a PET scan is asked to imagine he is listening to a symphony, the same part of his brain will light up as if he were actually hearing a symphony. The same is true for someone imagining a visual object. Ask her to imagine doing something with the object and a different part of her brain becomes most active. However, though it's possible to locate some specific mental tasks on the map of the brain, the capacity to muse is not one of them. Not yet understood by philosophers and neuropsychologists is the magic that converts auditory and visual images, and the accompanying synaptic activity, into felt experience.

Many of our concepts of imagination can be traced back to Aristotle, who believed it was connected with perception. His term *sensus communis*, or common sense, represented the part of the psyche responsible for combining impressions from different senses into a single coherent and intelligible representation. Specifically, Aristotle saw imagination as the mechanism that blends the perception of seeing your hands holding a cup of coffee, feeling the warmth of the cup, and tasting the java into a single unified experience. Thus, the imagination is the great integrator, bringing together the multifarious aspects of physical reality.

The integration of senses is a central function of our inner life, resulting from the brain's constant activity. We take this integration entirely for granted, but imagine how different our understanding of the world would be if our sensations were disconnected.

The Vivid Image

In the Imagination Economy successful businesses capture the imagination by creating vivid images. Marketers have an implicit understanding of the power of imagery to stimulate the minds of consumers. Think of some of the most popular products—the iMac, the VW bug, the PT Cruiser; each conveys an image that the imagination can easily grasp. Making something visually stimulating so that it may be readily captured and held in the imaginaion is the goal of marketers.

2. Connection: Compare and Contrast

University of Toronto cognitive psychologist John Kennedy describes imagination as operating between two mental functions: the representation of finite elements and the mixing of these elements into new combinations. The human brain is remarkably adept at identifying finite elements. Our mind naturally identifies things, largely through the language instinct, our built-in tendency to give names to things. According to Kennedy:

> The other function is the assimilation of those finite elements into innumerable combinations. Every discipline has at its disposal a finite collection of elements or symbols that form an operational foundation. Chess has six types of playing pieces arranged on an eight-by-eight board, and it has rules of engagement. English has twenty-six letters, ten digits, a handful of punctuation symbols, and rules of syntax. A business has customers, products, research, marketing, manufacturing, distribution, and accounting, as well as numerous other corporate and industry-specific elements. The point is, there is a finite collection of variables that we are aware of and operate from.[1]

Imagination links images and other representations through a variety of means: logic, feelings, and free association, among others. This capacity enables the imagination to combine old thoughts to make new ones.

Connection Exercise
Imagine a $10 bill in the middle of a large dining room table. Now on the table imagine three objects you could buy with the $10.

We naturally combine known finite elements into endless patterns and situations. Everything from faces to food, notes of a song to product plans, becomes part of a whole. Mathematicians estimate that the possible variations in a game of chess number about 10^{80}; that's several orders of magnitude larger than the number of atoms in the known universe. The twenty-six letters of the English alphabet are combined to create words, and those words are then manipulated to create all the thoughts and expressions that have ever existed in our language.

Music has **seven letters,** writing has **twenty-six** notes.

Joseph Joubert

In his classic 1965 book *The Act of Creation*, Arthur Koestler called the dynamic interaction between two normally distinct frames of reference *bisociation*. According to Koestler, all creative thought is bisociational, and insight is the impulse to bring two things together. The creative and inventive power of imagination is to imagine new combinations of one object in another context. Koestler's central metaphor is that a person working in a particular field is like an ant crawling around a two-dimensional plane. Everything the ant does and experiences happens on that particular plane. The ant has built-in and learned mechanisms for staying on the plane, but when it encounters another intersecting plane (a building, for instance) the ant can crawl up into another frame of reference.[2]

Neither the poet's words nor the inventor's things have any remarkable properties of their own.
They are everyday works and things.
It is the **juxtaposition** of them which is new.

David Pye

In business, many radical innovations have come about when finite elements from very different worlds were brought together. One of Sam Walton's fundamental breakthroughs at Wal-Mart emerged when he took the cash register and connected it to a database. This changed the face of retailing. Suddenly, everything on his shelves was trackable with minimal human intervention because he connected two things. Walton's idea eventually led to Wal-Mart turning over $130 billion a year globally—close to the GDP of Greece.

Art, science, and business are filled with examples of **intersecting** planes.

Alan Kay is one of the inventors of the Smalltalk programming language, a father of the idea of Object Oriented Programming. He is the visionary behind the laptop computer and the architect of the modern windowing graphical user interface. He is an Apple fellow, a Disney fellow, and a professional musician. He is also best known for saying, "The best way to predict the future is to invent it." Kay stresses the importance of being able to connect finite elements from many planes to the problem you're working on:

> Of course you can have quite a bit of imagination walking around the flat plane. You can imagine things before you've seen them on the flat plane. And you can imagine things that might be there without realizing that you're limiting your context. Any art, such as music composition or serious writing, is trying to get multiple planes all at the same time without being too obvious about it. You try to get some balance between technique and art. Let the art rule, but the more technique you can bring into it without killing the art, the better the total effect is. That's partly a skill, but if you have tendencies to minimalism, it helps.[3]

Kay believes that most really good imagings are analogies. If a person doesn't have a lot of knowledge, she won't find a lot of cross-contexts. An individual without a lot of experience can't imagine anything beyond the plane he is on. Kay also believes that the capacity to recognize good ideas is critical. Experience and intuition provide the gut response that distinguishes combinations that work from those that don't. Letting your imagination make combinations is like taking a trip to the flea market. "It's an incredible experience to see how much junk there is in the world ... Most of the ideas are junk."[4] But then again, all it takes is one pearl amidst the ocean of sand to make an enormous difference.

The Vivid Connection

In the Imagination Economy the goal is to create products and services that connect to what's important to customers. This concept is familiar to marketers, but it is useful in other areas as well. For the creators of the economy, the more access they have to a wide range of connections, the richer their imaginative ideas can be.

3. Emotion: Responding to the Mind's Theater

Mental imagery is deeply connected to emotion. Powerful images such as the attack on the World Trade Center or the birth of a child instantly evoke a forceful response. The flow of mental images continuously establishes emotional context and inner dialogue.

One reason images produce such strong emotions is that the cerebral cortex has direct connections to the limbic system—the part of the brain that manages feeling. What we see in the mind's theater determines what we feel. Imagination very quickly becomes sensed reality.

Marketers have a keen sense of how to stir the emotions in fifteen seconds or gain impact through a forceful image. Benetton continues to create an international buzz with its United Colors of Benetton ad campaign, which has in the past displayed photos of people dying of AIDS. Its 2001 campaign revolved around volunteering and features real-life volunteers in lurid situations: Nelson Gomez, who distributes condoms to prostitutes in Guatemala; William Huveso, who works against gang violence in Salvador; and Sarah Leval, who helps disabled children in Afghanistan. The photographs and situations are authentic, moving, and haunting.

Emotion is both an entry point to, and a result of, imagination. Emotion provides the power with which the imagination creates felt experiences, lasting impressions. The experiences of the imagination are sparks from connections between different planes of reference— the feeling of insight when you have an intellectual breakthrough, the satisfaction when you get a joke, the sense of profoundness when you understand and appreciate aesthetic beauty. Images drive feelings. Feelings drive imagination. This creates the power of the experience.

Imagination is closely intertwined with feelings.
The images we see in our mind,
what other images we connect them to,
and how we interpret them,
create a felt reality.

Emotional Exercise
Imagine opening your wallet and
unexpectedly discovering a thick wad of $100 bills.

The Drive of Emotion

Emotions are an important part of any creative work. When you ask creative people why they do what they do, they usually say it comes from a desire to undertake something for the sheer pleasure of it rather than for any prize or compensation. This internal motivation is passion. Without passion, how could the poor artist continue to dream, the entrepreneur to work eighty-hour weeks, or the archaeologist to travel to impossible dig sites?

Finding Your Passion

Passion makes a person hungry for new ideas and experiences. Without the desire to penetrate, explore, unravel, contribute, and tinker, the imaginative mind would not, and could not, elevate itself to new heights.

Mike McCue, CEO and co-founder of Tellme Networks, a California Internet-based telephone portal, puts it this way: "Do what you love to do, and surround yourself with people who also love to do that thing and who are full of talent. If you do that, you can build a great business, you can build a big business, or you can build a small business. But you will be passionate about it, and you will be innovative as a result."[5] McCue's employees and investors remark that his spirit is contagious and that his meetings make you feel good about yourself.

Passion is what drives us to shatter the invisible barriers that dominate the field of human endeavor. In 1903, the *Times* reported that machines heavier than air could not possibly fly; at the same time, the U.S. government was spending $600,000 to demonstrate scientifically and irrevocably that motorized air travel was impossible. When people believe they can make something happen, when they are passionate about a personal core truth, ideas and dreams move from the realm of fantasy to become possible. Truth forwards possibility and enables imaginative energy to continue to circulate. Douglas J. Cardinal believes

we are magical beings, as human beings, because we have this power of creativity.
No other beings on this planet have this gift because their patterns of existence are
set, and just as a deer is always a deer, a bear can only be a bear, a fish only a fish.
But we can re-create ourselves and create the tools to be anything we want—faster
than a cheetah, fly higher than a bird, stronger than an elephant. We're not limited.
All we have to do is declare our intention powerfully and keep our word, not operating on reason but on a total commitment, and we make our vision happen.[6]

Communications and public relations specialist Maureen O'Donnell puts it simply and eloquently: "Imagination is passion supported by courage."[7]

What is your truth?

4. Interpretation: Deriving Understanding and Meaning

The mind's inner theater not only makes representations of objects and abstractions, establishes connections between them, and sparks emotional responses to them; it also infuses them with an underlying sense of meaning. Steven Pinker calls this *mentalese*—the inner language by which we create a sense of how things work.[8] We each devise our own mentalese, with its own syntax and sense of logic and feeling, to fit things together. The abstract images you see in your mind enable it to create pictures, maps, and charts of the way the world works.

You've probably never seen an atom, but you have a sense of the size of one, what it consists of. You've probably never seen your entire business in action either; whether you're part of a home business or a multinational, there are simply too many aspects to experience in a single sweep of vision. Mentalese fills in where there are gaps and creates an abstract model that does its best to reflect reality. The imagination is working continuously to establish meaning.

The capacity to make sense of representations and connections is our inner language of mentalese. The imagination organizes experience into meaningful contexts.

Interpretation Exercise
Imagine the essence of a $10 bill without linking it to purchasing a product or service.
What do the connected concepts of worth, exchange, and money mean to you?

The Value Chain
of Understanding

The language of imagination creates the representations and connections that make sense of experience by adding meaning and context through the "value chain of understanding." The chain begins with what we are incessantly exposed to: *noise*. As the mind seeks to find meaning, it processes *noise* into *data*, then into *information*, then *knowledge*, and finally *wisdom*. Increased understanding—a move to the next link in the value chain—comes about by the imagination establishing an increased number of connections and contexts. The interpretation becomes more personal and sophisticated—and more valuable—as it approaches wisdom. The more contexts, connections, and education your imagination has to draw from, the more able it is to discriminate between noise and data, to put data into a useful context that converts it into information, and to connect the information with practical experiences, which leads to knowledge and personal wisdom.

In *The Experience Economy*, Joseph B. Pine, James H. Cilmore, and Joseph B. Pine II create a commercial analogy for the value chain of understanding. It is organized this way: *commodities* (value resides in the raw materials), *products* (value moves to tangible things), *services* (value is found in activities), *experiences* (value is derived from the time you share with your customers), and *transformations* (value is the demonstrated outcome the customer realizes).[9] In the Imagination Economy the goal is to develop products and information that lead to customer insight—or, to use Gilmore and Pine's terminology, experiences and transformations. Imagination has a natural desire to understand and interpret, and the more thoughtfully the experience is designed and presented, the more likely it will be to capture the imagination of the customer along the entire value chain of understanding.

Music is noise submitted to order by wisdom.

Giacomo Puccini

Data Is Not Information

Though we use the terms interchangeably in the context of business, they in fact mean very different things. *Data* refers to the raw elements that our brains are bombarded with—facts, figures, conversations, articles, sound bites, factoids. We obtain data from sources as varied as electronic and print media, formal meetings, and water-cooler conversations. Data surrounds and envelops us. It is easy to find but has little value unless placed within a larger context.

Information Is the Start of Meaning

Peter Drucker tells us that information "is data endowed with relationships."[10] Data becomes information when it is organized and placed in context for the intended users. A list of stock prices exists as raw data until it is sorted into useful information about the stocks we own. The key to providing good information is to organize and present data in contexts that add value to the customer's experience.

Basic Categories of Information Organization

magnitude – ranked by size, cost, distance, whatever is important
time – duration or date
number – sequences
alphabet – the artificial but easy-to-access arrangement by letters
location – identifying on a map or in a qualitative arrangement
category – color, shape, demographic
randomness – no arrangement other than haphazard

Amazon.com creates enormous value by organizing its product database into a web of relationships. Consider a certain book and you are able to look at a range of reviews, a list of books that have been bought by customers who liked the book you are considering, links based on themes, and even links to enable you to purchase a used copy of the book. Amazon.com is not so much a bookseller as a tool to enable purchasing decisions.

We naturally gravitate to articles, charts, and photographs that present information we consider relevant to our lives. Each of us both consumes and produces information. To stimulate the imagination we need to make sense of the data in front of us as well as present data to others so as to help them make purchasing decisions *and* enliven their experience.

Knowledge Is Personal

Unlike data and information, knowledge is not easily digitized, copied, and distributed. Knowledge emerges through personal interactions with information. A business-school grad may have digested a great deal of textbook information about marketing, but she will have little direct knowledge until she launches and grows a product line of her own, and sees how the information she has learned meshes with her actual experience. The mechanisms that convert information into knowledge are conversations, stories, experimentation and improvisation, trial and error, and connecting to other experiences.

As knowledge becomes deeper and more personal, it is the imagination that takes it through the processes of representation, making connections, establishing a mental map of relationships, interrelating memories and feelings, and using the language of mentality, which lies beyond words, to establish context. And because of the restless nature of imagination, our knowledge builds upon itself, establishes more connections, and generates further knowledge. A person who is informed about building a Web site can follow a template and place in content, but one who is deeply knowledgeable about Web creation can build general solutions.

Wisdom Is Private and Intangible

Defining *wisdom* presents us with the same problems as defining *imagination*: we have a sense of what it is, but delineating it is difficult. Wisdom can't be easily shared. We create our own wisdom through introspection, musing, contemplation, and imagining. Wisdom has qualities in common with good sense, insight, and judiciousness, but it also has a tolerance for ambiguity. Wisdom grows through the conversations and conscious interplay of imagination.

You can tell whether a man is **clever** by his **answers**. You can tell whether a man is **wise** by his **questions**.

Naguib Mahfouz

The Imagination
at Play

As part of its interpretive aspect, imagination can, if given permission, make things up in the absence of facts—often at lightning speed. Imagination interprets the ambiguous by filling in apparent gaps or making the flat three-dimensional. This ability to fluidly interpret allows imagination to thread together events and create a sense of meaning in what we see. The imagination's interpretation then becomes more real than the lived experience, as it creates the context in which we view events.

Imagination really shines when it goes beyond intellectual interpretation. Imagination spends time uncovering what may be *behind* a particular question. Imagination looks *into* a painting and *feels* the color rather than staying close to the details, the tangible. Imagination thrives on information that is fleeting, inconsistent, ephemeral, ambiguous. Imagination likes to sit on details that don't jibe with other facts, and revels in the space between the details. Imagination is relaxed, open, leisurely, and playful, willing to explore without knowing what it is looking for.

For imagination, ignorance and confusion are the ground, even the promise, from which understanding and invention may spring. Imagination loves to visit the worlds of myth, fantasy, and dreams, and is willing to take seriously hunches, concerns, and intuition, without needing a rationale to justify them. The search for meaning through the invention of stories is hard-wired into our brains.

Our experience of, and reaction to, an imaginative work is most powerful when its creator's voice speaks directly to us. This occurs when the creator has successfully connected with some inner personal truth and expressed his authentic voice through the creative medium. Works in this self-expressive mode invoke in the observer the truth of his own voice, even though the activity is more passive than active. In this way, imagination might be considered the voice of the soul. In *Care of the Soul*, Thomas Moore expresses the notion eloquently: "Soul lies midway between understanding and unconsciousness, and its instrument is neither the mind nor the body, but the imagination."[11]

Two Modes of Thinking

The World of the Undermind

The idea of thinking as a deliberate, conscious act—as the sole way to learn and make decisions—might seem natural and self-evident. But modern cognitive research tells us that the brain has different types of intelligence, which simultaneously process information in different ways, at different rates, and at several levels of organization. Deliberate, conscious thinking is only one color in the mind's rich palette.

English psychologist Guy Claxton has introduced the notion of the "undermind," a part of the psyche that learns, processes information, makes intuitive leaps, identifies patterns, and comes to decisions well below the level of conscious, deliberate awareness.[12] This undermind is not the same as the unconscious mind identified by Freud; rather, it is unconscious *intelligence*, with the capacity for generating images, absorbing information, making connections, and originating feelings.

**Nothing can be in me,
that is, in my mind,
of which I am not conscious ...
I think, therefore I am ...**

René Descartes

Cogito ergo spud.
I think, therefore I yam.

Popeye

Each of us is familiar with the rhythms of the undermind. The solution to a nagging problem pops into your head in the shower. You un-busy yourself with a walk to let ideas percolate through your subconscious, and you feel something heating up in your mental furnace. You have to immediately jot down or sketch an emerged idea or risk it fading away like a dream. We know to wait for inspiration rather than press for it.

The undermind goes along at its own pace. It tolerates ambiguity and complexity. It derives meaning from abstraction, and is able to detect, learn from, and apply patterns of information that the deliberate, conscious mind cannot even see, let alone register and recall. Simply by attending and responding to a situation without consciously thinking about it, your undermind can detect complex patterns of information.

Stories telling of solutions that come in a flash—such as the one about Newton devising his theory of gravity after an apple fell on his head—are misleading in that they emphasize the sudden realization of ideas that fit in just the right way. But ideas come and go according to your focus. An accountant is unlikely to have an insight into how to optimize the fluid flow of a chemical plant; nor is a physician likely to have insight into the nature of anti-aliasing on a computer monitor. Each person's imagination, and therefore his undermind, is occupied with the ideas that are most relevant to his profession, art, or craft.

The undermind is largely underrepresented in mental maps. Business tends to overlook it entirely, instead regarding conscious, articulate understanding as the exclusive foundation for action, and logical thought as the sole problem-solving tool. Claxton calls this the *deliberate mode*. He describes its ways of working and how it is emphasized in everyday life and in education, from elementary to business school, as the default way of operating.[13]

The Deliberate Mode

The world of deliberate thinking—the dominant modus operandi in business—prefers explanation to observation. It focuses on *how* over *why*. In deliberate mode it's vital to be able to explain what you are doing, but if the "always-show-that-you're-busy" approach becomes the default mode of the mind, it can suppress other ways of knowing.

The deliberate mode prefers unambiguous situations. It also sees problems as inherent features of situations. When tackling a problem, it treats it as a collection of nameable parts. The idea that the way a situation is perceived or "framed" contributes to the problem does not come naturally to the deliberate mode. It tends to be suspicious of what it sees as the slippery and evocative world of metaphor, allusion, and imagery. There is little room for poetry in business. The continuous sense of being under time pressure, of having to stay focused, perpetually seeking solutions and quickly providing answers, soon becomes the only way we know how to operate.

The deliberate mode of thinking operates by:

Figuring Things Out: The deliberate mode weighs pros and cons, develops decision matrices bound by measurable criteria, talks things through with colleagues to develop logical and consistent stories, draws flow charts and equations, and formulates sales pitches.

Determining Solutions: Rather than ask questions, the deliberate mode treats unwanted and inconvenient conditions as problems to be fixed. It treats the world like a machine in which complex symptoms, like changing market conditions, staff morale, and product development, are technical malfunctions to be solved by hitting the hammer in just the right place.

Maintaining a Sense of Urgency: In business there are never enough resources, people, money, and above all, time. Deliberate-mode thinking likes to have things sorted out quickly and gets irritable if confusion reigns. If you're not up on the latest market trends and changes in the competitive landscape, you're not a serious contender.

Operating on Clock Time: The deliberate mode operates at the speed at which language can be received, processed, and produced. If you slow down words or speed them up too much, communication becomes impossible. The business mode likes to maintain a pace of thinking that is controlled and deliberate rather than spontaneous.

Valuing Precision: Business, like science, mathematics, and accounting, works with propositions composed of clearly defined symbols, where every term is agreed upon and complete. A financial model of projected yearly revenue and operating expenses provides a complete picture of an organization based on probability, and is taken more seriously than a vision based on possibility.

Seeking Clarity: The deliberate mode abhors confusion. Because business focuses on plans, it prefers to move along the well-lit path from problem to solution, holding on to the mental handrail every step of the way.

Exploring the
Unknown World

It could be said that each of us lives in three worlds.

The first is the world we know that we know. It is vast, filled with a lifetime of experiences. It could be described as the combination of all the data, information, knowledge, and wisdom you are aware you hold within you. It is the ability to look at a balance sheet and connect to a clear image of a business's financial health. This is the stuff you know, and you know you know it.

The mind loves the **unknown.** It loves images whose meaning is **unknown**, since the meaning of the mind itself is **unknown.**

René Magritte

Then there is what you know you *don't* know. This domain encompasses solutions to the problems you've defined; for example, what you need to do to make your products less expensive or more efficient. This world includes that mathematical formula which lies just outside your grasp, the one you know would solve your problem; you haven't discovered it yet, but you're fairly certain you'll be able to figure it out. This is the zone we typically travel to when we don our imaginative "hat," the part of imagination that speaks mostly in logical "if … then" statements. Though the resulting innovations can be imaginative, and insights can occur in sudden jumps, the overall process is primarily linear.

You are lost the instant you know what the result is.

Juan Gris

Finally, there is what you don't know that you don't know. This is the world outside your current knowledge, experience, understanding, and awareness—essentially, the endless universe. Imagine the world of subatomic particles that phase in and out of existence, the hundred thousand nutrinos that pass through each square centimeter of us every second; the five thousand languages spoken on earth; known and unknown mathematical equations; the nature of time; everything posted on the Internet that you have never read—the scope of the unknown is beyond words.

Although the realm of imagination encompasses this unknown world, we tend to overlook it, preferring to stay within the bounds of our comfort, closer to what we know. We structure much of business and our personal lives this way—around the known, protected from what lies outside our conscious realities. But if we fail to expand outside the familiar world, we restrict the power of possibility. By believing that something is within the realm of the possible, we give ourselves the power to create it.

Do not go where the path may lead, go instead where there is no path and leave a trail.

Ralph Waldo Emerson

Zen wisdom teaches us about the power of the beginner's mind. Habitually, we put labels on things—a coffee cup, a lamp, cash; and in labeling them, we think we know them. However, removing the labels and putting yourself into the frame of mind of the unknown is to experience the world without the straitjacket of words, to be free to try out some new concepts. The point is to be open to the idea that the context of your life is infinitely larger than you are consciously aware of. In order to make all the worlds of the imagination part of our lives and our work, we must be willing to explore unfamiliar places in unfamiliar ways, and trust in the value of what we will find. You can never get to know someone if you leave him standing on the doorstep. You must invite him in for a chat.

The Map Is Not the Territory

Unfortunately, because of their perceived contradictory nature it is rare that the many aspects of imagination are combined in the business world. Imagination can appear to be counterproductive to the business mind. The very essence of imagination makes it impossible to contain and define—a perceived drawback in a business climate that favors stability and predictability. But it seems business might be better served by making room for imagination. After all, the world was flat only until we headed out to sea.

imag·i·na·tion \e-maja'na-shen

1: an act or process of forming a conscious idea or mental image of something never before wholly perceived in reality by the imaginer (as through a synthesis of remembered elements of previous sensory experiences or ideas as modified by unconscious mechanisms of defense); *also:* the ability or gift of forming such conscious ideas or mental images esp. for the purposes of artistic or intellectual creation. **2a:** creative ability: genius **2b:** the ability to confront and deal with a problem: resourcefulness **3:** a plotting or scheming esp. of evil: plot **4a:** a mental image, conception, or notion formed by the action of imagination **4b:** a creation of the mind: esp. an idealized or poetic creation **4c:** fanciful or empty assumption **5:** popular or traditional belief: usual or accepted conception.[14]

What Imagination Values

Imagination values experiences. It is driven toward insight, pleasure, and connection. Imagination values freedom and exploration, the big idea and possibility, play and energy, ambiguity and realization.

The Languages of Imagination

Imagination converses through many forms of mental representation, imagery, poetry, music, allusion, metaphor, simile, and abstraction. Imagination "gets" modern and hears in ways that do not necessarily follow the rules of logic.

Ways Imagination Operates

Imagination operates spontaneously, making connections through random associations, feelings, aesthetics, and a sense of design. It is comfortable with intuition, contemplation, and just plain wandering around without a specific destination.

busi-ness \'biz-nes

1. Purposeful activity: activity directed toward some end. **2**. An activity engaged in as normal, logical or inevitable and usually engaged in for an extended period of time. Role. Function. **3a**. An activity engaged in toward an immediate, specific end and usually extending over a limited period of time: Task. Chore. Mission. Assignment. **3b**. A usually commercial or mercantile activity customarily engaged in as a means of livelihood and typically involving some independence of judgment and power of decision and sometimes contrasted with the arts or professions. **4a**. A situation. Matter. **b**. A difficult or complicated matter. Project **5**. Something that is so put together as to be not easily classified or felt.[15]

What Business Values

Business values what sustains and fosters economic activity, including profits, results, achievement, growth, shareholder value, market share, and stability.

The Languages of Business

Business prefers explicit and well-defined discrete elements and symbols, found in spreadsheets and PowerPoint presentations, as well as in stories.

Ways Business Thinking Operates

Business tends to prefer operating through deliberate and conscious logical analysis. Business needs to tell stories, make arguments, and create equations that support decisions and rely on logic as their essential tool.

is irresponsible.

doesn't come naturally.

doesn't get you anywhere.

is high-energy.

can't be serious.

has no practical application.

is a waste of time.

Imagination

is expensive.

is only for the weird.

is unproductive.

is something that you do away from work.

belongs in the playground.

Business

kills imagination.

is only about making money.

is more important than imagination.

is no fun.

requires complete control.

success means continually increasing profits.

is the center of the world.

has to be serious.

is productive.

is responsible.

inspires invention.

defines reality.

Can you
come out
to play?

Innovation

is the child
of imagination and
business.

What inspires you?

1.

2.

3.

4.

5.

History Anyone?

Aristotle called the imagination **phantasia** and believed it was the mind's inner theater, playing an essential role in all forms of thinking. **"The soul never thinks without a mental image,"** he wrote. Aristotle also believed another mental organ, called the **sensus communis**, brought the perceptions of sight, scent, taste, hearing, and feeling into a single integrated impression. If the mind received impressions from what was around the body, it used the **sensus communis**; if the mind created impressions independently through daydreaming, it used the **phantasia**. In either case the mind generated **phantasma**—mental images.

Medieval anatomists located Aristotle's **sensus communis** at the front of the brain's first ventricle and the **phantasia** at the rear second ventricle. They surmised that as nerve impulses flowed from various sense organs, the **sensus communis** consolidated the resulting impressions, then passed them back to the rear ventricles, where they could be used in thought or stored in memory. The anatomists thought this process of passing impressions back and forth between various mental holding areas enabled the mind to freely and idiosyncratically create new images. Whereas all the brain's other faculties were governed by reality and constrained by the laws of logic, the tossing of sensory data back and forth enabled the imagination to retrieve images from memory or create fresh ones never experienced in reality.

For Aristotle and other early Greek thinkers, **inspiration was divine**, literally breathed into one's soul by the gods or the nine Muses, and **imagination had no special connection to inventiveness or creativity.** The medieval anatomists were the first to try to explain how the mind might operate in terms other than divine intervention.

Timeline of Imagination

Plato: Everything is becoming, nothing is. ⓥ Aristotle: Such stuff as dreams are made of. ⓥ Boethius: A person is an individual substance of rational nature. ⓥ St. Thomas Aquinas: The soul is known by its acts. ⓥ Sir Francis Bacon: Words are but the images of matter. To fall in love with them is to fall in love with a picture. ⓥ René Descartes: I think, therefore I am. ⓥ Søren Kierkegaard: The supreme paradox of all thought is the attempt to discover something that thought cannot think.

A leech has about 350 neurons, an octopus about 300 million, and the human brain 100 billion.

Since each neuron has from 1,000 to 10,000 synapses connecting it with other neurons, the total number of connections in the human cerebral cortex is estimated to be about 240 trillion.

(About 5 billion blades of grass cover a football field.)

Imagination doesn't actually exist in three-dimensional space, but it creates the experience of three-dimensional space. Mental images appear from somewhere, play out in your mental theater, and then go somewhere else.

What form do the images take *before* they enter consciousness?

What happens to images *after* they leave conscious attention?

Where do dream images come from?

Where do your thoughts reside?

How does your mind come up with solutions and then inject them into consciousness?

Watching your imagination leads to the essential conundrum:
how can we possibly step outside our imagination to look into it?

In 1880, Sir Frances Galton, a cousin of Charles Darwin, set up a laboratory in South Kensington, London, to measure people's performance on a variety of psychophysical tasks, such as sensitivity to musical pitch. In 1905, French psychologists Alfred Binet and Théodore Simon developed tests to measure judgment, comprehension, and reasoning, in order to determine placement of children in various Parisian schools. A Stanford University psychologist, Lewis Terman, revised the Binet-Simon Scale to create the Stanford-Binet Test in 1916. Revised frequently, the Stanford-Binet is still in use. This test, and others like it, assign an intelligence quotient, or IQ. Originally calculated as the ratio of mental age to physical age, psychological tests are now usually measured by statistical distributions.

Since Binet formulated the I.Q test, psychologists have devised a spectrum of profiles and personality assessments—including the International Personality Item Pool, the popular Myers-Briggs, and the Keirsey Temperament sorter-in an attempt to categorize, analyze, and measure every aspect of human character and mental capability. Among them are creativity tests. They pose questions like these:

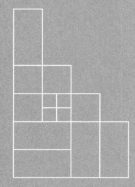

1. How many four-sided figures can you find in this diagram?
2. Interpret the sentence 90 = D. in a R. A.
3. If two ladybugs crawl in opposite directions for three inches, turn right, and then crawl an additional four inches, what is the distance between them?
4. Invent twenty different uses for a brick.

It's curiously disheartening to take such tests, because the very act of setting a measurement puts constraints on the imagination. These tests are less revealing about imagination than they are unsatisfying. In trying to capture imagination through a series of questions, they only faintly detect the shadow of creative capability. Creativity assessment tests typically aim to measure mental flexibility, originality, elaboration, and resistance to closure.

Rules: 1. Make fewer

2. Break more   3. Forget the rest

Tell yourself a story.
> *Be present.*

Converse with your imagination.
> *Make up new words.*

Focus on truth and beauty.
> *Try different questions.*

Build bridges.
> *Invent new rules.*

Un-pop the cork.
> *Unpack the feelings.*

Let it flow.
> *Be extravagant.*

Take a random walk.
> *Find out what's missing.*

What could you do?

Where is the soul of your business?

What is the business of your soul?

Do you have a burning passion?

4

Measuring
the
Intangible

Business and imagination
    operate in different worlds.
    The challenge is to find ways
        to bring together successfully
an expansive sense of possibility
        with the pressing need for order,
results, and profit.

The Tangible

It's no surprise that business values what it can measure. The oldest business rule in the book is to make money; and to make money, you need to know how money comes in and where it goes out, the amount of each, and what the difference is. Since double-entry accounting was invented in Renaissance Italy, business has developed a wealth of indicators to describe the overall health and performance of a company and its employees. Financial metrics pinpoint everything from inventory and cash flow to bottom-line results. Customer measurements track market share, trends, and overall satisfaction. Sales reports tally identified leads, probable deals, and closed sales. Human Resources assesses company turnover, employee satisfaction, absenteeism, salaries, and a host of other factors.

Every business sector has unique and specialized ways of tracking the flow of activities that lead toward its goals. Web statistics, for example, have grown from a simple "number of hits" metric to a sophisticated science that traces everything from number of unique visits to average duration of a visit and the visualization of customers' journeys through a site. These measurements not only provide essential feedback on how to improve a customer's experience by, for example, simplifying a purchase transaction, but they also establish benchmarks for the site's value. The advertising rate card is directly correlated to the number of people who will see the site, how long they use it, and what demographic they represent.

Part of the goal of metrics is to tell a company's story. Employee satisfaction describes the state of the company's culture. Stock price divulges the market's assessment of future performance. But the mother of all measurements, common to every organization and the very foundation of commerce, is the simplest—the measure of profit and loss:

ROI = NET INCOME / OWNER EQUITY

Invest $100, make $120, and the return on investment is $20, or 20 percent. The bigger the number, the better. Organizations make every effort to maximize their returns, tracking as many relevant factors as possible in order to decrease costs and increase income. But trying to measure the intangible with the usual metrics of commerce leads to assessments that just feel wrong or miss the point, like assessing a suit jacket primarily by how much it weighs.

The debt we owe to imagination is incalculable.

Carl Jung

Eight hundred years ago, in medieval Europe, a patron of the arts would commission a work and have a formal contract drawn up with the artist. The contract described the dimensions of the painting, the type of wood to be used as a base, the date the painting was to be delivered, where it was to be prepared, and who would prepare it. The most detailed part of the contract focused on the pigment. Pigments were remarkably expensive and derived from all kinds of objects— roots, berries, crushed minerals, seeds, and gold—many of which were rare and needed to be imported from Africa or Asia. The patron and the artist also agreed upon the subject matter and how much area of the painting each color would cover. However, the composition, the aesthetic, the expression—the *art,* in other words—was accorded minimal attention and value in the contract. For medieval patrons a painting was more about demonstrating wealth and patronage—usually religious—than artistic appreciation.

Times have changed. Just over a century ago Vincent Van Gogh painted the *Portrait of Dr. Gachet* with readily available oil paints on a regular canvas while living in poverty. The painting was auctioned at Christie's in New York in 1990 for $75 million, the highest amount paid for any work of art to date. Value is no longer contained in the raw materials but in what the work means and represents, the feelings it delivers. In the case of the *Portrait of Dr. Gachet*, the painting has value because of its rarity; it is, after all, one of a kind, and there was only one Van Gogh.

So how do you measure imagination? How do you size up the value of ideas? What are the metrics for quantifying a company's ongoing capability to generate products and services that will engage its customer base? How can you measure a company's sense of possibility, vision, or hope for the future?

THE FIVE STRATEGIC ARTS

The situation gives rise
to measurements.
Measurements give rise
to estimates.
Estimates give rise
to analysis.
Analysis gives rise
to balancing.
Balancing gives rise
to triumph.

Sun Tzu

In the Imagination Economy the value of the new range of businesses, products, and services lies not only in the thought and expertise people bring to the situation, but in the unseen potential that can only be felt through the active imagination. Beyond accepted, even inventive, monetary metrics, business needs to extend more credence to descriptive and qualitative assessments. Something every successful entrepreneur knows is how to fly by the seat of her pants on a hunch or feeling. Even if all your accountants can prove you're headed for certain failure, sometimes that intuitive place of knowing holds more power and promise than any spreadsheet ever could.

The Value of Ideas

In an economy shaped by intellectual property, it's vital to know the value of intangibles. According to John Howkins, author of *The Creative Economy*, about 6 percent of the total US$30 trillion global economy—approximately US$2.2 trillion—is directly responsible for producing creative content. Fifteen industries—from film production to R & D—contribute to this economy.[1] This may seem a small portion of the entire economy, but its impact mustn't be underestimated. Just as capital- and machinery-intensive industries—automobiles, chemicals, and steel—drove growth in the 1950s and 1960s, the creative industries are the growth engines of today. And with a growth rate of 6 percent, double the global economy's 3 percent rate, these industries will have a growing impact.

The problem with valuing intangibles is that it requires subjective judgment, something accountants tend to despise. In 2001, *Business Week* and Interbrand went through an exhaustive process to rank the top one hundred global brands, measuring them the way analysts value other assets: by future earnings. It was no surprise which brands topped the list. But what was surprising was the size of their value. Coca-Cola's brand was valued at almost $70 billion. Others that topped the list were: Microsoft at $65 billion, IBM at $52 billion, G.E. at $42 billion, and Nokia at $35 billion. Keep in mind that this does not include any physical assets, such as manufacturing plants or distribution infrastructure; it includes only patents, customer lists, goodwill, and what the market collectively agrees is the brand.

Creative Economy by Industry

Sector	Global Market	U.S. Market
Advertising	45	20
Architecture	40	17
Arts	9	4
Crafts	20	2
Design	140	50
Fashion	12	5
Film	57	17
Music	70	25
Performing Arts	40	7
Publishing	506	137
R & D	545	243
Software	489	325
Toys and Games	55	21
TV and Radio	195	82
Video Games	17	5
		$US Billion

Source: Howkins, The Creative Economy, 2001.

Few concepts in business are as elusive and powerful as the *brand*. In a typical grocery store there are thousands of brands to choose from. Years ago a brand was little more than a product line with certain characteristics that fit the preferences of a specific consumer group. Today the concept of the *brand* has evolved into an image that is infused with meaning and associated with a certain lifestyle.

A brand does not exist anywhere except in the collective consciousness of producers and consumers, and in brand character documents. It possesses abstract qualities and emotional connections that go well beyond the products and services it represents. With Nike the connection is with sports, fitness, and the exhilaration of winning. Starbucks is associated with the experience of coffee as an oasis of pleasure and decadence in a rushed day. In the case of Apple and the iMac the connection is with individual empowerment: the common person can easily be more industrious, creative, and fashionably computer savvy. Patagonia is linked with finding solutions to the global environmental crisis and keeping the planet healthy while maintaining a solid personal relationship with nature.

Brand management has become an art, and an increasingly important part of business. Branding is the creation, care, and fostering of an image, a promise of or commitment to a level of quality, a representation of a set of intangibles that the customer can aspire to. Car safety: think Volvo. European excitement: it's a Maserati. Ostentatious road presence: it could only be Hummer.

Brand management has evolved from overseeing products' features and performance to managing image through advertising and lifestyle associations. The latter can be measured through a host of psychographic profiles and market share data. But as the economy shifts into a mode characterized by stronger connections, the brand is becoming an ever more important part of the organization, incorporating ideas that are not only about advertising and marketing but about leadership, authenticity, and the human spirit.

Tom Peters, in *Brand You*, says that individuals are brands. He promotes writing personal mission statements, clarifying and promoting what you value, and giving the world a clear picture of who you are.

In the Imagination Economy the measurement of intangibles requires the inclusion of *real* intangibles—like spark, inspiration, unseen potential, history, feelings, values, and connections. Most accepted metrics address only one aspect of imagination, that is, the act of representation. Through complex thinking and elaborate formulations we can tangibly represent something as intangible as a brand by assigning a monetary value to some of its components. But the other aspects of imagination that in the past have gone unmeasured—emotion, connection, and meaning—are growing, and represent a significant value in today's economy.

Historically, business may have paid little attention to these more vague aspects of imagination. But the increasing value assigned to them by our markets, our customers, and our employees tells us it's time to make room for the fuzzy stuff in our evaluation processes. This is not to suggest that we begin assigning monetary value to the intensity of emotional response. Rather, it is a call to seriously consider these more nebulous and qualitative concepts alongside traditional metrics.

Kevin Roberts, CEO, Saatchi & Saatchi, describes what is happening to the brand as an evolution into the *trustmark*. Because consumers nowadays are more savvy, suspicious, and discriminating, and everyone has access to massive amounts of information about any organization, companies need to be authentic. "We all know what a trademark is," Roberts says.

It's what differentiates. It's a distinctive name, symbol, model, or design that legally identifies a company or its products. But what's a trustmark? A trustmark is a distinctive name or symbol that emotionally binds a company with the desires and aspirations of its customers. It's an emotional connection, and it's bigger and more powerful than the uses that we traditionally associate with a trademark.[2]

Brands that are in tune with the Imagination Economy are smart and savvy. They wow and impress the customer, get his attention, amuse and inspire him, and capture his imagination. But beyond all the smart, slick marketing talk needs to be a core of real substance—a message, a value, an ideology, a company that connects to something solid and truthful, not just a big pink puff of candy floss. Today's consumers won't buy illusions any more. It's time to get real.

What does your business **stand for**?

Every business has a brand or trustmark. From small Web-page production companies to the restaurant down the street, each has a reason for being and presents an image to its customers and partners. But the evolution of a strong brand does not happen of its own accord. Whether or not a company is large enough to support brand managers, each organization has the opportunity to formulate the intangible brand character that creates a lasting and evocative image in the customer's imagination. And brand character has now become more than just a marketing tool: it is an expression of the company's vision, of what it really stands for. The brand is the focus of the organization's efforts to provide value to the customer and reflect employees' core values.

Brands are more and more being measured by intangible qualities: longevity, authenticity, self-awareness, the ability to tap into emotions, a capacity to reinvent categories, relevancy, and how well the brand and the trustmark can travel through a target population. These aspects are useful not only as indicators of the effectiveness of the brand, but as tools to paint a picture of what the organization stands for and how it presents itself. Measuring the intangible is now less about product functionality and performance and more about spirit. The backlash embodied by Naomi Klein's book *No Logo* is a response to the brand bullies, the large organizations that intentionally manipulate their message while dealing in unfair trade—being inauthentic. Anti-globalization, the voice against unfair trade, has become a powerful social force.

Owning Ideas

Few concepts have such a wide influence and are as broadly debated as the ownership of ideas. Proprietorship over intellectual matter has a history that dates back thousands of years, but it has evolved into a subtle and esoteric area of law. The original legal intent behind the protection of intellectual property was to foster creativity, innovation, and competition. However, as the range and content of protected ideas becomes broader, more complex, and increasingly infringes on what once would have been considered publicly accessible, the opportunities for creative expression and the sharing of research and information are being ever more restricted.

Opinions about the ownership of ideas range from support for the public domain, where ideas are free to circulate and benefit humanity, to favoring the private domain, where ideas are protected for the benefit of their creators. In an 1813 letter Thomas Jefferson described the essence of the problem of trying to possess an idea:

If nature has made one thing less susceptible than all others of exclusive property, it is the action of the thinking power called an idea, which an individual may exclusively possess as long as he keeps it to himself; but the moment it is divulged, it forces itself into the possession of everyone … Its peculiar character, too, is that no one possesses the less, because every other possesses the whole of it. He who receives an idea from me, receives instruction himself without lessening mine; as he who lights his taper at mine receives light without darkening me. That ideas should freely spread from one to another over the globe, for the moral and mutual instruction of man, and improvement of his condition, seems to have been peculiarly and benevolently designed by nature, when she made them, like fire, expansible over all space, without lessening their density at any point, and like the air in which we breathe, move and have our physical being, incapable of confinement, or exclusive appropriation. Inventions then cannot, in nature, be a subject of property.[3]

However, recent economic trends have led to the emphasis on intellectual property as a fundamental principle that enables organizations to create and own the expression of their ideas, adding millions to their asset value and holding the innovation potential of their competitors hostage. Intellectual property, or IP, is an artificial construct, which did not exist until governments and the courts invented it.

Intellectual property is generally organized into two categories. The first, industrial property, includes inventions, trademarks, industrial designs, and geographic indications of source. The second category includes copyrights and a wide range of artistic and literary works, such as novels and Web articles, music and painting, architectural works, photographs, drawings, artistic performances, and movies.

What I think we often do is confuse artifacts of the medium with where the creative element is. For instance, a great work of music is not what's written on the page. It's what's heard by the listener or heard in the head of the composer. A great work of literature is not how it is scribed on a page but is the meaning of the words. I think we so very often get distracted and seduced by thinking the interface medium—the way the information, knowledge, wisdom—all of these things up the semantic ladder are transferred from one person to another are what matters. Writing is not about physically writing and reading. It's about how you code the information on one end and how it's interpreted on the other.

Bran Ferren

An Idea by Any Other Name

It's important to note that ideas cannot be copyrighted but their expression can. Ideas live in the realm of imagination and therefore outside legal jurisdiction. The author, however, has to use skill and effort to take the imaginative idea and express it in a specific form or work. From the point of view of commerce, an idea must be useful and actionable. Patent law requires that the creator take an inventive step; without this, no patent is awarded.

Consider an everyday object such as a refrigerator. The mechanical elements—the parts and processes that keep food cold—are patented inventions, which means that competitors can protect their specific manufacturing techniques. Aesthetic elements, such as the design of the handle, the shelves, and the style and appearance of the temperature controls, can be protected as industrial designs. Even the fridge manual is copyrighted.

The explosive growth of patent applications, trademarks, and copyright is a testament to the Imagination Economy, and to the value of the expression of an idea as a competitive tool. If you measure the economy by the growth of intellectual property, there is no downturn.

Intellectual Property

Inventions and Patents

The word *patent* comes from the Latin word meaning "to open" and was used for letters and documents that could be easily opened. The city council of Florence awarded the first recorded patent in 1421 for glass-making. In the 1460s John of Speyer brought one of Germany's printing presses to Venice and filed letters of patent to the council to protect his business. The city council granted him a five-year exclusive contract to publish books, though the writers themselves had no copyright on their work.

Over the next centuries the concept of protection was developed and granted by monarchy, councils, guilds, and enterprising entrepreneurs. The idea was eventually enshrined in law. Modern patent law had its origins in England in 1624 with the Statute of Monopolies that granted awards to "new manner of manufacture." As the concept of intellectual property became more sophisticated, the laws evolved into more useful and focused regulations, and have been described as "the metaphysics of the law where the discussions are, or at least may be, very subtle and refined and sometimes almost evanescent."[4]

An invention is a product or process that provides a new way of doing something or offers a new technical solution to a problem. Inventions are protected by patents, which provide exclusive rights to the owner of the patent. This means that the patented invention cannot be made, used, distributed, or sold without the patent owner's consent. Patent protection is granted for a limited time, usually twenty years from the filing date of the patent application. Once a patent expires, the protection ends and the invention enters the public domain, where it is available for commercial exploitation by others.

PATENT QUALIFICATIONS

1. NOVELTY: Is the idea new? Can a skilled person deduce it from an existing idea?

2. INVENTIVE STEP: Is there a non-obvious discovery?

3. USEFUL: Does it have a use or utility?

Patents not only provide an incentive to individuals by ensuring recognition and material reward; they also enrich the total body of technical knowledge in the world. Patent owners are obliged to publicly disclose details about their inventions, thus providing valuable information for other inventors, as well as inspiration for future generations of researchers and inventors. This leads to further invention and innovation, generating fresh ideas for copyright and patent protection.

The number of patent applications is skyrocketing. According to the World Intellectual Property Organization, the number of patent applications is growing at the rate of 12 percent annually.

The range of patents spans the ultra-technical to the deceptively simple, and even the curious. Patent number US5443036 is a method for exercising a cat. It reads as follows:

> A method for inducing cats to exercise consists of directing a beam of invisible light produced by a hand-held laser apparatus onto the floor or wall or other opaque surface in the vicinity of the cat, then moving the laser so as to cause the bright pattern of light to move in an irregular way fascinating to cats, and to any other animal with a chase instinct.[5]

Patent authors range from corporate giants like IBM, which submits thousands of patent applications each year, to individuals. Technical patents now require armies of review staff to sort through the massive amounts of comparative and related data and to offer judgments. With each new patent, one change, one innovation added to an existing product, gives you the edge that prevents competitors from copying your technique.

Other examples of patents include the simple expression of an idea and how it reframes a problem in a new way. In some cases this may prove to be controversial, as exemplified by the debate surrounding Amazon.com's patent on its 1-Click ordering. As a *New York Times* article by John Schwartz states "Patent has been criticized in the high technology industry as part of a trend that extends property rights to inventions and ideas that critics say do not merit the protection and that squelch innovation."[6]

In the world of Internet innovation, the sharing of ideas has been paramount. A belief widely shared amongst pioneers in the Web community is that the opportunity for developers to build upon the ideas of Internet leaders like Amazon.com is what has made the Internet so amazing in its evolution, what has allowed such exponential growth. From this point of view, ideas are best shared, as they break the ground for further innovation and far-reaching possibilities, all in the name of creating something better. The argument goes that when patenting of small innovations like 1-Click begins, companies will start hoarding their ideas as a means of protection and defense.

On the one hand, this is not difficult to understand when you consider the fate of Netscape and the possible alternative had it registered a few patents in the name of protecting its business. From this perspective, looking after your interests seems the intelligent thing to do, particularly for the small innovator who may not have the massive legal team and revenue source to engage in endless legal battle.

On the other hand, the belief exists that when a company begins to patent these kinds of innovations the entire process becomes cheap, defensive, and closed. Opportunities for sharing, growth, and development across an industry are thwarted, and it becomes a game of who can outwit, outlast, and outmaneuver whom. Sharing innovation openly for the sake of possibility, growth, and something better for all stakeholders gets traded in for paranoia, playing it safe, protecting your turf.

It does seem unfortunate when the big players who have the power to lead entire markets in innovation instead choose the default mode of muscling out competitors, all in the name of market share. What would be lost in choosing to leave room for all stakeholders and channeling energy into pushing innovation, in an effort to raise the bar ever higher on things like quality and service? This approach is one that speaks more to the spirit of the Imagination Economy. This is the true spirit of innovation, where ideas and progress come from players all across an industry rather than as a result of a series of legal maneuvers.

But what can happen if you don't patent an invention? What's the potential loss in revenue and valuation? According to Alan Kay, Xerox Parc gave up $5 trillion worth of wealth. He says, "That's how much the inventions from the first six years of Xerox Parc have translated into. The mouse. The personal computer. The bit-map screen. Overlapping Windows. The laser printer. The Ethernet. Desktop publishing. Object-oriented operated system. In today's economy the investment would equal US$60 million." Instead, the revenues went to those companies that took and tweaked the innovations, thus making them "their own."[7]

Trademark

If you want to start looking for trademarks, you'll find them everywhere—from grocery stores to coffee shops to shopping malls. A trademark is a distinctive sign that identifies a particular good or service as belonging to someone. A registered trademark can be any combination of words, letters, numbers, drawings, images, symbols, even musical sounds, and it provides the owner of the trademark the exclusive right to use it or authorize another to use it. Trademarks date back to ancient times, when craftspeople reproduced their signatures or marks on their products. The products don't require any creative expression, as for a copyright, or special inventive skill, as for a patent. The purpose of the trademark is to identify the origin of the product.

The process of trademarking is straightforward enough. A person or company makes a search to ensure their proposed trademark is not already in use, provides a description, pays the fee, and the product is protected for seven years (the exact period may vary in some countries). The duration of the trademark can be extended indefinitely.

What is interesting is how trademarking is extending into a much wider range. Despair Inc. is an Internet-based company that creates "Demotivational" posters and other products. Master satirists, the company's vision as posted on their Web site, Despair.com, is to be

> a company that would create dissatisfied customers in the process of exploiting demoralized employees while selling overpriced and ineffective products to remediate the problems caused by the very process itself. A company that would become the bold embodiment of every shortcoming rife within corporate America. A business dictatorship with draconian tendencies. A company grossly obsessed with margins. A peddler of absurdly embellished corporate publicity.[8]

True to their vision, Despair Inc. filed for and received trademark no. 2347676 for the commonly used Internet "frowny" emoticon **:-(** , after which they posted a press release stating their intent to file a lawsuit against the millions of Internet users who infringe on their trademark every time they type the "frowny" in an e-mail message. The mock press release was Despair's satirical response to developments in the world of intellectual property as exemplified by the Amazon.com 1-Click patent.

The intent of the trademark system is to help consumers identify and purchase a product with confidence, based on its reputation as

indicated by its unique trademark. But it does get stranger and stranger. According to the *Financial Times*, Chilean businessman Eduardo Arevalo Mateluna applied to industrial property authorities to register the name "Osama" as a trademark. Mateluna believes this to be a commercially astute move given the name's popularity and his past success exploiting the name Pinochet for financial success.[9] But is this true innovation?

Industrial Design

To be protected, industrial design must be primarily aesthetic in nature and not involve the technical features of the product whose design is being registered. In other words, design is the ornamental aspect of an article. The design may consist of three-dimensional attributes, such as shape, or surface features, such as patterns, lines, or colors.

Industrial design makes an article attractive and appealing, and adds to its commercial value. The owner of a registered industrial design is assured of protection against unauthorized copying or imitation of the design by a third party. Registration typically lasts for an initial five years, after which it can usually be renewed for fifteen years. Industrial designs include such things as the shape of a car fender or the arrangement of knobs, dials, and buttons on a television. The intent is to assist economic development by encouraging fair trade and creativity in industry as well as in traditional arts and crafts through the design of more innovative and aesthetically appealing products.

Geographical Indications

The words *Champagne, Chianti, Darjeeling,* and *Roquefort* are not only the names of places; they are also geographical indications of source that are applied to particular products, in this case sparkling wine, red wine, tea, and cheese. These items have particular characteristics that are closely identified with their geographical place of origin.

Because these names and the products associated with them often acquire a valuable reputation for a particular quality or characteristic, they are protected by various national laws and international agreements. For this reason sparkling wine from the Champagne region of France is called Champagne, while similar products from elsewhere are called sparkling wine.

©opyright

Copyright is the right of creators to benefit from their literary, musical, and artistic works and covers a wide range of artistic output, from novels, short stories, screenplays, poems, and plays to paintings, computer programs, databases, drawings, photographs, sculptures, films, videodiscs, and architectural works, including designs, drawings, and plans. Copyright provides an exclusive right to creators to use or authorize others to use their work. The creator of a work can prohibit or authorize its reproduction in various forms, including printing, recording, broadcasting, public performance, translation, and adaptation.

The intent of copyright is to encourage human creativity by recognizing economic rights of creators, which allow them and their heirs to benefit financially from their work, usually until fifty to seventy years after the creator's death, depending on the country. This provides not only recognition for existing work but an incentive to create more. As they create, we all benefit, through a greater access to and wider variety of culture, knowledge, and entertainment.

Patents and copyrights are quite different. Whereas copyright is granted automatically and does not require registration of any kind, a patent has to pass stringent tests requiring it to be novel, non-obvious, and useful before being approved. None of these tests apply to copyright. Once registered, however, a patent gives stronger protection than a copyright.

Open Source

An alternative way to drive innovation is through collaborative creativity, where ideas are made freely accessible. Collaborative creativity works by open discussion and development around a common vision, without anyone claiming intellectual property rights. This way of working can be far more efficient and produce surprisingly elegant results.

In open source creativity, every participant has free access to the same body of knowledge and is encouraged to contribute to its improvement in a free, open, and shared manner. What often happens in these environments is that, since ideas flow freely and fluidly, any single person's approaches are quickly accepted, modified, altered, and then replaced by others.

This openness is central to the Internet. Flexible and accessible, the Internet operates by a universal, non-proprietary standard of data transfer that operates on infinitely changeable pathways. Individuals can own computers, servers, and the fiber connecting them, but

nobody owns the system. This is clearly one of the reasons it has grown at such a remarkable rate.

The flagship of Internet collaborative creativity is GNU/Linux, an operating system first developed by the Finnish programmer Linus Torvalds while he was a university student. Torvalds did not claim a patent for Linux and gave away the source code for free. Thousands of people contribute to Linux, and Torvalds acts as editor, managing the improvements. Several companies, such as Red Hat and VA Linux, sell packaged versions of the software and make their profits primarily on services, but nobody owns the rights to the source code. One might think that this approach would produce second-rate software, but Linux is Microsoft's biggest competitor. According to IDC, Linux owns 27 percent of the server market, compared with Microsoft's 42 percent.

Richard Stallman, leader of the Free Software Foundation, has developed a concept called "copyleft" that takes the opposite position to copyright. His General Public License encourages people to distribute software freely and features quirky legalese: "You may not copy, modify, sublicense, or distribute the Program except as expressly provided under this License. Any attempt otherwise to copy, modify, sublicense or distribute the Program is void, and will automatically terminate your rights under this License … You are not required to accept this License, since you have not signed it."[10]

The driving principle behind open source is that making a technology, discovery, or invention freely accessible to everyone will promote a spirit of sharing and return yet more technologies, discoveries, and inventions. The debate circles around the issue of ownership and the right to profit for an investment of time versus the responsibility to share information and knowledge openly.

Open source did not begin with the digital age. One of the greatest works of scholarship in the English language, the *Oxford English Dictionary*, is the result of open source. In 1879, James Murray, president of the English Philological Society, began the impossibly gargantuan task of tracing the history of every English word ever written in every book, letter, journal, or periodical ever published. No individual or organization could hope to accomplish this task alone. Murray used the network of booksellers, libraries, and literary magazines to solicit thousands of contributors to read and send their research to Oxford University, where the data was compiled on cards. Though Murray never lived to see the completion of the project—he edited about half the dictionary, the letters *a* through *d*, *h* through *k*, *o*, *p*, and *t*—the entire project was completed over fifty years and published in 1933 with over 2,400,000 entries.

The case for open source is compelling. In an internal Microsoft report the organization acknowledged: "Linux and other open source advocates are making a progressively more credible argument that open source is at least as reliable, if not more, than commercial alternatives. The ability of the open source process to collect and harness the collective IQ of thousands of individuals across the internet is simply amazing."[11] Open source creates a self-sustaining ecology of individuals who are focused on a common vision. The order and equilibrium that emerge from the thousands of participants is as rich and productive as a centrally co-ordinated system.

Peter Martin, deputy editor of the *Financial Times*, wrote about the impact of the Internet on business:

> The Internet's ad hoc, flexible, consensual structure offers powerful lessons to everyone in business. It is, in some ways, a prototype of the way companies will have to operate in future. The consensus stems from a shared purpose: the creation of a network that allows easy communication. This is in part a technical vision, and it requires deep knowledge of computer science. But it is also an ideological one, requiring a humanistic commitment to freedom of expression and to a medium of communication that rises above the interests of government and commerce ... An ethics of collaboration and open discussion around a common purpose is an extraordinarily powerful and creative force.[12]

The impact of technology may be greatest in redefining how intellectual property is measured and possessed. John Howkins writes that new technologies "allow us to bring in authors (and to wave goodbye to them, too) at all stages of the creative process, from the thinking of the original idea to its design and marketing. In turn, this has led us to act like editors and impresarios of other people's work; to be tenants, rather than owners, of property rights."[13] In the Imagination Economy we need to explore our relationship to the worth of ideas in ways different from what we have done before.

Measuring the Qualitative Side of the Imagination Economy

In 1975 Richard Dawkins, writing in *The Selfish Gene*, introduced the concept of the *meme*—a virus of the mind. Memes take on a life of their own and propagate through the mental activity of populations. Memes are contagious ideas, everything from popular television shows to dance fads and fashion trends, even religion. They compete for a share of our imagination through a kind of Darwinian selection process.[14]

In a way, intangible properties are memes. Since ideas are contagious, the measure of a fertile idea is how widely and quickly a market's imagination accepts it. The meme blends images, feelings, connection, and understanding to make a real impact. This is quite a departure from the traditional approach to measuring value. Rather than sizing it only by its features, a product is measured for what it represents and how it promotes and supports the ethereal experience.

Examining intangible assets brings us to a fork in the road, where traditional ROI business thinking and imagination diverge. Fundamentally, trying to assign a measurement to imagination is like trying to nail Jell-O to a wall. Each world converses in its own language, is guided by its own values, and operates according to its own rules. Bringing together the true potential of imagination and the rational, practical side of business means dancing the left-brain/right-brain tango. The challenge for the traditional business mind will be to respect imagination's wild, artistic, what-if thinking. For imagination the challenge is to focus on practical application, to connect to the traditional values of business.

The ideal process is one that converses alternately with the domain of imagination and the world of business. By maintaining a focus on the integrating experience, the ideas shape each other in different contexts and the circulation of ideas is strengthened. The key is to make it not a democratic process so much as an integrative one where, rather than make compromises that lead to losses in both camps, the two worlds of thinking come together and synthesize into something totally new. Imagination + Economy. Possibility + Commerce. The whole-brain tango.

The magic is in the synthesis. The big win lies in being able to create something completely new, like a disruptive technology that follows the path of truth and blasts forward through barriers into a previously unknown domain, rather than inching along in predictable increments. Real synthesis changes the value of the component parts.

The true intangible in the imaginative business is like the core of imagination in ourselves. That which we cannot see or touch is the very thing that makes us most who we are. Where is the heart and soul of your business? Who are the people who embody those intangible qualities? What qualities do they possess? How do you assign a quantitative value to the "Aha!" experience?

The challenge in business is always to connect clients to something with commercial value. If you can't, then you're creating art, not conducting business. The difference between art and business is that art (at least in its purest form) creates and expresses ideas regardless of their potential commercial value. If, in business, an idea cannot be developed to have any commercial value, it is theoretically valueless. If you can make an idea make sense by uniting the left-brain and right-brain sides of it, simultaneously inspiring with the imaginative aspect of the idea while staying rooted in pragmatics, then any client will buy the idea.

Measuring Return
in the Imagination Economy

Imagination offers us a sense of limitless possibility. Business offers stability and security. Measuring imagination is subjective and intuitive, relying largely on feelings and emotional intelligence. Measuring business requires objective, quantifiable components and metrics. Imagination longs for freedom and play. Business requires order and seeks control. How, then, do we begin to bring together the expansive sense of possibility with the pressing need for order, results, and profit? How do we assign a value to the quality, spark, or potential of an idea? How do we measure spirit? How do we determine the worth of a happy, healthy, self-aware community infused with passion and purpose? How do we measure the quality of the human experience? How do we measure the realization of a dream?

We know that in order to be sustaining, business requires black ink on the bottom line. Spin it any way you like, financial viability is an integral part of the equation. It is possible to assign a concrete value to things like patents, trademarks, brands, and other types of intellectual property. But there is so much more to imagination. And while the power and expression of imagination may produce tangible, measurable results, its essence, its true nature, its humanness, is largely invisible.

So, where do we begin?

We begin with the decision to fuse imagination with business. Support this decision with the understanding that we can have an imaginatively vibrant *and* profitable organization. This is not an either-or proposition. Being imaginative does not preclude profitability, or vice versa. Rather, the synthesis of imagination and business is what creates a world for the full expression of human potential and the realization of dreams.

No one knows this better than Gary Hawton. Hawton struggled for years over how to meld his personal beliefs with his desire for success in the business world. He found that balance as CEO of Meritas Mutual Funds, an organization offering socially responsible investing. When considering an issuing company, Meritas's fund managers evaluate financial strengths and outlooks as well as performance against social and environmental standards. The standards that must be met are:

1. Respect the dignity and value of all people.

2. Build a world at peace and free from violence.

3. Internalize a concern for justice in a global society.

4. Exhibit responsible management practices.

5. Support and involve communities.

6. Practice environmental stewardship.[15]

For the skeptics who think socially responsible investing means financial disaster, consider the more than $50 billion invested during the fifteen years the product has been available in Canada. And the big news is an annual growth rate at a whopping 40 percent—about double the rate of regular mutual funds. As for how the funds are performing, the Jantzi Social Index Fund (the first socially responsible index fund offered in Canada) outperformed four established Canadian benchmarks (S&P/TSE 60, TSE 100, TSE 300, DJC 40) over a one-year period.

Hawton says: "We are definitely a for-profit business and expect our funds to perform competitively and successfully. Our fund managers know the performance of their investments will be measured against market performance." So what's the difference? For Hawton, it's being able to leave for work each morning and come home at the end of the day with a smile on his face, knowing his organization has made a positive impact through its choices. It's the knowledge that "I have had the opportunity to accomplish so much more than I will ever see."[16]

Criteria for Measuring Returns

Begin by designing criteria for measuring your own success. The criteria will be a reflection of your corporate vision and culture, an expression of the collective personal and professional values of your people, and, ideally, a balance between the human spirit and quantifiable results.

What are your concrete goals? A zero-balanced budget? An annual growth rate of 5 percent? A 15 percent return? To take your company public? To move to a new building? To hire two hundred more people? To be the market leader? To have a globally recognizable brand? To introduce five new products each year? To invent a disruptive technology? To gain 5 percent market share? To complete a successful merger?

What are your qualitative goals? To create a community of energy, creative expression, and fun? To have the ability to generate thousands of new ideas? To support the communities where you do business? To make the world a better place? To have a happy, passionate, and loyal staff? To reduce stress and encourage inspiration? To uncover, explore, discover, dream, grow, learn, wonder, and play?

How will you know when you've achieved success? When it comes to measuring financial goals, that's fairly straightforward. But as for the big picture, the broad view, consider the aspects of imagination: representation, connection, emotion, and meaning. Investing in imagination means our experiences are richer and fuller; our understanding is more connected and profound; opportunities are boundless; ideas are infectious and plentiful; and possibilities are brought closer to reality.

Here are some of the returns you'll realize by investing in imagination:

Creation of new opportunities

Non-linear break-throughs

Deeper experiences

Nourishment

Balance and harmony

Flow

Energy that mobilizes

Integration

Ability to effect lasting and positive change

Trust

Self-awareness

Application of inspiration

Rich and rewarding experiences

Empowerment

Authenticity

Openness

Ideas that drive profit

Growth and learning

Positive contribution, positive experience, positive attitudes

Excitement

True invention

Representation

Can you tell your story in a way that captures the imagination so that, once the stimulus stops, your story endures despite all the surrounding noise?

Connection

Do you have the capacity for many diverse connections that bring relevance and a sense of shared meaning?

Vivid
Experiential
Sensually stimulating
Memorable
Captivating
Unique
Enduring
Sticky

Quantity
Intensity
Variety
Relevance
Diversity
Metaphors
Similes
Storytelling
Meaning

Emotion

What you imagine is real

Do you have the ability to raise and inspire passion?

Meaning

Are you able to inspire deep understanding by connecting to a core truth?

Range
Intensity
Immediacy
Lingering
Passion

Authenticity
Clarity of purpose
Definition of values
Depth of understanding
Meaning and purpose
Impact

Discovery and invention

Vision, leadership, and followership

Sense of purpose

Shared values and goals

The continuous flow of ideas

Energy of possibility

Alignment of values

Play

Breakthroughs

Increased productivity

Participation of the whole person

Inspiration

Clarity

Buzz

Respectfulness

Commitment

Synchronicity

Loyalty

Enjoyment

Fun

Loyalty

Personal power

Spark

Uniqueness

Individuality

Reduced stress

Perpetual energy

Vibrancy

New strategies for profit

Soulfulness

Mentors and champions

Talking
about art is like
dancing
about
architecture.

Steve Martin

If all we try to do is have fun,
we won't make any money.
But if all we try to do is make money,
we won't have any fun.
a) Happy but broke (and out of a job).
b) Financially stable (but bored and unfulfilled).
Hmm… Here's an idea…
Have fun and make money.
Can it be done?

**When the bottom line
closes the door,**

**imagination
opens a window.**

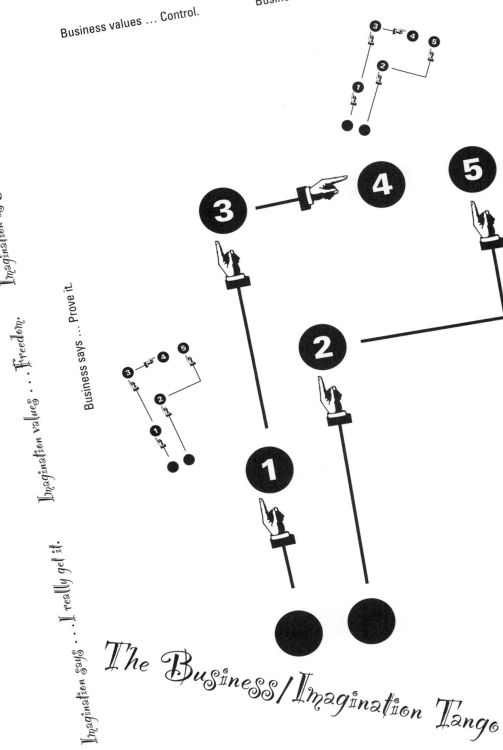

Business values … Control.

Business asks … How much?

Imagination asks … What does it feel like?

Imagination values … Freedom.

Business says … Prove it.

Imagination says … I really get it.

The Business/Imagination Tango

To **imagination**, success means …
floating, being, exploring,
expressing, experiencing, feeling,
connecting, understanding.

To **business**, success means …
meeting defined
quantitative objectives.

To **business**, success means …

meeting defined

quantitative objectives.

To **imagination**, success means …

floating, being, exploring,

expressing, experiencing, feeling,

connecting, understanding.

connecting, understanding.

expressing, experiencing, feeling,

floating, being, exploring,

To **imagination**, success means …

meeting defined
quantitative objectives.

To **business**, success means …

To **imagination**, success means …

floating, being, exploring,

expressing, experiencing, feeling,

connecting, understanding.

meeting defined

quantitative objectives.

To **business**, success means …

Imagination Institute
714 Undermind Dr.
Metaphor
Republic of Possibility
427527

To: Imagination Recruits
Re: Challenge, Commitment, and Chutzpah

Let's face it: what we are suggesting here is not a walk in the park. Just because you decide to bring your imagination to work one day doesn't guarantee everyone else is going to be willing to play. The truth is, this is a challenge. But it is *so* worth it.

There's no question you will be faced with resistance. And it will be disguised in forms ranging from apathy to aggressive confrontation and everything in between. When you set about changing things (whether you are the leader or especially if you're not), people get nervous. We all get into our regular groove of zooming along in life, peeking up over the familiar comfort of our deskscape only once in a while. Making real, fundamental change is hard work, and it makes people uncomfortable. That's just a fact of life. The point is, be prepared. Resistance will strike, and it may be discouraging and even disheartening. Hark back to the wisdom of the change management gurus: it takes time. Expect challenge. Be patient. Hang in there.

Changing the status quo takes guts. Especially if the status quo is most enthusiastically supported by those who sign the paychecks. But if you're going to be committed to living an imaginatively rich life, it's going to take plenty of chutzpah. You have to be willing to zig when everyone else is zagging. You have to be willing to put yourself on the line, to stand by your beliefs, your values, and your vision. In the best of times you'll be able to make changes to your environment, rallying supporters and like-minded teammates around you. Given the choice, most people want to be more imaginatively inspired—if for no other reason than it just feels better, more alive, and more human.

Being true to your vision may mean leaving the organization you're with if there's no room for change, growth, or possibility. It takes courage to move on, but sometimes there is no other choice. Remember the words of Theodore Roosevelt, who said:

> It is not the critic who counts, not the man who points out how the strong man stumbles or where the doer of deeds could have done them better. The credit belongs to the man who is actually in the arena, whose face is marred by dust and sweat and blood, who strives valiantly, who errs and comes up short again and again because there is no effort without error and shortcomings, who knows the great devotion, who spends himself in a worthy cause, who at the best knows in the end the high achievement of triumph and who at worst, if he fails while daring greatly, knows his place shall never be with those timid and cold souls who know neither victory nor defeat.

Pack light and wear comfortable shoes. It's going to be hard work, but it will be loads of fun.

Trust us. Orientation starts whenever you're ready.
See you there.

When people started taking MBA seriously, that was the beginning of the ruination of the North American industrial society. When all decisions are based on an MBA's concept of numerical reality, you're in deep shit, because the only thing that can be judged as real is that which can be proved by a column of figures. And when all aesthetic decisions are turned over to these kinds of people, who use these criteria to make steering decisions for a company with no regard for people and no regard for what the product really is, and the only thing that matters is maximizing your profit, you have a problem.

Frank Zappa

New Metrics
         Profit: advantage or benefit financial gain excess of returns
                 over outlay
   Profiterole: small hollow choux bun usually filled with cream and
                 covered with chocolate

         Pay me in cream puffs!

You already know what it costs to ... run a department ... hire an engineer ...
license some software ... outsource your distribution ... participate in a trade show ...
... rent a studio ... downsize ... hire an agency on retainer ... train your people ... conduct a brainstorming session ... buy a building
keep an agency on retainer ... train your people ... conduct a brainstorming session ... restructure your workforce ... and work around the clock.
... hire a fleet ... redesign your corporate identity ... restructure your workforce ... and work around the clock.

But do you know what it's worth?

Keep your eye on the big picture.
Shift your focus from
what's right in front of you
to the l o n g view.

inspires

What   you?

5

Fostering
Imagination

No one has a single formula for
uncovering the Next Big Idea.
But making time,
granting permission, and having
available mental space
go a long way toward
fostering innovation success.

The Big Idea

As a young broadcaster, president, and executive producer of Toronto's CityTV, Moses Znaimer searched for ways to reinvent television and make it more personal, interesting, and relevant. He spent years traveling through Europe in search of new approaches to television. The studios he visited were all alike: "big grey buildings with large sound stages and lots of expensive production equipment. And what came out of those studios from places as far apart as Spain and Bulgaria all looked the same."[1] Though the languages were different, the television shows felt similar because they were all developed with the same tools, the same infrastructure, and the same management approach.

Znaimer's creative journey took him "away from the idea that programs are invented in little boxes called offices and executed in big expensive boxes called studios. That's why we wired the building to shoot itself."[2] In creating this new model for production, Znaimer reinvented television. The main production facility in downtown Toronto was gutted and wired with over sixty video spigots that enable camera operators to plug into the building's nervous system. The production offices, editing suites, and open theaters were transformed into movable studios, creating an ultra-flexible production and broadcast environment. This strategy enables CityTV to produce four times as many hours of programming as similarly sized competitors.

The building itself has a video kiosk where the public can vent their opinions, and the videos are subsequently broadcast. Located in the heart of the downtown scene, it now houses six channels and is considered a cultural hub, opening its doors to live music acts. Teams of hip anchors and broadcasters give the shows strong personality and a multicultural flair.

Rather than follow traditional models for creating new programs and channels, CityTV tests every idea. Program ideas start off as ten-minute spots on an existing show. If successful, the format is expanded into a single program, then a three-show run, a full series, and ultimately a new channel. This approach has successfully created series specifically focused on fashion, music, science fiction, technology, media, and sex. CityTV's series *FashionTelevision* is now broadcast in seventy-four countries.

The Myth
of Inspiration

In business, art, or science, the journey of imagination is the quest for inspiration. Suddenly, a revelation of what you're thinking about, the opportunity you're exploring, the problem you are trying to solve, fits together and makes sense. You see the business prospect. The solution comes in a flash. The situation becomes clear. It is an experience that arrives in any size package, from a series of little insights to an eye-opening realization that changes your life.

The Nine Muses
Calliope: Epic Poetry
Clio: History
Erato: Love Poetry
Euterpe: Music
Melpomene: Tragedy
Polyhymnia: Sacred Poetry
Terpsichore: Dancing and Choral Song
Thalia: Comedy
Urania: Astronomy

This quest for inspiration is as old as humanity. The early Greeks described how the union of Zeus and Mnemosyne gave birth to the Muses, who brought the gift of beauty and joy to mortals. The earliest myths told of three Muses—Melete (meditation), Mneme (memory), and Aoede (song)—but with retellings the Muses grew to nine in number. They brought music and theater, invented the letters of the alphabet, and taught mortals to combine these letters into poetry. Though the skill to put letters, words, and notes together was taught, the primal impulse was a divine gift.

Aristotle believed that imagination had no special connection to inventiveness or creativity. For Aristotle and other early Greek thinkers, inspiration was divine, literally breathed into one's soul by the gods.

**The concept of creativity as an internal human activity was devised in the seventeenth century.
The word *originalité* first appeared in French in 1699, and *originality* in English in 1742.**

This concept of inspiration is shared by many cultures. In Hinduism mental work is shared by the divine and cannot be owned privately. Islam's *Sharia* dictates that the properties of the mind are the properties of God. The Latin roots *creator* and *creare* refer to God and his actions: God alone could create; people could merely rearrange. In fact, the word *inspiration* originally meant "the breath of divinity" or "a transfusion of soul from the gods to a mortal individual."

In our culture it seems inconceivable, even ridiculous, that thoughts and impulses could come from anywhere except inside our own minds. Today, *inspiration* means the experience of something that produces a sudden insight which leaps across the usual steps of reasoning. Normally a deeply pleasurable moment, it is an impulse that creates an idea.

**It is not the mind that controls
the moment of inspiration. It is the idea,
or the suddenly articulated power
of our inner energies. New ideas
capture and possess the mind that
births them: they colonize it and renew its laws.
The expansion of any idea is thus
also an expanded self.**

Robert Grudin

What Is
an Idea?

An idea is an organizing principle, a mental event that blends elements of the imagination—images, a sense of connection, meaning, and feelings—and wraps them up into a single mental object. Ideas come in all shapes and sizes, from passing notions that come and go as quickly as fads to more substantial ones that make a true and lasting difference. Substantial ideas are expandable and pliable, and often take on a life of their own—joining, competing with, organizing around, and imposing themselves on other ideas.

The word *idea* is derived from the Latin *idein* and the Greek *eidos*, which both mean "to see."

And then, of course, there are *big* ideas, the ones that create new ways of thinking, seeing, and relating to the world. Charles Darwin's idea of evolution through natural selection, formulated over almost thirty years of study and analysis, overturned the common views of humanity's origins. It was not only an extraordinary scientific achievement; it was a dangerous idea, one that toppled some of the most cherished beliefs and longings of the human psyche. Before the publication of Darwin's *Origin of Species* in 1859, much of biology consisted only of naming and classifying living organisms. The idea of evolution through natural selection provided an overarching context for all subsequent research using a physical mechanism to unify and explain how life works. Darwin's theory reset the agenda for all of biology, as well as for many other sciences.

Plato believed in a physical world and the world of ideas. In the famous myth of the cave, Plato compares the ordinary person to a man sitting in a cave looking at a wall of shadows of real things behind his back. The enlightened philosopher is one who has got out into the open and seen the real world of ideas.

Other big ideas, such as democracy—government for the people, by the people—have resonated with millions and grown into ideologies that define entire societies. Big ideas in commerce, such as assembly lines for manufacturing (Ford), on-line auctioning (eBay), and carrying your life in your hand (the Palm Pilot), unleash an imaginative impulse that organizes commercial activity and drives business forward.

The quest for the Big Idea is a central preoccupation of the Imagination Economy. The curious thing about inspiration is that it can't be hemmed in without being diminished. But even if we can't command it, we can prepare our minds and situate ourselves in ways that will make the lightning of inspiration more likely to strike.

Personally, I always preferred inspiration to information.

Man Ray

A Metaphor
for the Growth of Ideas

Many metaphors describe approaches to finding ideas and bringing them to light. We can mine them, excavate for them, or travel to an archeological site and dig for them. We can hunt for ideas in the outback or wait for them like the rain. We can borrow ideas, tweak them here and there, and then make them our own. We can build them, like a house, first creating a foundation, then framing the overall structure and filling in the walls, fixtures, and other aspects. Though each metaphor emphasizes certain nuances, none is as rich as the concept of *gestation*.

Having an idea is like growing a garden. You begin with a seed. You put it into the ground, nourish it, water it, give it room and light, and the idea will germinate, take root, and flourish. You need to protect the idea, and if it has the right conditions, it will develop and emerge.

**If we all did the things
we are capable of doing,
we would literally astound ourselves.**

Thomas Alva Edison

Gestation metaphors express the complex nature of our mind's relationship with thoughts. Gestation has its own timetable, psychologically and physically. Once the process starts, however, the entire mental machinery is set in motion and continues to fruition through its own momentum. A gardener cannot engineer the development of a rose, but she can influence it through caring attention. Nutrients and weather patterns, stresses and soil conditions, appetites and available light affect what emerges from the garden of imagination.

**No amount of skillful invention
can replace the essential
element of imagination.**

Edward Hopper

This metaphor illustrates a difference between two related activities of imagination: invention and discovery. Invention is the world of problem solving and engineering, where one defines the parameters of a challenge and works through to the optimal solution. Discovery is the world of exploring the unknown. It is the realm of wandering through uncharted territory and being open. At times you may have a destination, at others you don't.

Where Do Ideas Come From?

Perhaps no question in the Imagination Survey brought as wide a range of answers as this one. For some the question led to a torrent of abstract language: "I look deep and I go far"; "I ask myself a series of questions"; "I change points of view"; "I try to put myself into the mood where I can converse with my imagination." Answers went from the practical to the philosophical, but they all touched on the possibility of *doing* something.

Where do you get your ideas? I don't. They get me!

Alan Fletcher

For some the question was nonsensical, even meaningless. "What do you mean, 'What do I do?' I just do it. It takes no effort. It is who I am. I become open to the possibility and ideas flow. I look and see. I listen to what's in front of me. In fact, I can't stop thinking."

For others, the question was an insult. Talking about how ideas emerge is like opening the kimono, akin to sharing their deepest dreams and personal ideologies, as private as the details of their sex life or bank account.

Most people described their ideas as coming in odd places and at unlikely times: browsing through magazines at the hairdresser's; hearing a sentence fragment that connected to something; strolling through a hardware store; chopping vegetables. Rarely did ideas come while sitting at a desk.

When asked how they generate ideas—big or little—most people said, "Well, not easily. It's not something that I can force or direct." The results of the Imagination Survey are quite telling. The largest factors stimulating personal imagination were identified as time to let the imagination flow, a sense of freedom, and actions, states, or activities that induce a flowing state of mind. Specifically, the survey indicated that the key factors promoting the flow of imagination are time, conversation, freedom, reading, and goals.

Questions Direct Imagination

A question puts you into a ready-to-learn frame of mind by stimulating your curiosity. The Latin origin of the word "question" is *quaestiio,* which means "to seek." Inside every *question*—simple or complex—is the opportunity for a quest, an adventure, a pursuit, which leads to the unexplored.

Questions Tap Into Imagination

You don't get better ideas by mentally pushing twice as hard; you get better ideas by becoming interested, by mentally leaning forward into your work, by finding aspects of the problem or opportunity that speak to the part of you that really cares. Starting a project by thinking of all the things you don't know about it opens you to the don't-know world and the don't-know mind.

Questions Start Connecting Ideas

A question creates a state of tension. Like a puzzle box ready to be taken apart and put back together, a good question can engage your mind for days, months, or a lifetime, driving you to find answers and to explore further afield. This feeling of irresolution is gratifying, the impulse almost irresistible, and it explains why people pursue answers to their questions.

Questions Focus Intention and Meaning

The questions you ask yourself set the course your thoughts take and determine how your imagination is stimulated. Intelligent businesses focus on questions.

Questions can enlighten us, expand our understanding of the world, create a sense of awe and mystery, and clarify what we need to do on a practical level. Creative minds continually ask and answer questions in an ongoing mental conversation. A mechanical engineer looks at a bridge and asks, "Can that be made with less material?" The product manager wonders, "What if we changed the packaging?" Many people we interviewed in the Imagination Survey mentioned the ongoing conversations they have with themselves.

Synonyms for the word *question* include *problem, difficulty, issue,* and *uncertainty.* We endure the uncertainty and the conflicts our questioning minds sometimes inspire because we have hope of a reward for our determination when the work is complete. And there is no end to asking questions. Since there is no book with all the answers, we continually reformulate and refine ideas, which gives rise to new questions.

We know that questions are tools for understanding. The Socratic method of learning is based on the notion that we already know all the answers; we hold within us all we need to know. Questions then become a medium for exposing the truth.

For people focused on solutions, answers provide more value than questions; for people focused on learning, questions are more important than answers. If you focus your attention on the solution rather than the question, it is impossible to change your mindset. The truly imaginative approach is not one of mapping the route to a predetermined outcome, but of exploring the territory, being willing to challenge the beliefs you hold to be true, and discovering a perhaps unforeseen, unimagined outcome.

Our educational system encourages students to supply answers to predetermined questions, not to pose new questions. Imagine how much more we could learn, how much bigger the world would be for us, if we were experts at asking questions.

Three decades ago Dr. Judah Folkman recognized that developing tumors require angiogenesis—the growth of their own blood vessels to supply them with nutrients. He theorized that certain molecules could be used to inhibit angiogenesis, starving tumors of their blood supply, and ultimately stopping and even reversing their growth. This thinking represented an enormous change from the mindset that was the basis of cancer research at the time, which was focused on destroying cancerous cells. In a lecture Folkman gave at the Gairdner International Awards' first-ever public lecture in Toronto in October 2001, he reflected on how lonely this work was in the early years. It wasn't until he received the prestigious Gairdner Award in 1991 that his field of research gained attention and interest. And by the time the press jumped the gun in 1998 and attributed to Folkman the cure for cancer, most of his former critics were undertaking similar research.[3]

The important thing is not to stop questioning.
Curiosity has its own reason for existing.

Albert Einstein

A good question is never answered. It is not a

bolt to be tightened into place but a seed to

be planted and to beget more seeds toward

the hope of greening the landscape of ideas.

John Ciardi

Find the right question: you don't invent the answers, you reveal the answers.
Jonas Salk

It takes a very unusual

Nobody ever came up with a really

brilliant answer to a really stupid question.

Bran Ferren mind to make an

In all affairs, it's a healthy thing now and then to hang a question mark on the things you have long taken for granted.
Bertrand Russell

analysis of the obvious.

To find the exact cause, one must ask the exact question.
S. Tobin Webster

Alfred North Whitehead

The greatest gift is not being afraid to question.

Ruby Dee

A prudent question is one half of wisdom.

Francis Bacon

Not to know is bad; not to wish to know is worse.
Nigerian proverb

Good questions outrank easy answers.
Paul Samuelson

Ignorance never settles a question.
Benjamin Disraeli

The Imagination Survey

Factors Encouraging Personal Imagination

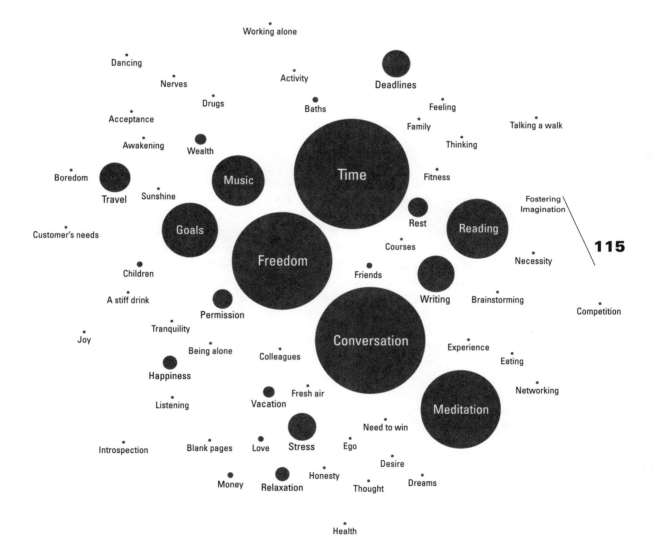

The larger the word and circle, the more frequently the factor appeared in the survey as a significant influence promoting imagination.

Time

Without making time to disconnect from daily pressures and plug into, listen for, or open ourselves to imagination, there is no breathing room for new ideas to form. Time provides the opening that allows the under-mind to emerge.

Warren Pratt is chief operating officer of Silicon Graphics Inc., a billion-dollar high-performance computing and graphics hardware company based in Mountain View, California. He understands the importance of making time for innovation, professionally and personally.

I can tell you there are many people who, for whatever reason, get so locked into the details of the everyday grind that they don't give themselves the space to think, to innovate, to connect ideas. That's a problem. You need some people who will give themselves the space to do that. It means that, to be successful, they have to be pretty reasonable at delegating, and not micromanage everything, or they will never get the freedom to really do that kind of thinking.[4]

Pratt makes this kind of thinking a priority. Each quarter he takes a team of senior managers out of the office environment to focus on long-term thinking. Short-term issues are dealt with only at the start of the meeting, or ignored altogether. "Being able to pull together, collect ideas, and look at cross-functional aspects is very helpful. To do that with a group of people is the first rule. To set aside some time for long-term thinking, as opposed to the issues of the day, is a second rule."[5]

Making time for imagination is essential, whether it's an hour at the end of each day when you look in new places, a couple of days every quarter when you review strategic plans and big-picture goals, or a longer vacation or sabbatical when you recharge your batteries. It is well known that Bill Gates takes two weeks off each year to think about long-term vision; and organizations such as SGI have implemented programs that encourage employees to replenish their minds and bodies.

Pratt sets aside some time in his own calendar to stay abreast of the broader issues and reflect on essential business wisdom. "I think, for all of us, we should spend a little more time dealing with the important, and a little less dealing with the urgent."[6]

Conversation

Richard Saul Wurman, who has written and published over thirty books as diverse as analyses of information architecture and diagnostics guides, is the founder and host of the TED (Technology, Entertainment, and Design) conferences. In a typical conference, sixty world-class participants talk freely on subjects relevant to their field of work, from the design of creativity, to the experience of religion in today's world, to the fine art of juggling. The conferences are breathtaking, moving, stimulating, and challenging.

At the heart of Wurman's philosophy is the art of conversation. He writes that conversations "are organic, constantly changing, and people are continually exploring ways to communicate with one another because conversation is not governed by any established set of rules. A conversation goes from story, to joke, to incident, to fact, to story, to issue—all in a natural, organic way."[7]

While conversations with others are an inexhaustible source for ideas, many people converse continually with themselves, believing this to be equally important. When William Thorsell became editor-in-chief of the *Globe and Mail*, his goal was to increase readership and enhance the quality of the newspaper's content. He recalls, "At first I didn't know how to make this happen. It took me about a year just to find my feet. And then I started coming up with ideas about what it should be."[8]

How did he come up with ideas? Basically, he did it by sitting around and not thinking awfully hard about it. He did it at home, pondering, asking himself questions. It was largely a solitary act. As various ideas emerged, he would write or draw them out and give them a rationale. Then he would take them to his colleagues and pass them around.

Eventually, I learned that getting new ideas is sort of like change management. Where does imagination come up with new ideas? In my case, I always put myself into the shoes of my reader—the consumer of my product. If I were a newspaper reader, what kind of paper would I like to read? If I come into a building, what kind of experience would I like to have? It's very personal. Very personal. I don't do it for other people. I do it for me. And if it works for me, it will work for them.[9]

Thorsell took six columns from the paper, moved them to the back page, and called the page Facts and Arguments. In that space he did three things every day: an essay on real life; tidbits on all sorts of interesting stuff; and Lives Lived. The page was written not by journalists but by ordinary people. This was a bold act. He took over some of the most valuable real estate in Canadian journalism to make room for real people to talk about real things of importance to them, rather than stories traditionally considered to be newsworthy. He broke the journalists' monopoly in the newspaper's pages so that it could become more personal, more relevant, more important to its readers. As a result, readership went up significantly and the page has been a remarkable success.

Freedom

At the heart of freedom, we find permission. Whether the permission comes from another person, an external source, or a wonderful opportunity, or is simply a personal decision, you will never act freely on your imagination if you don't make the choice to begin.

On granting that permission to self and others, Richard Saul Wurman says:

The only thing I feel I have some expertise on is myself—and my wife would challenge that. And that's not a trivial comment, and the reason it isn't is I very quickly say that I don't do TED for the audience. The measure of it is myself, because I'm the only person that I know. And the measure of who I choose to speak, of what's interesting to me, can only be myself; it can't be a committee. It is interesting to me that a number of other people think the things I'm interested in interest them. And it's also fascinating that other people find similar connections between speeches, and some even find more fascinating connections between things I wouldn't even have thought of. TED really comes from my interests. The only imagination I really know is mine.[10]

Wurman underscores the parts of imagination that are inventive, that give rise to radical alternatives and the risk of flying solo.

When I decide to do a conference called Geeks and Geezers, I just decide. Or if I decide to do a conference on design and I decide to call it simply The Greatest Design Conference That Ever Was, I'm not consulting with anybody to say, "Is this a good idea to do? Will that offend people? Is it OK to do a conference on design?" I really have that conversation with my imagination and give myself permission to fail.

For Wurman, permission means "to have and celebrate your interests, see interest in connections, to fail, to give permission to fail, to have curiosity, and to explain things to other people. These are all kissing cousins to each other."[11]

Reading

When it comes to reading, business people are most frequently engrossed in business books and trade magazines in search of more data, information, or knowledge to keep themselves abreast of the fast-paced markets. But literary critic Harold Bloom believes that serious literature has fundamental truths to reveal. "By reading great imaginative literature, you can prepare yourself for surprise and even get a kind of strength that welcomes and exploits the unexpected."[12]
Works other than those with a business focus carry important messages for us. Storytelling teaches and shares knowledge through the language of imagination, and gives the mind a rest from structured mental work while imparting captivating lessons. Literature speaks to us in a personal way that business writing cannot. Perhaps the most striking recent example of a story's ability to capture the popular imagination is J.K. Rowling's Harry Potter series—now second in sales only to the Bible and Chairman Mao's *Little Red Book*.

How Do You Engage
Your Imagination?

There are more ways to engage the imagination than you can think of. The activities that do so are as varied as your moods. And for most, mood has a lot to do with it. Some prefer quiet stillness; others crave noise and excitement. Sometimes, setting goals is essential to get started, while at other times, nothing will open imagination's door as well as spontaneous, unfettered play. Even if we are unable to point directly to our imagination, each of us has a preferred path when we want to find it, and a different way of knowing when we have connected to it.

Start anywhere

Start anywhere

Start anywhere

The Imagination Survey

Absolute Quiet. *I listen to music, dance, read and write, or doodle to really get my imagination flowing. None of the things I do require rules or for me hardly any thought at all. It is also really fun, so it is like relaxing while having a ton of fun!* **When I am alone, taking a shower or driving to work alone in the car, my mind wanders. I usually do a "What if ..." analogy and take it from there.** *ARE ANY OF THESE REAL QUESTIONS?* **Reading, and being able to relax the mind—especially at work.** *Primarily just do stuff; get caught up in the flow at the time, and typically end up leading some sort of conversation, an activity that includes exploring through imagination.* **Pictures and images—I tend toward more conceptual/abstract and have recently found that using real images helps to direct and focus thinking. This is odd, I haven't figured out a way to get my imagination to participate at will, but I do find that quiet meditation or time are helpful. The way it happens for me is, ideas just come, whether driving in the car, sleeping, or just plain out of nowhere. I consider helpful ideas a gift from the world beyond. Conversation and research.** LONG DRIVES. **So that would mean time to do so.** *Role-play in the mind.* **Quiet setting. No real interruptions for at least a few minutes. Reading or playing music.** *I have a hot bath filled with satsuma bubble bath. I write a piece of poetry and release all my thoughts on paper. I take a long walk or hike somewhere outside of the city to regroup and draw strength from the nature around me.* **Take a walk, surf, read quotations/poetry, listen to birds/observe nature; start writing anything and edit later.** *I LIKE TO LOOK AT BEAUTY. IT MAKES ME DREAM. Sometimes I listen to music to get into the mood. Most of the time my imagination just flows. Comes and goes. Don't really know how it comes and why it goes. Wish it stayed around longer than it does.* **Music, conversation, brainstorming sessions over a glass of wine in a non-work setting. Long drives and loud music.** I start to associate things, memories, words, and create new things. I don't set out to use my imagination, it just happens. It's part of my being. **I read, I meditate, I listen to good music, I wash dishes, I do housework. I just live life.** *Quiet time; running; cup of tea alone; talking to my husband; most of all,* solitude; bath with essential oils, especially a blend of clary sage, lavender, cedar wood and geranium and green tea and chamomile, while listening to Chopin nocturnes by candlelight; a walk down the street to a patch of woods; art institute on a weekday (less commotion) with a sketch pad; lying down on the grass with my son, sky-gazing or star-gazing; playing the piano just for fun; listening to music of primitive cultures; Argentine tango with someone who can make you dream for three minutes. **Most of the time I'm lucky, I don't really need an artificial tool in order to stimulate my imagination ...** *I just begin reading the sources I use to write my books, then apply them to the question at hand, and then the ideas come to me.* **I go kayaking, I walk the dog, or I just sit in the sun. It is hard not to feel creative and alive when you are outside. But by the water I find that my spirit is the happiest and the mind dance has a hundred partners.** *Listen to music to get in the mood; write whatever comes to mind to dance with my mind; gather information and feed off it piece by piece. I just do stuff ... gardening, hiking, taking a shower— great ideas can happen there! Peace and quiet and fresh air seems to stimulate.* **Go for a walk, go horseback riding, go swimming.** *Conversations with like-minded forward thinkers!* **BRAINSTORMING!** *Garden! Paint! Do stuff!* **I just engage in quiet time to be at peace with my inner soul; usually starts off with exploring my spirituality.** *Imagination, and its cousin creativity, come from God. Closer communion with Him requires effort, but it's worth it. A pocket pad helps too. You've got to have some ready way to record ideas as they come.* **A pocket pad is the butterfly net of the imagination.** *I just do it. Paper and a pencil helps. I'll often use whatever is available (napkins work).* **Peace 'n' quiet, stimulating thought ... I just do it like smiley :-) Sit and don't do anything.** *I actually do a couple of things. One is I try not to use my imagination in a conscious way. I study my problem or concern or desire and then I stop thinking about it—usually my subconscious will come up with something that I can work with or on later. Another method is using the teachings of my Rastafarian rabbi.* **Reading, and listening to music, as well as exercising and eating really good food get my imagination going.** *It just flips into my mind.*

Renaissance Man

Since the discovery of his notebooks two centuries ago, Leonardo da Vinci has been the poster child for imagination and creativity. Leonardo represents our cultural ideal, with a mind equally at home in science as in art, versed alike in pragmatic thinking and aesthetic appreciation.

Iron rusts from disuse, stagnant water loses its purity and in cold weather becomes frozen; even so does **inaction** sap the vigors of the mind.

Leonardo da Vinci

Leonardo was born in 1452 and lived in Renaissance Florence and Milan. His genius in painting, drawing, sculpture, military design, invention, scientific speculation, map-making, architectural design, human anatomy—the list goes on—is now legendary. The *Mona Lisa* and *The Last Supper* are among his greatest artistic masterpieces. He consulted on cathedrals in Milan and Pavia. Leonardo designed plans for a helicopter, a parachute, the extendable ladder, the snorkel, the bicycle, locks for canal systems, a water-powered alarm clock, a ditch-clearing crane, the three-speed gearshift, folding furniture, and the olive press. He developed the principle of automation, including the automated loom. Leonardo's advanced military engineering foresaw the armored tank, the machine gun, the mortar, the guided missile, and the submarine. He contributed to the sciences of anatomy, botany, geology, physics, and optics. He was a friend and partner of Machiavelli, and developed plans to divert the Arno River in a massive military campaign to deprive Florence's arch-rival, Siena, of its water supply. In almost every conceivable way Leonardo was a man of expansive and luminous imagination. His was a mind that was curious, forceful, energetic, and articulate.

Though Leonardo did not write a complete autobiography, he did record elements of a personal philosophy. Author Michael J. Gelb has distilled and unified these elements into seven principles:

- An insatiable, curious approach to life and an unrelenting quest for continuous learning.

- A commitment to test knowledge through experience, persistence, and a willingness to learn from mistakes.

- The continual refinement of the senses, especially sight, as a means to enliven experience.

- A willingness to embrace ambiguity, paradox, and uncertainty.

- The development of balance between science and art. Whole-brain thinking.

- The cultivation of grace, ambidexterity, fitness, and poise.

- A recognition and appreciation of the interconnectedness of all things.[13]

To the extent that a Renaissance man or woman is a person versed in all the key disciplines, there are few, if any, alive in our era. Why? The body of knowledge in our times is so vast that no single person has the time to master any single discipline, let alone many. However, Renaissance teams composed of passionate, bold, open, and questioning individuals have the potential to bring real imagination to business.

The Imaginative Mindset

If we try to define the imaginative mindset, we can look to the habitual traits or attitudes of those who are productive, generate ideas, and successfully propel new concepts in the business world. What are the characteristics of the lively mind? Most would agree that imaginative people are curious and interested, and have a passion for learning. They travel and seek out new challenges and diverse experiences. Their minds make connections. Many look for new ways to express and re-express ideas. Imagination is a quality that makes them feel good.

The following is by no means an exhaustive list of traits that characterize the inner imaginative mind. It is built from interviews, the Ideakit Web site, and other sources.

Passion

Passion is simply a sense of joy at being in one's own element. It is the feeling of identifying with your work and seeing it as an expression of who you are. Entrepreneurs and artists live lives of passion, as do those who feel a strong responsibility and ownership in their work.

Passion, like imagination, leaks beyond the workday into the wee hours. Passion makes its ways into dreams, vacations, and weekends. In off-hours the mind is free of deadlines and open to its natural energy. Leisure not only relaxes the mind from its work but allows the work to be appreciated more fully.

The nature of passion is that it dissolves the normal distinction between work and leisure. Though the business world sees leisure and work as opposite poles, imaginative individuals don't recognize that divide. In imaginative work the mind does not confine its operation from nine to five. It operates when it wants to operate—without regard for time or place. Creative work is self-expression, self-fulfillment. Leisure is not the opposite of work, but a complement to it or confirmation of it.

Curiosity and Love of Problems

Each of us enters the world with boundless curiosity. From birth, every moment is geared to learning, exploring, and growing. All parents are familiar with the young child who rolls out an inexhaustible stream of questions.

Great minds continue this impulse, regarding the world with inquisitiveness and wonder. What is striking about highly imaginative people is the number and diversity of their apparently inexhaustible interests, and how far they pursue these interests. Bill Buxton, a leading expert in human computer interface design, is passionately interested in the history of Nepalese and Tibetan mountaineering, voraciously acquiring and reading all related books, regardless of their accessibility. Alan Kay is interested in new musical instruments but also has a passion for old astronomical instruments.

Curiosity loves problems, and enjoys seeing them expand. It loves problems because they represent an opportunity to venture into something new, a way of engaging and exercising the imagination, of finding new meaning and understanding, of making connections. Often, imaginative people are seen as troublemakers because their perception and sense of potential expose problems others may overlook or choose to ignore.

The pessimist sees difficulty in every opportunity. The optimist sees the opportunity in every difficulty.

Winston Churchill

Openness and Willingness to Experiment

In business we tend to see the world as an enclosed space, filled with other people's ideas and opinions, and offering only limited opportunities for our business or personal contribution. To be imaginative is to see the world as an unfinished house of light and shadow, with the process of construction of equal if not more value than the finished work. Rather than intimidating, incompleteness and emptiness beckon and encourage exploration.

Imaginative people live with trust that the next idea to come along will be totally new. The possibilities contained within the world they don't know are a source of excitement and inspiration. The process of synthesis and connection, as opposed to fixedness on individual elements, also intrigues them. The imaginative mind doesn't get bogged down by the component parts of an idea but uses them as touchstones, points of departure, realizing that the greatest solution, the big idea, lies somewhere in the spaces between.

I love fools' experiments. I am always making them.

Charles Darwin

Tolerance of Ambiguity and Love of Beauty

Uncertainty and ambiguity are formidable and familiar strangers. But imaginative people have a tolerance for and are at ease with confusion, and see the unresolved as part of the learning process. Why does the imaginative mind do this? Simply, it fills itself with the energy and excitement of possibility. The search for truth, simplicity, and elegance is grounded in the appreciation of beauty, because those qualities come closest to the essential nature of imagination, and to the nature of truth.

When I am working on a problem, I never think about beauty. I only think of how to solve the problem. But, when I have finished, if the solution is not beautiful, I know it is wrong.

Buckminster Fuller

Innocence and Playfulness

No matter how many products they have designed, books they have written, or business plans they have formulated, those we consider deeply imaginative have a way of wiping their mental slate clean when they begin a new project. Preconceptions get in the way of new insight. Most of us assume, largely involuntarily, that the world is the way it is because, well, that's the way it is. However, when applying itself to a problem or opportunity, imagination does not see the world as a statue or machine, but as fluid energy, something that is flexible, changeable, malleable, capable of variation, and open to possibility.

Inventors and discoverers have a knack for using their past well while opening themselves to new wanderings. This commitment to novelty is a driving principle. Innocence is the child who picks up a toy and grasps it, feels it, turns it over and over, without knowing its purpose or even which end is up or down. The object is mysterious and the discovery fresh and alive. This freedom of mind can enliven any situation. Innocence is without preconception or embarrassment. The mind that is open to simple truth is the one that is open to inspiration.

If I have seen farther than others, it is because I was standing on the shoulders of giants.

Sir Isaac Newton

If I have not seen as far as others, it is because giants were standing on my shoulders.

Hal Abelson

Memory and Forgetfulness

Growth is only possible as an artifact of history. Whether the history is personal or collective, we use our past experiences to create connections and understanding from which wisdom develops. Without memory as a springboard, innovation is merely novelty. History provides a reference point for our explorations. The idea of standing on the shoulders of giants is a deeply entrenched metaphor.

But just as memory and history are a point of departure for our imagination, that is all they should be; for the truly inquisitive are those who forget the experience but remember the lesson.

Boldness, Determination, and a Pioneering Spirit

We think of imaginative people as being extroverted, willing to state their mind and their beliefs. But the real boldness is the inner counterpart: the courage to look at, examine, and confront ideas. To enter into the world of imagination is to risk chaos and ridicule.

Inspiration visits people who have an ongoing contact with their work and who keep their involvement with it open. Trusting in their skills, they know that their ideas are constantly flowing, that there is no end of them. With this mindset they can accept setbacks, confident that they are temporary.

Concentration should be expansive, full, extended, and generous so that the idea, opportunity, or problem fills the mind. Creative people say the idea becomes a world in itself, so connected that it fills the rest of experience.

To be bold and determined requires a pioneer's spirit. It is the love of the imagination's potential and the belief in the importance of its contribution that keep the truly imaginative from being paralyzed or intimidated by fear. Judgment is irrelevant—creation is divine.

The River of Imagination

Author and creativity facilitator Joyce Wycoff, a founder of the Innovation Network, has been teaching creativity for twenty years. She feels that connecting to imagination is about tapping into the raw energy that courses through everyone's mind. "There's an energy flow within us that is just always there, like a river that's going along. This river is something that we can dip into and do something with. This is the creative-process output. The energy or river is always going to be there, and the process of creating something with it doesn't take anything away from it. It doesn't alter it.

It's like we're all sitting on the bridge and we're watching the river of imagination go by. And every second that it goes by, it's gone. And there's no way we could ever bring that river back. But what we could do every once in a while is get off that bridge and go stick our toe in the water ... When we talk about creativity, we talk about how we can increase it or decrease it. When we talk about imagination, I'm not sure that's something that gets increased or decreased. It gets sopped up.[14]

Just as the rivers we see are much less numerous than the underground streams, so the idealism that is visible is minor compared to what men and women carry in their hearts, unreleased or scarcely released. Mankind is waiting and longing for those who can accomplish the task of untying what is knotted and bringing the underground waters to the surface.

Albert Schweitzer

Tapping into imagination is not just about being more creative. It's about giving your mind and feelings the room to reconnect with the raw and natural impulses that flow through your system. This authentic energy is often hidden in us, mossed over with years of conditioning. Although imagination, make-believe, and a sense of fantastic possibility flourish in children, they quickly wither away as the mind's focus conforms to the business world's gray representation of reality.

Toronto designer Bruce Mau talks about connecting with this imaginative impulse as a way to connect to the energy of growth.

Forget about good. Good is a known quantity. Good is what we all agree on. Growth is not necessarily good. Growth is an exploration of unlit recesses that may or may not yield to our research. As long as you stick to good, you'll never reach real growth. Growth is fueled by desire and innocence. Assess the answer, not the question. Imagine learning throughout your life at the rate of an infant.[15]

Connecting to our personal imaginative impulses means being open to the energy flowing inside us without continually evaluating it. It means being sensitive to the ideas that are already percolating through us and providing them with a mental environment where they can flourish, where the undermind can connect with the deliberate mind.

The experience of connecting to our core, our inner, authentic voice, in a feeling way largely means slowing down, letting the pressures on the busy mind relax away, and allowing the imaginative energy to bubble up. This side of imagination is deep and quiet. It calls for exploring and opening the source of ourselves, and experiencing the energy within. This is the land of metaphor, intuition, poetry, and profound knowing. This side of imagination, for which there is little room in the business world, feels most personal.

Architect Douglas J. Cardinal feels that creative expression connects to a primal energy inside all of us. He says:

Silence voices so that you can be a luminous body, a strong creative force that can make a difference. When you regard yourself as more than a physical being, when you see yourself as a powerful light housed in a physical container, then you can truly release your creative energy and bring humanity one step closer to their evolution.[16]

Fostering the connection to personal imagination requires creating an environment in which your deeper ideas can flow. Understanding this river is a prerequisite for growth, which is an internal process. Real growth is a response to experiences and events that connect with that intangible part deep within each of us to bring forth real change.

George Spencer Brown wrote in *Laws of Form*: "To arrive at the simplest truth, as Newton knew and practiced, requires years of contemplation. Not activity. Not reasoning. Not calculating. Not busy behavior of any kind. Not reading. Not talking. Not making an effort. Not thinking. Simply *bearing in mind* what it is that one needs to know."[17]

I put down on the canvas the sudden visions which force themselves on me. I don't know beforehand what I shall put on the canvas, even less can I decide what colors to use. Whilst I'm working I'm not aware of what I'm painting on the canvas. Each time I begin a picture, I have the feeling of throwing myself into space. I never know whether I'll land on my feet. It's only later that I begin to assess the effect of what I've done.

Pablo Picasso

Create mental environments where you can **connect** and **converse** with the river of imagination.

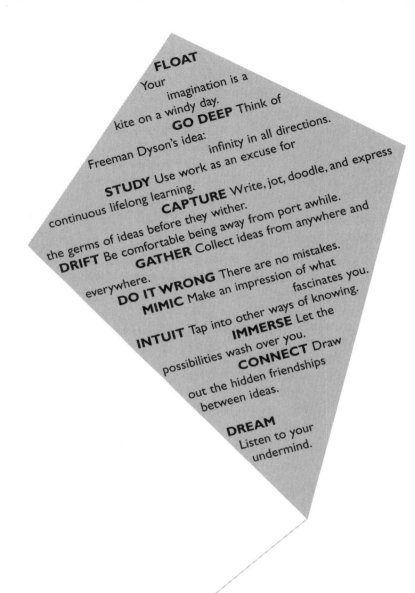

FLOAT Your imagination is a kite on a windy day.

GO DEEP Think of Freeman Dyson's idea: infinity in all directions.

STUDY Use work as an excuse for continuous lifelong learning.

CAPTURE Write, jot, doodle, and express the germs of ideas before they wither.

DRIFT Be comfortable being away from port awhile.

GATHER Collect ideas from anywhere and everywhere.

DO IT WRONG There are no mistakes.

MIMIC Make an impression of what fascinates you.

INTUIT Tap into other ways of knowing.

IMMERSE Let the possibilities wash over you.

CONNECT Draw out the hidden friendships between ideas.

DREAM Listen to your undermind.

Soak Everything Up:

Art, fashion, music, architecture, film, graphic design, books, magazines, electronics, technology, colors, cars, cellphones, toys, holiday packages, coffee, retail spaces—anything that connects (or anything that doesn't) to your field.

Then s i
f
t
t
h
r
o
w
o
u
t
t
h
e
j
u
n
k

Do the obvious.
Do the next obvious thing.
Keep going until you've exhausted
your stock supply of ideas.
Then, dig deep
and do something really

NEW.

Psychology 101

Psych yourself out: get over yourself to the point
where you can just let the energy flow.

You want to be evaluated when you are at your
creative *best*, but the acid test is how good you are
when you are at your creative *average*.

Learn ways to dip into the creative well when
you don't feel like it.

Persistence can open new forms of inspiration.

**Follow your bliss and what look like walls
will turn into doors.**

Joseph Campbell

EXUBERANCE!

See
meaning
in Clouds

See meaning
in Emoticons

See meaning
in products,
members,
trends

IMAGINK TION

IDEA GARDEN
IDEA MATRIX!

TRAINING YOUR IMAGINATION:

- VIVIDNESS.
- CONTROLLABILITY.
- FREEDOM
- 'IMAGINATIVENESS'
- VISION + FUTURE
- AUTHENTICITY.
- RECEPTIVITY to AUTHENTK
  DEEP IMPULSES

650 M
cell phones
on world

Where to
inspire imagination
Look at details
in between:
the cracs

"SANDRISMS!

DIALED on
WILD.

IMAGINATION
GONE WILD.

NOT TOO
MUCH
BUSINESS IS NOT
ABOUT I' only

BE A CHAMPION FOR THE IDEAS THAT MATTER TO YOU.

Develop an infallible technique and
then place yourself at the mercy of inspiration.

Zen maxim

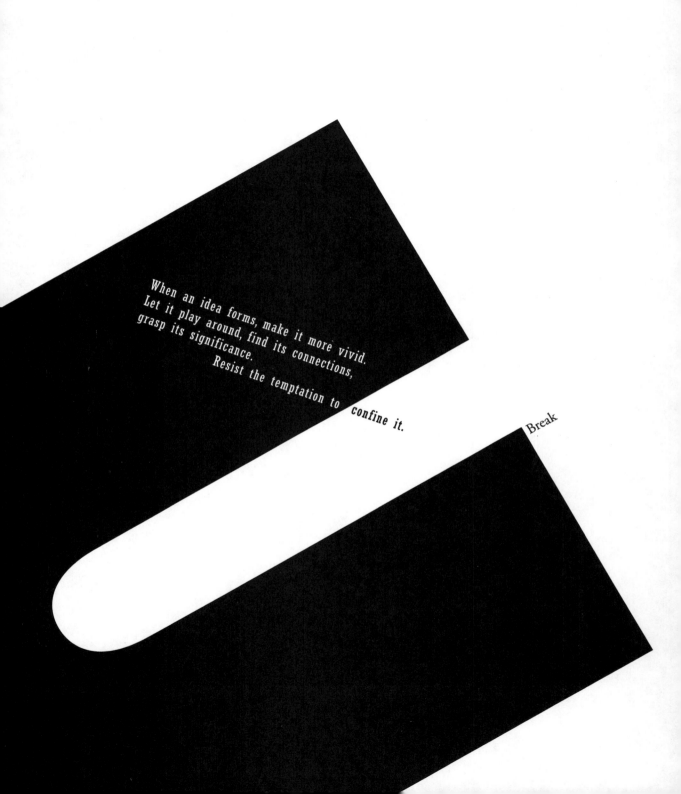

When an idea forms, make it more vivid.
Let it play around, find its connections,
grasp its significance.
Resist the temptation to confine it.

Break

free of the pull of past learning and immerse yourself in the doing. Don't lust after quick solutions. Relax.

Cultivate ideas. Edit applications. Build bridges.

Un-pop the cork. Let it flow. Unpack the feelings. Find the shape that unifies. Find out what's missing.

Ideas need dynamic, fluid, generous environments to sustain life.

Applications benefit from critical rigor.

Produce a high ratio of ideas to applications.

Contemplation
Zone

Shared
Imagination,
Inspired
Vision, and
Open Ideas

6

Creating an ecosystem
where people actively
participate in shared vision,
entertain possibility, and
invest in ideas
brings forth
true innovation.

Engineering
Imagination

When Vladimir Lenin took power during the Bolshevik revolution in 1917, he aimed to put the socialist economy on a level playing field with the Western world and to cultivate a workforce that was excited, passionate, and productive. Based on the ideas of Henry Ford and Frederick Taylor, Lenin envisioned high factory production and innovative scientific and technical development through a state-run system that promoted the continual gathering and implementation of good ideas. This vision led to what was perhaps the largest organized attempt ever to create and foster imagination and creativity.

The task of making the vision a reality was given to Felix Dzerzinsky, who later founded and ran the KGB. The system revolved around a central authority called the Ministry of Rational Proposals, which established an infrastructure of mandated creative solutions. The authority set monthly "idea quotas" for every factory in every industry in each geographic region. Factory directors were responsible for ensuring that their employees proposed a certain number of ideas that saved the factory time and money. If the managers fell short on their quota, they lost their bonuses—often a sizable chunk of their annual income. Periodically, the Ministry held national competitions where factories, cities, and regions squared off to see who could generate the largest number of creative improvement plans.

Though the system of rational proposals had a consistent internal logic, it created an unintended world of emergent behaviors. One of these was the development of the "spoof idea." As the end of the month drew closer, employees submitted impractical and sometimes ridiculous ideas that their managers would be forced to accept. Replace metal drive shafts with wooden ones. Remove safety mechanisms because they get in the way. Duplicate one idea over and over with tiny variations. In a printing press factory one employee suggested changing a particular screw in one machine. Change the screw in sixty machines and *voilà*, you have sixty ideas.

The spoof and duplicate idea problems did not *officially* exist. But to ensure that proposed ideas were implemented fully, a parallel ministry was created to check up on factories and their workers. This meant that many of the spoof and duplicate ideas had to be put into action. In one large car factory a worker suggested that a metal cutting machine could be improved by disabling one of the two safety buttons that would normally be pressed to activate the machine. The idea was adopted and the worker was rewarded. Six months later he lost a hand.

It gets even stranger. The Ministry of Planning employed armies of economic engineers to measure the value of ideas. They established prices based on what the cost *would have been* if there were a market economy. A gallon of gasoline cost less than a penny and an airline ticket for a thousand-mile trip less than two dollars. The engineers applied enormously complex rules to set prices and used dozens of telephone-sized books filled with arcane formulae and tortuous equations to establish market value. In fact, the overseeing Central Committee issued an edict that ideas must be evaluated and implemented within two years of their submission—an attempt to stimulate innovation still further.

These stories are at once funny, tragic, and instructive. Clearly, real innovation does not emerge naturally through legislation or the offer of a reward. If the only reason for generating ideas is to meet a quota or win a bonus, the emerging idea ecosystem becomes constrained and hemmed in, limited by conditions that hinder the real flow of imagination. These conditions fly in the face of what imagination values: vision, connection, passion, and the intent to make a real difference. In politburo economics there's no room for real inspiration.

Many well-intentioned and respected Western companies have made the mistake of setting idea quotas. 3M is known for its well-publicized policy that each division should generate a quarter of its sales from products introduced within the previous five years. This policy, developed in 1974, reflects the company's commitment to research and innovation. In 1992, CEO Livio DeSimone upped the ante: 30 percent of revenue had to come from products less than four years old, and management's compensation—bonuses and promotions—depended on reaching these goals.

Applying pressure to generate new products for the sake of producing new products created an artificial economy. New products were old products in different colors, slightly larger or smaller, with different finishes, in packages of three instead of six. R & D pushed product ideas into manufacturing before they were fully developed and their kinks ironed out. R & D no longer had the time to let ideas soak. In 1996, with product quality measurably dropping, 3M began to downplay the innovation policy. In the Imagination Economy quantity alone doesn't guarantee success.

Creating a culture of innovation is not about making people more imaginative, but about creating environments that allow for authentic imagination to thrive. The problem with many business environments is that they create conditions that actively discourage imaginative interchange from occurring.

The social context has enormous influence over the flow of imagination and innovation. If an organizational environment values one aspect of imaginative work over another, then that is the culture that will emerge—loose or stiff, uptight or free, fluid or structured. People produce in response to how they are rewarded—and rewards can range from monetary compensation to a sense of ownership and personal accomplishment.

Norm Simon, former VP of several major Canadian Crown corporations, puts it succinctly when he describes the failure of the "out of the box" thinking phase of the 1990s:

When they said "think out of the box," they didn't mean "act out of the box," "let your personal style be out of the box," "let your relationships or your style as a boss be out of the box." What they meant was "give us innovative ideas." So they weren't willing to pay the price—and the price was that they'd have to cope with a little deviance. If you really want out-of-the-box thinking, you have to have out-of-the-box trappings. You can't suddenly come up with this strange, new, wonderful idea in an environment where you have hierarchy and structure and have to be corporate and behaved. There's a danger in proclaiming you want out-of-the-box thinking if your intent is shrouded in hypocrisy. Really investing in imagination to see its returns is not just about nourishing and encouraging or even rewarding creativity; it's about being willing to deconstruct the conventional environment and all of its rules, or it doesn't work.[1]

The Imagination Killers

The Imagination Survey highlighted the key factors that interrupt the flow of imagination.

Anger
Pain
Angry Bosses
Bad living spaces
Bureacracy
Power
Change
Ego
Coversation
Micromanagement
Conflict
Telephone
When dream dies
Idiots
Reality
Budgets
Thinking I know it all
Deadlines
Negativity
Scales – Arpeggios
Confusion
Noise
Fear
Opposition
Lack of bandwidth
Ignorance
Multitasking
Distraction
Money
Stress
Boundaries
Work
Shoulds
Rules
Criticism
Limits
Cold water
Frustration
Boredom
Relationships
Boss
Annoying challenges
Distress
TV
Opposition
Self-doubt
Trends
Clutter
Apathy
Dull People
Exhaustion
Repetitive Work
Habits
Business
Lack of time
Finances
Lack of Incentive

The larger the word and circle, the more frequently the factor appeared in the survey as a significant influence interrupting imagination.

According to the survey, the top factors that kill imagination are rules, stress, fear, conflict, bureaucracy, exhaustion, and ego. Each has the effect of stopping the interchange of ideas cold.

Rules

An organization defines the way it does business through its policies, procedures, and processes. Organizations are always looking for ways to improve and optimize these methods of building and delivering products and services. Rules provide structure and organization to the workplace, producing measurable and quantifiable results. In this way, rules and imagination don't mix. And in fact, imagination is not always desirable in every aspect of business. You wouldn't want all the people on an assembly line to leave their personal imprint on a computer circuit or the molecular structure of a prescription drug. You would want every circuit to be the same one that was designed by the engineer.

However, for the imagination, rules usually reduce the sense of possibility. "That's the way we've always done it." "There's a reason we do it this way." "That is the way we develop it." "We've tried that and it doesn't work." Rules create barriers that hem in potential, having more to do with the rule-makers themselves than with serving any defined purpose.

Stress

The pressures that we face in business occupy our mental world with the urgent, the short-term, what needs to get done today, now. There is little room for conversations connecting us to the river of our imagination. Besides, in this kind of fast-paced, results-driven environment, the floating and meandering mind appears unproductive and wasteful, even absurd. Stress is the mind-killer.

And yet stress can be a powerful motivator and catalyst for imagination. A practical and pressing need, a problem to be explored or addressed, a task at hand, give framework to what might otherwise be random daydreams. The key with stress is to achieve a healthy and reasonable balance.

Fear

Fear has a paralyzing effect on individuals as well as entire departments and organizations. In fact, the reason most of us do not exercise the full capacity of our imagination is that we operate from fear. We are terrified of looking bad, of failing, of being ostracized from the group, of losing the security of what we currently have. Fear is enormous, and it keeps us small.

Fear of change locks us into repeating what we've always done because it's more comfortable. Piero Carcerano has created a sophisticated training facility for automobile managers and designers in Turin, Italy. Using advanced visualization hardware and software, he helps organizations convert their traditional design process into a digital one. The process is entirely different from what managers are accustomed to, employing technology such as PowerWalls and complex visualization equipment. Managers lose control because they are not familiar with much of the vocabulary of design in this new context, and their skills and strengths are thus largely unused. Leaders are accustomed to change and know its value; and at the junior levels of an organization people tend to be younger, have lots of energy, and can deal with change. But those in the middle are faced with managing both upward and downward. Caught in the middle, they are often the slowest to change. Says Carcerano: "The middle managers are the most difficult to introduce change [to]. They are the ones who worry."[2]

Fear of being laughed at insulates us from our co-workers by discouraging us from asking questions or introducing ideas that travel against the grain. We don't want to appear unwise, especially at senior-level positions. The result: we leave our authentic selves at the door. Similarly, fear of rejection keeps our ideas from circulating and the connections from being established.

I am wise because I know I am not wise.

Socrates

Fear of the unknown precludes us from traveling to a world we don't know and dipping into the river of imagination. The desire to know each step of the process beforehand, to have a plan or map of the route that lies ahead, may provide us with the illusion of safety, but it thwarts the imaginative impulse. Whereas the deliberate mind needs a story with a start, middle, and finish, the imaginative impulse can start anywhere and end anywhere.

The school system has had a huge impact in creating a collective mindset of fear. School highlights who has the "right" and who the "wrong" answer. The thousands of tests we've taken train us to look for the one right answer rather than explore alternatives. People feel stupid if they have the wrong answer. Post-secondary institutions too seem to be increasing the pressure on students to focus in tighter and earlier on an area of specialization. Degree programs seem more often designed to slot people into job functions rather than allow for exploration, experimentation, and expansion.

Why do we run our lives with fear? Why do we give up responsibility for the individual power we each possess? Why do we have such a lack of trust in others and in ourselves? I believe it is tied to the fact that we are mortal beings. We're terrified of our own death, of our own demise ... This life is a gift to make a contribution to your own growth and development and [that of] those around you. Why be a coward and die a thousand times, each time you sacrifice your potential out of fear?

Douglas J. Cardinal

Conflict, Bureaucracy, Exhaustion, and Ego

Corporate politics and the reality of business pressures cause imagination ecosystems to stagnate. The clash and intolerance of people with diverse ways of thinking turn new ideas into challenges rather than ways to stimulate thinking and consideration of alternative options. The cost of overhead and the minutiae of reports and presentations prevent people from just rolling with their ideas. The sheer fatigue of keeping pace with the pressure to deliver keeps us occupied with what's not that important, and it's easy to slip into busywork under the guise of productivity. Confrontation with people who are more concerned with ownership of their ideas and being "right" than learning and considering alternatives drains the lifeblood out of interaction. Together, these factors are the dirt in the gears that slow down the whole idea process.

Informed decision-making comes from a long tradition of guessing and then blaming others for inadequate results.

Scott Adams

Fostering the
Circulation of Ideas

In the Imagination Economy the successful organization strives to foster the imaginative impulse and to increase the value of the ideas it gathers, filters, analyzes, blends, selects, and implements. Organizations can manage this process in very formal ways, using market-driven product development schemes with rich decision-matrix criteria, or with more informal networks of personal relationships. Formal processes usually miss the disruptive, innovative ideas that are needed to survive in a fast-paced environment, while personal networks are limited in influence.

In any environment where ideas take center stage, several behaviors emerge:

• Ideas evolve through ongoing conversations.

• Ideas develop through continual renewal.

• Ownership of particular ideas becomes less important.

• As ideas are represented more fully, they grow in value.

• The more connections ideas have, the more valuable they become.

• The more people see an idea and are given an opportunity to evaluate it, improve it, and apply it, the healthier and more powerful that idea will be.

• Ideas grow when they connect to the collective vision or significance of the organization, to its reason for being.

• Ideas grow in value when they are authentic at their core and resonate with the truth that people really feel, that's connected to their core.

Organizations have infinitely complex systems for exchanging all kinds of data and information, involving conversations, e-mails, memos, reports, spreadsheets, videos, Web pages, presentations, and many other media. Creating an environment of trust, collaboration, and shared values, where the importance of the idea takes precedence over the position or power of its author, means establishing a safe haven for the free exchange of ideas.

Have a Vision

People come together when they have a common purpose, a sense of possibility, and a passion for making change. To generate new ideas there must be clear, identifiable objectives. The vision is the North Star, the guiding light that determines the overriding reason for the company's existence, as well as the measure for what is rewarded, what ideas percolate to the top. This may seem like old news, but it is as current as ever. People are charged when their ideas have a home.

Create a Community

The idea that people need to learn to be more imaginative is basically nonsense. Rather, what organizations need to learn is greater tolerance for diversity of thought. Efforts can be made to hire more "talent" or train people to be more creative, but that's not going to affect the trajectory of a corporation. A corporation should aim to create a culture that accommodates and encourages diversity, and is conducive to conversations between people who normally wouldn't interact. An organization with a shared imagination is a community with a common purpose, a defined set of values, and a language that everyone understands. Most of all, a community is a set of people who have relationships and conversations and who keep a balance between discipline and anarchy.

Have Flexible Teams

An organization with rigid work teams and hierarchical structures is like a painter who can use only one brush and one color of paint. The work will get done, but it is what it is, never changing to adjust to the task at hand. Letting people work in teams that are organized around the nature of the work and that produce ideas as the needs of the organization change is far more realistic. Teams that come together for project work keep things fresh and alive for both the organization and themselves. Mixing diverse stakeholders can promote creative abrasion and lead to greater understanding across divisions. Interdepartmental teams directed by clear and unified objectives break down the wasteful politics of "us vs. them" and free up energy that can be channeled into more positive work. Creative organizations capitalize on their employees' talents by forming temporary teams to focus on specific tasks. Like good jazz bands, they play with both structure and freedom.

Identify Roles

In a community, different people have different roles. There are big-idea people, money people, and get-it-done people. There are creators, evaluators, editors, and users. Making these roles explicit helps a team understand how it will function and where to find support and expertise. But the roles shouldn't be so fixed as to prevent people from bringing all of themselves to the table. In *The Tipping Point*, Malcolm Gladwell identifies three main types of idea facilitators: mavens, who originate ideas; connectors, who see and develop applications for ideas; and salespeople, who champion or promote ideas.[3] Imaginative job titles support a lively environment and focus activities on ideas.

Focus on Simplicity and Clarity

Nothing hinders imagination in quite the same way as confusion. Intricate, convoluted, and conflicting instructions block the flow of imaginative ideas. The KISS rule (Keep It Simple, Stupid) is as valuable in fostering a connection to the imaginative impulse as it is in implementing a project. Give people the tools they really need to do the work they really do. Enable them to connect quickly and concisely to the essence of corporate work. Free up time spent wrestling with the minutiae, the irrelevant, and the superfluous to leave room for thinking.

Produce Artifacts

Artifacts are objects—business plans, sketches, models, QuickTime movies, magazine articles, or videos—that prototype the project and move it forward in increments. Creating a culture based on ideas and their expression through artifacts provides the team with complete experiences around which to interact. Teams should be free to build new artifacts and make new categories of artifacts. As enticing as a concept is while in the mind, holding it, touching it, and playing with its material manifestation is an empowering experience. Prototypes are tools of change that bring ideas to the tangible world.

Create an Environment That Promotes Imagination

The physical environment, from the layout of desks and the placement of windows to the kind of lighting and the nature of the noise, has a profound effect on the way people communicate, relate, and work. A mix of open space, where ideas can intermingle, and hiding places and cozy cubbyholes, where people can go off and tease out germinal ideas without interruption and work with focused concentration, helps keep imaginative conversations alive. War rooms, collaboration spaces, and what-if rooms are physical expressions of imaginative thinking.

Use Technology to Promote Idea Flow

The tools we use—e-mail, voice mail, video conferences, intranets, and other technologies—open us to a new world of creative collaboration. Making them easy to use and supportive of what people actually do increases the chance that they will be used.

Requirements vs. The Big Idea

Fundamentally, business ideas can progress along two paths: requirements or the big idea.

Requirements Process

In the requirements process you put together a team of people and task them with generating an idea for a new product, service, or venture. They conduct market research, competitive analysis, customer research, and analysis of internal core competencies with the intent of producing a requirements document. This document provides a snapshot of a product's features and intended market, how much it will cost, and how long it will take to build. The document is then circulated to other departments and stakeholders, such as engineering and marketing, for assessment. Generally, the process tends to be too expensive and takes too long.

There are two kinds of people in the world. There are the people who believe there are two kinds of people and there are the people **who do not**.

Big-Idea Process

The big-idea process begins with a vision, an inspired concept of what a product or service could be. Usually, a big idea is the work of an individual who champions a simple but powerful organizing principle that drives the venture. The big idea is a charismatic idea that, ideally, connects significant principles. This mindset prefers to move forward quickly, with minimal process requirements.

Putting It Together

The successful venture of the future requires a combination of big-idea thinking with requirements process execution. But bringing the two together produces a powerful clash of cultures. Bran Ferren puts it succinctly:

> So what's the problem? You bring big-idea and requirements people in the same room and you're done. These people hate each other. Requirements people think big-idea people don't belong in big organizations. Big-idea people think that requirements people drain the life force out of the organization and their participation precludes creativity.
>
> Still, there has never been a big idea that came out of a requirements process. You can spend as much time as you want doing due diligence, I don't believe that you can or will (unless it's a complete coincidence) end up with a big idea. And if you do, it will be killed in the value-engineering phase.[4]

The ideal is to merge the two processes, recognizing there is a need for both. The challenge is achieving a balance between the two mindsets so that ideas aren't strangled by processes that are so intensely focused on quantifiable measurement that they completely overlook the inspirational and intrinsic value of the idea spark. This requires the right mix of people to achieve a core of mutual respect, starting from the team's leadership so that the players understand its importance.

Leadership goes a long way toward fostering environments where people can respect each other even if they disagree. Part of the challenge is remembering that there are basic human needs to be addressed. While our technology may be driven by rules of thumb like Moore's Law, we as human beings are not. And the same human needs, such as love, companionship, warmth, culture, art, food, and shelter, that have governed us for the past few million years will continue to govern us in the future. Giving permission for people to be more human means they don't have to spend so much time hitting the deck running, and can spend more time hitting the deck thinking, feeling, and caring.

Along with solid leadership, we need vision. Vision is something that we will not achieve through an internally generated evaluation process or any equivalent. Let's face it: vision is aspiration.

Vision

Few terms in business create such a complex reaction as *vision*. In the past two decades of corporate business life the vision thing has been implemented and re-implemented, worked and reworked, packaged and repackaged. The majority of the Imagination Survey respondents were skeptical about their company's vision: many had gone through several consultant-led vision exercises, often on a yearly basis with the arrival of new management teams. New guy, new view—no big deal. The process becomes insignificant and meaningless. No wonder the vision thing produces a sour taste in the mouths of most employees.

Martin Luther King did not say, "I have a strategic plan." Instead he shouted, "I have a DREAM!" and he created a crusade.

Bob Kreigel

But the fact is, vision does matter. It's difficult to know how to make the right decisions without the guiding star of vision. If you don't have that one most powerful tool to align, enliven, and spark the imaginations within an organization, how can you focus your effort? In *Built to Last*, authors James Collins and Jerry Porras identify the single factor that determined which organizations survived longer than twenty years: a clear and well-articulated vision.[5]

If you don't know where you're going, any road will take you there.

Vision is an intersection between business and imagination, a way to connect the thinking and the energy of the two mindsets, even if the ways you get where you're going are quite different. A clear, well-thought-out vision provides a framework for understanding the kinds of ideas that will be explored, worked, adopted, implemented, and rewarded within an organization. This framework helps employees channel their creativity and imagination toward ideas that will have a chance of making it to the light of business. And it defines corporate purpose, speaking to the imagination's need for meaning and business's need for quantifiable metrics.

Doug Walker is president of Alias|Wavefront, a division of Silicon Graphics Limited and a 3-D computer graphics software company whose vision is to create the world's most compelling digital visual experiences and become the standard by which 3-D visual experiences become pervasive and interactive. He believes that generating support for the company's values is an important part of getting employees to buy into the company vision. He describes it this way: "The more we can create a framework, so people know where we're trying to go through our mission and vision, the more successful we will be. If people see their peers being rewarded for creativity, they will step out of their way to be more creative."[6]

Walker says that understanding where the customer "is going or could be going informs the vision. If you have too much freedom, then chaos becomes its own form of bureaucracy. You want all of these good ideas to channel in certain ways so they drive business results. You don't want to bridle those ideas so they can't bubble to the top."[7]

A mission statement should articulate the fundamental purpose of the company. It should send a signal as to why it's worthwhile to be part of the organization.

Ted Davis

How do you reward these ideas? You want a rewards and recognition system that's based around the company's goals. Ralph Christensen, senior vice-president of human resources for Hallmark Cards, believes that vision is the idea factory: "Everyone might not get the words exactly right, but everyone here gets the spirit right. The mission statement has a lot of power to move people. People come and stay at Hallmark because they want to be part of the mission. It helps us stay focused."[8]

Don't give people goals, give them direction.

A handful of companies have distilled their strategy into a simple, single phrase and have used it to drive consistent strategic action throughout their organization:

America Online Consumer connectivity first—anytime, anywhere.

Bombardier Moving People

Dell Be Direct.

eBay Focus on trading communities.

FedEx People—Service—Profit

General Electric Be number one or number two in every industry in which we compete, or get out.

Hallmark To help consumers express themselves, celebrate, strengthen relationships, and enrich their lives.

Southwest Airlines Meet customers' short-haul travel needs, at fares competitive with the cost of automobile travel.

Vanguard Unmatchable value for the investor-owner.

Wal-Mart Everyday Low Prices

Fostering Ideas in a Culture of Creativity: ICE Corporation

Doug Keeley is founder and president of ICE, a Toronto-based creative services organization that produces branding, digital media, and corporate events. With customers internationally, ICE is an agency whose lifeblood is the generation of creative ideas that customers will buy. ICE focuses on three things: customer satisfaction, employee satisfaction, and profitability. But underlying these corporate measurements is the credo *No more same old, same old here.* Keeley says, "Our credo is reflected in how we think, in how we deal with clients, how we treat each other, and in the kind of work we do."[9]

This approach is one of the essential elements of ICE's culture, itself an important part of ICE's success.

I think business is life. I don't buy that you wake up in the morning of your life and you exit through a door to do something called business, where you have a certain set of behaviors, and then you return back through a different door and continue with your life at night. Most of us spend more time doing business than we do with our families or doing whatever we want to do on our own. And so I think that the most important perspective of business is to realize that it is the greatest expenditure of the waking hours of your life and you'd better treat it appropriately. This is a belief that doesn't necessarily go well with the stock market.[10]

When Keeley started ICE, he and his partners wanted to do "cool stuff" and be "the coolest company in the world." When they expanded and brought people in from IBM, the new people said, "It's not customer-focused. It's hokey and corny." Keeley has had time to think about this and he concludes: "They're wrong. People want to be inspired. They want to go to work and say, 'God, I love being here. If I have to be apart from my loved ones, this is the only thing I want to be doing.'"[11]

So what is business about? Is it about doing something amazing or is it about making money? When great organizations like Apple, The Body Shop, and HP started, they were about something amazing. The stuff in the bottles is just a by-product of the passion. Unfortunately, this is something you don't learn at business school. It's a huge challenge to have a goal and a mission that is really exciting, and to make money doing it. And as you grow as an organization, it's harder to match those two things.

For Keeley, coming up with ideas is the heart of the process, and having a creative culture is what's important.

You need to make everyone in the company feel like they are part of the creative process ... You've got to be able to create an environment where everyone feels that they own the creative, an environment where communication is open, where there is no fear and there's not a lot of ego. Bring people with different skills together and that forms a team. If you've got two good heads looking at a problem, then two heads are better than one. And five heads can be way better than two.[12]

In the context of a culture that promotes the circulation of ideas, based on the values of mutual respect and authenticity, any type of idea-generation process will work. Some of ICE's people go away and lock the door and imagine on their own, brainstorming by themselves, even meditating quietly. Others prefer to go the other way, and tap into their imagination by getting a group of people in a room to create energy around possibilities and to throw ideas around. Keeley describes it as "a collective play process where you throw a piece of imaginative clay on the table and everyone whacks at it and carves at it and you end up with something a few hours later and everyone thinks, 'Hey, that's good.'"[13]

Understanding Risk and Making Connections: X-Corporation

X-Corporation is a Toronto-based brand management organization that develops creative material. Founder and president Sabaa

Quoa attributes his capacity to flip between strategic and creative mindsets to his background in both business and design. Imagination contributes to his business thinking because it helps to break assumptions and to generate fresh approaches. At the same time, business focus provides the necessary structure that allows the effective implementation of imagination. Business constantly scrutinizes, while the imagination continuously looks around and out for possibilities.

According to Quoa, imagination and business

are very complementary as long as you know when to switch gears between non-linear and linear. You need to have a sense of how to switch gears. Creative types don't always know how to get structure and vice- versa because each camp accepts clichés such as "We're 'creatives' so we don't accept structure," and the business-minded say "Those creative types!" They all get stuck in their own paradigms.[14]

One of X-Corporation's areas of expertise is minimizing its clients' sense of risk. According to Quoa, most clients are mired in their corporate politics and have a low comfort level when it comes to introducing new ideas to their organization. For them, because success lies in reaching a team consensus, they continually manage upward, downward, and to the side, anticipating the way new ideas will be judged by their peers. The further an idea progresses along the path of implementation—the more ideas, dollars, and resources get attached to it—the riskier the idea becomes. The perceived risk increases as new ideas have to be sold to the boss or the board. X-Corporation provides clients with tools to keep anxiety and risk to a minimum. It manages the meeting of objectives and is careful to structure ideas and package its approaches as ideas move along the path from possibility to implementation.

As a part of managing his clients' comfort, Quoa often omits them from the idea generation phase, because it's easier for outsiders to come with naive and fresh minds to ask the "obvious" questions that internal employees might overlook or not dare to challenge. Additionally, clients' anticipation of the future risks associated with change can derail promising germinal ideas. But Quoa responds by posing the questions,

"What's the worst that can happen?" "What does it cost to put an idea on the table?" Brainstorming is an essentially low-risk activity. It costs virtually nothing to put ideas on the table. Ideas don't hurt because at this phase of the process there are no cost implications. It's OK to say, "We have to be linear in our delivery," but we don't have to be linear in our thinking and our approach."[15]

You have to be comfortable with chaos at the beginning.

Rather than rely on one individual to develop the creative brief, X-Corporation chooses the team approach. This way the project or "problem" is new and fresh to everyone, and ideas can be freely brainstormed, bounced off and picked up from each other, resulting in a good number of solid ideas that can then be filtered down. The more people are involved, the greater the chance of coming up with the best possible idea.

Throwing ideas on the table is the most unstructured part of the process, bearing the lowest risk and the greatest potential. Once there is a good pool of ideas on the table, they begin the process of narrowing them down to the one the client will connect most strongly to. Then they form, develop, and deliver the presentation. The process is akin to starting with scribbles, looking for good ideas to jump out, picking up the gems, and then balancing the business and creative modes to choose winners that are imaginative and also deliver on business needs.

According to Quoa, the role of imagination is critical in creative services because one has to come up with new solutions that match a particular brand, and that means doing something outside the norm of the client's experience. You have always to start from scratch, and to feel confident about putting something in front of the client without being intimidated by the need to come up with something totally new.

Tapping into imagination means drawing on all the influences, all the personal experiences one has as an individual, often in an unpredictable way. Working imaginatively means being willing to go back in order to access knowledge derived from past experiences. For example, in response to a particular packaging problem, Quoa was reminded of the way his mother used to fold the paper when wrapping presents. The connection was relevant and useful even though the source was completely out of sequence. The team took the idea out of one context and applied and adapted it to the project at hand.

Quoa and his organization operate with the belief that they'll never run out of ideas. If anyone gets stuck, they have resources immediately at hand. "Ideas are as close as the next desk ... I can ask the person next to me, 'What do you think of this?' Or look out the window. There's always a source for ideas."[16]

If there is an underlying way to bring the creative and business elements together, Quoa thinks of it as presenting an idea and imagining the right reaction. He envisions articulating an idea and sees in his mind's eye how it works. "The role of business is to bring structure to the ideas in a way that's useful or resolves some kind of problem in a way that makes sense for its audience."[17]

I have made decisions that turned out to be wrong, and went back and did it another way, and still took less time than many who procrastinated over the original decision. Your brain is capable of handling 140,000 million bits of information in one second, and if you take hours or days or weeks to reach a vital decision, you are short-circuiting your most valuable property.

Jerry Gillies

Authenticity, the People Experience, and Real-World Values: The Body Shop

Margot Franssen, founding partner and president of The Body Shop in Canada, attributes her organization's success to having a value system that is consistent twenty-four hours a day. Some people maintain one business-oriented value system from nine to five and switch to a family-oriented value system from five to nine. Franssen believes it is too hard and too draining and rather unrealistic to change values when stepping in and out of work. There was no template for this way of doing business when she, her sister, and her husband started The Body Shop, so they simply did what came naturally. They extended their home values and mode of living to their workplace and the business environment they created. When people join The Body Shop, they feel the freedom to be themselves. "When you're a business, you're not allowed to make mistakes; but when you're home, it's OK to make a lot of mistakes," Franssen says. "Your mom and dad are always saying, 'Way to go, pick yourself up, try again, that's a way to be!' You never find that in a workplace."[18]

A genuine opportunity to learn through encouragement is a key part of organizations that encourage the circulation of ideas. The Body Shop offices maintain open workspaces and no ceilings. The three principals have always shared an office and believe that people should hear their conversations. They have now added a fourth desk to their space and bring in a new person every six months. In this way, ideas and processes can be heard, understood, and shared freely, and even challenged first-hand. This can only work in an environment where it's OK to be your authentic self and to make mistakes.

Franssen says that running a business in this way is not just about leadership—it's also about "followership."

If you don't have followership in an office, you're dead meat. Oftentimes a leader can make a mistake and nobody knows about it. So you have to show your vulnerable side, that you make mistakes and that it's OK. And when you make a mistake, verbally apologize for it so other people can say, "OK, that person's making mistakes, so I can, too." If you're not making mistakes, you're not learning. You're not taking risks, and so you can't move forward. Nothing happens without a risk.[19]

The Body Shop lives by the principles of authenticity and openness, encouraging people to surf on their naivety. In the company's early years the management team put people into positions for which they had no experience. They had their corporate lawyer running the warehouse and distribution, while the warehouse manager ran the social values program. Every year or so they would switch everybody around because

the staff had to work on their wits or imagination or creativity to get over problems. An experienced person would say, "We can't do it that way because a year from now there's going to be this great big hole in the road and we don't want to have to encounter that." Whereas an inexperienced person would say, "Well, let's just go down this road as far as we can go, and if there's a hole, I'll just deal with it when I get there." So you tend to go a whole lot faster. You have to have intelligent people so that they don't fall into the holes, but I always think our business is a success because we were not experienced businesspeople. We had no formal training whatsoever except for our experience in life.[20]

Franssen stresses that there are certain life-sustaining areas of a company that you can't jive with—like your financials. But for the most part, experimentation, improvisation, and going by gut feel supported by thinking produce their own kind of innovation. Open and clear communication is a core part of The Body Shop's way of doing business. They created a department called Social Inventions that develops practical solutions for social problems. The Director of Values Campaigns, the Director of Community Services, and an Ethics Officer took a road trip from coast to coast, visiting the staff at all 120 stores. At the lunch meetings the employees brought food they felt represented the company, along with questions they wanted to have answered. The visiting team gave updates on the company's values and their stand on social issues, and allowed time for employees to ask any questions they wanted to help them feel better about where the company was at.

The road trip took a whole year, but the company came together because of the real belly-to-belly, person-to-person contact that Franssen says is so critical to creating relationships and teams. Then the Ambassador of Dialogue went out to speak with people across the country at customer evenings and to make presentations at universities, establishing contacts and "Friends of The Body Shop," making people aware of what the company values and stands for. According to Franssen, "That's how we do it—it's never a plan ... it just kind of happens from me sitting somewhere and then saying, 'I just got a great idea.'"[21]

Even a mistake may turn out to be the one thing necessary to a worthwhile achievement.

Henry Ford

Flexibility and Strong Leadership: Alias|Wavefront

An organization's culture starts with the people who lead. What an executive team considers important, how it communicates with its teams, the depth and extent of its integrity, and how it respects individuals have an enormous impact. David Wexler, director of human resources at Alias|Wavefront, says,

These core values flow up and down through all levels of management. If positive values flow up and meet with lack of integrity and honesty, they quickly hit a wall and sour into cynicism. If positive values flow down and meet honestly with trust, ultimately you can create synergy. When respect and trust flow down throughout an organization, the deeper communication, and the willingness to share and interchange, flow as well. The organization will "get it."[22]

Culture is ethereal, fragile, and a vital ingredient for organizations that depend on ideas. Culture reflects the way people feel, what they believe is important, how they communicate, why they make the decisions they do, what they notice, and what they don't notice.

It is a shared sense of something that is in alignment with personal values. You can put several people in the same environment with similar values—good or bad—and you instantly have a culture.

Universities are excellent places to examine the effect and self-organizing power of culture. People interested in mechanics and tinkering will congregate in places where they can pull engines apart and put them back together. People who want to discuss philosophical ideas will gather in graduate schools. People who are motivated by a desire to help others naturally congregate in volunteer organizations. Culture is the social, moral, intellectual, emotional, and spiritual glue that holds groups of people together.

It doesn't take much for imagination to flourish. It just takes someone saying, "Great idea! Would you like to run with it?" Then let them run to a certain point and check back in. Remember, not all ideas will be good ones. But one thing that will surely kill ideas and destroy spirit is an organization with no room for flexible structures. If every new idea that requires a flexible structure—such as a temporary research task force—is met with "Sorry, we're too busy," eventually most individuals will mentally check out, and some will check out of the organization altogether. In this way organizations lose immeasurable assets and potential. What would the view look like if we considered the cost of *not* doing something to be as significant as the cost of the ideas we do implement?

Wexler says:

I hire on the basis of two qualities: intelligence and attitude. I believe that experience can be acquired; but you either have intelligence or you don't. And you either have an attitude that will enable you to fit the culture and be part of a team, or you don't. If you have an organization composed of people of high intelligence and positive attitude, you have fertilizer for soil. You have many of the ingredients, perhaps not all. But without intelligence and attitude, you have no hope for having imagination flourish.[23]

We can only be truly great if we grow our revenues, our businesses, our markets, and the kind of talent we bring to the marketplace. Growth is an organic process, requiring flexible organizational structures, like task forces and project teams, made up of individuals who are passionate about their ideas and empowered to see them through.

Cross-Discipline Councils: Sony

When Sony embarked on the process of creating PlayStation 2, it felt the need to provide some structure, or the opportunity for structure, in order for real innovation to occur. To encourage faster development and bigger ideas, it brought together people from its thirteen different studios, each around their own discipline. The desire among the artists and designers for PlayStation 2 to be so much better than anything else on the market was so strong that they were willing to come together and share their ideas. They were united by a common vision of the potential for PlayStation 2. As a response Sony created the Artists' Council. This was followed by the Technical Council, a Graphics Council, and a Sound-and-Audio Council. Then these councils were brought together on a regular basis—and big ideas started to emerge. Says Rusty Reuff, Senior VP, HR, Electronic Arts Inc., "That's what we can do as leaders: provide the forum and the structure to bring people together who otherwise wouldn't have met."[24]

Self-Managing Work Teams: General Electric

When GE was faced with setting up a new domestic factory to comply with a revised set of government objectives, it turned to organizational development consultant Carolyn Gallagher. What followed was a long and intricate transition process, which resulted in a more complex environment with a greater variety of needs and a broader range of activities, populated by long-time employees who were accustomed to working in a certain way.

In the course of looking at productivity and work structures, production employees decided the best solution to the new work requirements would be self-managed work teams. But this suggestion met with some resistance from the VP in charge. Ultimately, there was agreement to set up a test run, which would give the VP the opportunity to evaluate whether or not he felt the team could handle self-management. The employees set up a production line and the VP role-played the product. The objective was to move the product (the VP) through the line to completion. The VP was allowed to ask questions about himself, designed to challenge and test the line, all along the way. The employees had to address his questions efficiently in order to pass him along successfully to the next phase of manufacturing. Needless to say, the questions were no walk in the park, and the VP pushed hard. But ultimately, the production employees' design proved successful, and they made the move to self-managed teams.

The advantage of self-directed work teams is that all the team members have and take equal ownership in the work, and their roles increase dramatically in scope. Management's role changes to one of facilitator and negotiator rather than taskmaster. There is a more holistic approach to knowledge, skills, and learning, resulting in greater transferability between roles and a more autonomous work environment. And it's no secret that when people are more self-directed, and have a greater stake in and a more direct impact on what they do, job satisfaction increases dramatically.[25]

Sharing the Responsibility and Privilege of Success: American Airlines

In 1989 Robert Crandall, CEO of American Airlines, launched the IdeAAs in Action system. It was an open program designed to control expenses, generate revenues, and tap into the organization's creativity, knowledge, and ideas. The program encouraged employees to share their ideas on better ways to run the business. Crandall set the bar high and defined a new corporate value when he said, "We will listen, will respond and we will provide rewards."[26] His priority was to reduce costs, and he was relying on his entire team to generate budget-cutting suggestions. Crandall got personally involved in making the reductions, and many of the stories are legendary.

Over years of gathering meal trays, American Airlines flight attendants had noticed that the majority of customers didn't eat the olives in their salad. Crandall initiated a study that showed almost three-quarters of passengers avoided them, and by eliminating the olives, the airline would save up to $500,000 a year.

During the Gulf War, business travel on transatlantic flights dropped significantly; often the first-class cabin was entirely empty. Nevertheless, each plane's provision list included one 200-gram tin of caviar valued at $250, most of which went to waste. Flight attendant Kathryn Kridel's cost-savings suggestion, to equip first-class cabins with two 100-gram tins of caviar in place of the more expensive 200-gram tin, was accepted. This seemingly tiny change affected 43,000 flights per year, saving over $567,000 from the $3-million caviar budget. Kridel received an IdeAAs in Action award of $50,000.

The IdeAAs in Action program percolated throughout the organization, resulting in tens of thousands of suggestions each year and the formation of an IdeaAAdvocates group to help promote participation in cost-savings activities. Virtually every part of the organization submitted cost-savings and revenue-generating ideas. Pilots, flight attendants, maintenance workers, and trainers, among others, came up with ideas that saved American Airlines hundreds of millions of dollars. The climax of the program was a drive to fund the airline's fiftieth Boeing 757 entirely out of employee cost-reduction savings. The campaign attracted over 48,000 suggestions, of which 4,600 were implemented, and together they produced $58 million in savings. The plane, called the *Pride of American*, is the only airship in American's fleet with a name.

The Buck
Stops There

Incentive programs, even those as successful as American Airlines', still have significant shortcomings. In that program ideas come from fewer than a tenth of the employees, and fewer than a tenth of the submitted ideas are accepted. Most of the value comes from the mechanics, who can often generate savings of $100,000 a year by their suggestions. It even got to the point where the mechanics worked secretly because their managers would look for the mechanics' ideas and then rush to submit them as their own.

From a business perspective the program has resulted in significant savings on expenses, but it has rarely generated out-of-the-box ideas. Since the company was oriented toward short-term cost reduction when it set up the program, this became the center of the employees' imaginations, automatically relegating other options to a secondary position. Though the successfully implemented ideas range from simple suggestions to complex reworkings of engine parts, the wealth of other potentially imaginative ideas—new business development, partnerships, joint marketing, elements that would change the way customers feel while traveling with American—has rarely been addressed.

From the point of view of imagination, the program serves as extrinsic motivation. The real challenge is to convert the extrinsic motivation of employees into the intrinsic motivation of imagination, which is not a simple or easy task. The fundamental goal is to create a productive environment that stimulates the core of imagination and aligns to the values of the organization.

Open
Dialogue

Considered to be one of the modern world's greatest physicists, David Bohm made enormous contributions to the worlds of both science and philosophy. He is also well known for his work on dialogue, which came as a result of extensive dialogue with the spiritual master and mystic J. Krishnamurti.

Along with associates Donald Factor and Peter Garrett, Bohm developed the concept of leaderless and agendaless dialogues among groups of twenty-five to fifty people. The purpose behind this format is to create spaces of time where people can come together to share openly and listen, and to suspend the opinions and judgments that are the usual results of a set agenda. Bohm made a distinction between discussion and dialogue, defining discussion as being akin to a ping-pong game: players bat their positions back and forth for the ultimate purpose of winning (and, of course, making someone else lose). Dialogue, on the other hand, is an equal participation, a sharing and exchange of thoughts and beliefs leading to a greater understanding. In this case there is no game, and everyone wins.

The rules for dialogue are:

1. Have no agenda.

2. Have no leader (only a temporary facilitator if required).

3. Have a large enough group for the presence of subcultures (twenty-five to fifty).

4. Make a time commitment that is generous enough to effect change (minimum one year).

In his book *On Dialogue*, Bohm states:

> In the dialogue group we are not going to decide what to do about anything. This is crucial. Otherwise, we are not free. We must have an empty space where we are not obliged to do anything, nor to come to any conclusions, nor to say anything or not say anything. It's open and free ... So we have here a kind of empty space where anything may come in—and after we finish, we just empty it. We are not trying to accumulate anything. That's one of the points about a dialogue. As Krishnamurti used to say, "The cup has to be empty to hold something."[27]

In an effort to get people talking to one another at the World Bank, Carolyn Gallagher initiated Bohm's dialogue process. The group met regularly for one- to two-hour sessions and followed Bohm's rules of engagement, with the addition of a tape recorder to record the dialogues. As a follow-up, the recordings were transcribed and passed along as items for reflection.

At first the idea met with skepticism: a two-hour meeting with no agenda seemed like a profound waste of time. But it wasn't. At the outset people were a bit awkward, not knowing where to start. But the small talk diminished as the number of meetings increased. And what Gallagher found came as no surprise. "Within forty minutes they were all talking about human values, who we are and why we do what we do. When this exchange of values began to take place, that's when the really creative ideas emerged. You could play back the recordings or review the sequence of transcriptions and really see the evolution of what had happened."[28]

To the skeptics, Gallagher has this to say: "People just want to talk to each other; they need shared air time. They do this anyway around the water cooler and by stealing away time from other meeting agendas."[29] Creating dialogue created relationships between diverse stakeholders and people who might otherwise never have spoken to one another. Because they had connected on common ground—that of human values—politics and personal risk were eliminated. That's when true innovation began.

The Imaginative Culture

Getting people to share ideas freely requires more than just dialogue. Fostering an imaginative environment means eliminating the barriers to creativity, the imagination-killers. Opening dialogue in a spirit of trust creates a culture that values sharing and thrives on the exchange of ideas.

This ongoing process of creating a community requires strong leadership, and a clear corporate vision to which all the stakeholders can set their compass. Organizations that have weakly defined vision, or no vision at all, or perhaps a vision that frequently changes direction, create cultures of doubt, filled with suspicious, demotivated employees.

If employees can look to a clearly articulated vision, they know where to set sail for. If they are empowered to run with and develop their ideas, they will be ignited by passion and commitment. If they have opportunities to work with diverse groups around varying tasks, the products of innovation will be broader and more far-reaching. If they are free to make mistakes and ask questions, they will be eager to seek answers and explore possibilities.

And if the employee can look to the team leading the journey and feel that its messages and actions resonate with truth and that there is shared meaning, the culture is built out of respect, even if there is disagreement.

Kerry Stirton, vice president, conglomerates investment research at Sanford C. Bernstein, has been involved in innovation teams with such global idea giants as Bombardier Aerospace, where he was vice president, strategic planning and business development, and McKinsey, where he participated in the groundbreaking work on the possible impact and direction of e-commerce. Contemplating the role of leadership, Stirton says:

There are those who might not be as attuned to the power of great new ideas that absolutely mobilize great energies on the part of the workforce. But wise leaders will almost never squelch good ideas, because if they have aspirations to grow and innovate, as they should have, then they understand the difference between an expense and an investment. And they ought to be facilitating the thinking process that gets a company to the point where a new idea could be a good investment, and not thinking about new ideas as irritating expenses.[30]

Invest
Wisely

Find your **VISION**

Openness

Individuality

COURAGE

Expression

Facilitate regular cross-functional meetings to get your teams thinking in new ways.

Facilitate regular cross-functional meetings to get your teams thinking in new ways.

Cross-Pollinate.

BRAINSTORMING DO'S

HAVE A FOCUS Clarify the reasons for brainstorming.

SET GOALS Keep in mind what the ideas are supposed to achieve.

BE PLAYFUL The best part of storms is the way they roll, crash, and surprise you.

GATHER IDEAS You'll never know when you have a juicy one. Record them all. Flip through your archives.

PLAY WITH CLAY Plop ideas on the table and let others shape them.

CONNECT IDEAS Let ideas build on each other. Yoke them together into new ones.

BRAINSTORMING DON'TS

THE BOSS IS ALWAYS RIGHT Let one person set the agenda.

ONE AT A TIME Go through ideas systematically, draining their energy.

CENSOR There are no bad … well, you get the idea.

NO FUN If it starts to get heavy, chances are so will the solutions.

THE LOUD ONES Letting the loud voices own the stage drowns out the quiet ones.

BRING YOUR EGO This is not about you.

What would it take
to create an environment
where it is safe to
— bring forth, talk about, and entertain new ideas?
— test and experiment with new ideas?
— implement and evaluate new ideas?

What are the bounds of safety
within your organization?

Where is the edge of its
imaginative comfort zone?

Set up a laboratory, a war room, a research center,

where your team has permission to be

outlandish.

Conversations

when was the last time you had lunch
with someone from work
Just foR fun
and you didn't talk business?
do you know the passion and hobbies of your colleagues?
(do you know your colleagues?)

where is your sandbox at work?

1. Hire opposites
   (for creative abrasion).

2. Create diversity
   (to get contrasting opinions).

3. Invite visitors
   (to hear fresh points of view).

4. Go outside
   (to escape cultural pressure).

5. Rally around ideas
   (aspire to aspire).

Meetings! **Bloody Meetings!**

Informational: What is the knowledge you want to share?

Brainstorming: What is the most **powerful** approach you can take?

Decision-making: What is going to make the **biggest** difference?

No-Agenda: What is on your mind?

Breakfast: Plenty of coffee.

To encourage innovation means to accept failure.

Expect things to blow up on you.

People learn by making mistakes.

Allow mistakes to happen.

Do not punish those who make them.

Strive to have a reasonable tolerance for things that don't go well, fall apart, or are imperfect.

Every mission is a discovery in the experiment of life.

Arming yourself with this attitude opens you to the freedom of creative experience.

Time in such a venture becomes less bundled up in beginning, middle, and end, and is more of a continuum.

"I only want ideas that are going to be successful."

SIMPLICITY AND CLARITY:

Establishing context lays the groundwork
for co-ordinated thinking and action:

CONTEXT

What is the background of the activity?
What is its purpose?

VISION

What are the desired outcomes? What will
the metrics be?

STRATEGY

What are the objectives aligning the context
and vision?

TACTICS

What are the approaches to reaching the
desired goals?

ROLES

Who is responsible for what?

SUCCESS

What constitutes successful completion?

Crisis Management Now
Adrenalin is not a cornerstone of good management.

The impresario is a powerful image of one who

inspires imagination. As director of a theater

company an impresario must deal with the

artistic temperament. Sometimes she acts as a

coach, coaxing the best out of her team, and

providing a framework and environment for

exploration and learning; and at other times she

is a drill sergeant, demanding the best possible

performance. The impresario makes the

environment safe, allowing each artist to do his

work without having to deal with the overall

structure and smooth running of the production.

7

From the Intangible to the Tangible

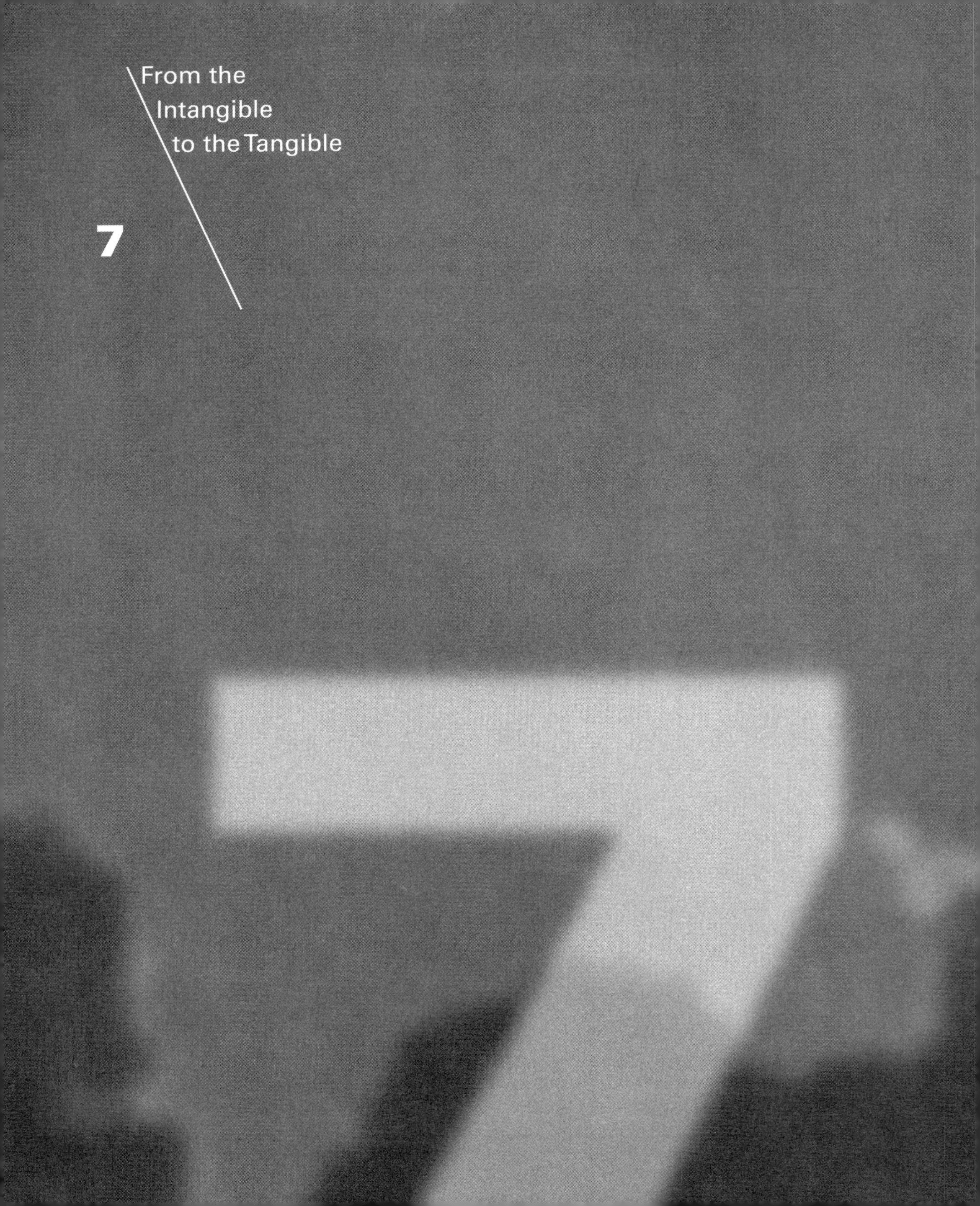

Bringing ideas from impulse
to reality in the Imagination Economy
calls for an organic process—a dynamic
interchange between possibility
and prototype, where concept, design,
production, and
experience blend.

Possibility
to Reality

Bill Gross is a well-known Silicon Valley entrepreneur. Starting in junior high school, where he sold candy bars, Gross has set up and sold companies his entire life. He has built parabolic concentrators that harness solar energy, designed loudspeakers to pay his way through Caltech, owned a high-end audio store, and written a natural language add-in program to Lotus 1-2-3. When his son entered kindergarten, Gross started Knowledge Adventure, an educational software company to inspire children to fall in love with learning,

The ultimate vehicle for Gross's entrepreneurial exuberance takes the form of the metacompany Idealab!, an organization that builds and sells prototype companies. One of the many business concepts Idealab! has developed focused on improving the experience of buying a car. Gross believed that a Web site that lets customers view, customize, and buy a car would be a viable and profitable opportunity. You select the car you want, customize it with drop-down menus, put down $1,000, arrange financing, and the car arrives on a flatbed truck. The customer never has to go through the hassle of dealing with the middleman.

When he pitched the idea, investors were skeptical. Would customers actually use the site? Where would the cars come from? How would the Web site affect dealer channels? When everyone was concerned about the reinvention of the business model, Gross said, "Why don't we just try it?"[1] and enlisted Idealab! to make a prototype.

Gross empowered an employee to be the executive of the idea and told him to just go ahead and make the site. If anyone orders a car, he instructed, then go to the local auto mall, buy the car, and drive it to the customer's house with an invoice. The money lost on the transaction would pay for the experiment and determine if customers would actually complete the transaction. The fact that the prototype didn't require raising any outside money or adding any new people to the company meant that Gross wouldn't have to lay anybody off if the idea didn't work.

The executive kept returning week after week to talk to dealers; he wanted to ensure a supply. Gross said, "Don't even worry about that. I just want to see if the idea would work."[2] Within sixty days Idealab! had bought the domain name Carsdirect.com and built a prototype site that was all smoke and mirrors—attractive graphics with no infrastructure. If someone ordered a car, the site sent an e-mail to the executive, who would print it out, order the car at the dealership, pick it up, and drive it over wearing a tuxedo.

The site was launched on a Thursday afternoon. By Friday morning they had sold five cars. With that, Gross knew his prototype was successful and could move forward on the larger implementation of the idea. He said to his idea executive, "OK. Hurry up and turn the site off!"[3]

The CarsDirect.com prototype lost $7,500 per car, but it satisfied five customers who got their cars at invoice prices. The point was, Idealab! proved that consumers would buy cars from a Web site. Within ninety days of the prototype test Idealab! had secured financing for CarsDirect.com, built a solid Web infrastructure, and created a real business model. A year later CarsDirect.com was selling two thousand cars a month at an average of $28,000 a car, and had grown into a $700-million business. The model continued to evolve, allowing the customer to choose between working with a local auto dealer or a CarsDirect.com vehicle specialist. In 2000 CarsDirect.com won the *Forbes* "Best of the Web" award, and it continues to grow and add services. The original prototype exercise cost about $80,000.

Gross's philosophy of creating businesses is predicated on rapid prototyping. "That's what I think the new world of business is going to be like. Look at problems in the world. Don't try to solve the whole problem perfectly, but try to make some kind of rapid prototype and see what happens. Learn from the customers and adjust ... adapt."[4] CarsDirect.com might not ever have grown into a business if it had listened to investors who said, "I don't know if you are going to be able to get the cars" and "I don't know if people will do it." But the proof emerged from the relatively low-cost market experiment: customers and investors could test drive and feel and make a decision on a tangible prototype.

**All truth passes through three stages:
First, it is ridiculed.
Then, it is opposed violently.
Third, it is accepted
as being self-evident.**

Arthur Schopenhauer

Bringing concepts from the realm of imagination, where all is possible, to the world of tangible reality is not an easy undertaking, especially when there are other people and groups involved. Steve Kaneko, director of design for Microsoft Windows, and responsible for bringing together the look and feel, engineering, and brand character of Windows XP into a single cohesive vision, puts it this way:

Innovation in itself is difficult. I think we've all been through that. A good idea is not enough. Actually getting an entire company, a manufacturing unit, or a production unit to embrace a new product concept, something that changes their standard mode of operation, requires someone internal to the corporation, who can actually carry the ball and make things happen.[5]

Ideas are easily shot down, discredited, and invalidated. Jerry Hirshberg, founder and CEO of Nissan Design International, writes in *The Creative Priority*, "A traditional bureaucratic structure, with its need for predictability, linear logic, conformance to accepted norms, and the dictates of the most recent 'long range' vision statement, is a nearly perfect idea-killing machine."[6] Part of the reason is that in most organizations pitching an idea is a verbal act. Conversations, memos, reports, e-mails, and proposals make up the bulk of the process. Since words are easily subject to misinterpretation, the success of the initial pitch depends as much on a promoter's communication skills and political savvy as on the merit of the idea.

Don't worry about people **stealing your ideas.** If your ideas are any good, you'll have to **ram them down** people's throats.

Howard Aiken

Words don't take a person's experience into consideration. Though you as a promoter have had the chance to play with and explore the idea from many points of view, the recipients are constructing the idea based on your story alone, one sentence at a time. However, when you *show* them something, the audience has room to create their own experience.

The Art
of Prototyping

Michael Schrage, a research associate at the MIT Media Lab and author of *Serious Play*, maintains that simulation, visualization, and prototyping are the keys to collaboration and innovation, and by extension to the fostering of shared imagination. Schrage describes prototypes as physical representations of ideas, which can include a very wide range of physical incarnations, from drawings and napkin doodles, spreadsheets and foam core mock-ups, to sophisticated three-dimensional digital models and simulations. A prototype demonstrates aspects of the concept in ways that words cannot. It may seem self-evident, but the simple act of representing an idea through a tangible mode engages the entire imagination, stimulating connections, feelings, and a sense of meaning.[7]

The CarsDirect.com prototype demonstrated to customers and investors the possibility and reality of purchasing a car over the Web in the early days of e-commerce. Schrage describes prototyping as

improvising with the unanticipated in ways that create new value. Any tools, technologies, techniques or toys that let people improve how they play seriously with uncertainty is guaranteed to improve the quality of innovation. The ability to align those improvements cost-effectively with the needs of the customer, clients, and markets dramatically boosts the odds of competitive success.[8]

Visualize, sensorize, and demonstrate everywhere possible: ideate, simulate, collaborate, then innovate, using the designer's most unique capability.

Bill Dresselhaus

Good prototypes produce conversations and encourage people to experiment, participate, and mess around. Charismatic prototypes emit the social and intellectual equivalents of a magnetic field. Innovative prototypes have the effect of generating innovative teams. Prototypes are tools for fostering collaboration, stimulating shared vision, and creating choices. According to Schrage, "You can't be a serious innovator unless you are willing and able to play."[9]

Tim Brown from IDEO feels that *showing*, not talking, is what drives ideas:

Don't just let them talk [in brainstorming meetings]—have them build things. The other key to innovation is that you have to build stuff. You have to prototype. As one of our employees says, "Never turn up at a meeting without a prototype." You've got to make it, draw it, act it out—do whatever it takes to describe your idea in more than words. When you start to make an idea tangible for other people, they can get a hold of it and start to participate in it. That sort of chain reaction makes innovation happen inside organizations.[10]

In the Imagination Economy prototypes are the currency for innovation. Each creative industry has its own tools and language for prototyping. Movie production begins as storyboard sketches that evolve to animatics, dailies, and edited scenes. Automobiles evolve from brand character and requirements documents to countless concept sketches and then into virtual-concept 3-D computer graphics models displayed on multi-projector, twenty-foot PowerWall screens for quick approvals and evaluation, and eventually to technical surface models, engineering representations, and full-size clay models. Most brand development organizations use their own methods to create ideas. The software, video game, toy, consumer product, architectural, and film and video production industries each has its own tools and techniques for bringing ideas collaboratively into the market.

The Linear Timeline

Even though prototypes are staples in many creative industries, they are still relatively unused in others. One reason is that the skills needed to produce prototypes are generally not distributed equally throughout an organization. The art of prototyping— sketching, building, fabricating, modeling, and presenting—does not figure prominently in MBA programs. Another reason is that, historically, production has been represented in a linear format. The Gantt chart, invented and developed from 1900 by consulting engineer Henry L. Gantt, was the first formal representation of workflow on a timeline. Gantt charts depict the difference between what needs to get done and what's been completed. They are easy to read, easy to use, and involved in practically every project.

Fifty years after Gantt developed his chart, the scale of large defense, aerospace, and construction projects had grown to an order of magnitude that required new forms of representation. In 1957 a joint venture of E.I. du Pont de Nemours and Company and the Sperry-Rand Corporation produced the Critical Path Method (CPM). Booze, Allen, and Hamilton and Lockheed Missiles and Space Company created the Program Evaluation and Review Technique (PERT) for the navy's Polaris submarine system. Both the PERT and CPM charts illustrate projects as a network of tasks connected by "must be completed by" arrows. The arrows represent the force of time. These visualizations organize and

ID	Task Name	Sep '99	Qtr 4, 1999			Qtr 1, 2000			Qtr 2, 2000			Qtr 3, 2000			Qtr 4, 2000	
			Oct '99	Nov '99	Dec '99	Jan '00	Feb '00	Mar '00	Apr '00	May '00	Jun '00	Jul '00	Aug '00	Sep '00	Oct '00	Nov '00
1	Stage 1															
2																
3																
4																
5																
6																
7	Stage 2															
8																
9																
10																
11																
12																
13																
14	Stage 3															
15																
16																
17																
18																
19																
20																
21																

Sample Gantt Chart

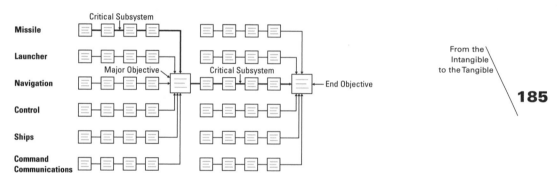

Sample Pert Chart

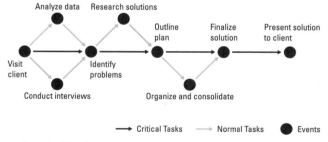

Sample CPM Chart

simplify the complexity and interrelatedness of tasks, while introducing a subtle bias into the flexibility of project management.

Linear timelines work extremely well for managing the production of Model Ts, airplanes, and missiles, but not so well for the development of intangibles. Gantt and PERT charts emphasize the sequential aspects of project management as well as the divisional nature of business. They reinforce the "toss the project over the wall" mentality as products progress from marketing to design to engineering to manufacturing. Each division has its own culture, priorities, tools, and language to propel concept to tangible expression.

In the Imagination Economy, where the value of a product or service is defined in the concept, experience, and design rather than in the production, organizations need methods to experiment, play, and give room for imaginative collaboration. The linear format provides little opportunity for innovation or space for the unexpected.

Linear development models can be distilled into the following basic format:

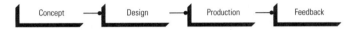

In this simple, general model you begin with the concept—formulating the idea, identifying the target audience, and outlining the features and function of the product or service—and this evolves into a requirements document. The ideas progress to the design phase, where they are developed into tangible shapes. The designs are then passed to production to be implemented and manufactured. Finally, the product is shipped and marketed. Clearly a gross oversimplification, this model emphasizes the sequential nature of much of business.

Lester C. Thurow, dean of MIT Sloan School of Management, makes the interesting observation that investment in innovation, and research toward improved process as opposed to improved product, give about a tenfold return on investment.[11] Investing in a way to manufacture or distribute a VCR faster or more efficiently than your competitor clearly pays enormous dividends.

Linear processes are slow and divisional, and leave little room for conversation and change. The Imagination Economy needs holistic ways to represent and manage workflow. It requires processes that encourage the ongoing clarification of vision, collaboration between diverse teams, experimentation, freedom to zig rather than zag, and the will to promote the flow of imaginative energy. The process needs to be simple, providing teams with the potential for their imaginative impulse to flow from concept to delivery.

Successive Prototyping

One of the most effective processes is the successive prototyping model. The essence of prototyping is simple:

Start with an idea, concept, or plan.

Build a draft, model, or trial.

Present it to those who have a stake in the venture.

Give them a chance to play, work, and interact freely with the prototype.

Watch and listen closely to their feedback.

Refine the concept and hone the prototype based on what you see and hear.

Then run through the entire process again, enhancing the fidelity and quality until it expresses the core idea.

Though the process is uncomplicated, managing it effectively requires finesse and rigor.

Iteration, conversation, clarity, and circulation are at the heart of this process. Though each organization that uses prototypes customizes its approaches to suit its market, the essential spirit of successive prototyping is distilled into a simple and easy-to-apply model represented by a spiral gyrating through four key areas: concept, design, production, and feedback.

Several features differentiate this model from linear and time-based workflow processes. Because work follows the path of a spiral, it cycles through and returns to each core activity several times. With each return, every aspect of the work can be refined and developed further. In the first iteration the team defines the initial core concept, builds conceptual prototypes, and plays with them, perhaps introducing them to stakeholders for feedback. The process can happen informally or formally, but ideally over a short period of time—days or sometimes hours. What the team learns in the first go-round is applied to the next iteration, clarifying the concept still more, even redefining it if the prototype and feedback tell them to, and building a higher-fidelity prototype, introducing other technologies to move the project down the pipeline. At the concept stage the focus is on intangibles—the clarification of the idea. At the production phase the focus moves to tangibles—fabricating the object. As the team iterates between the two, each redefines the other.

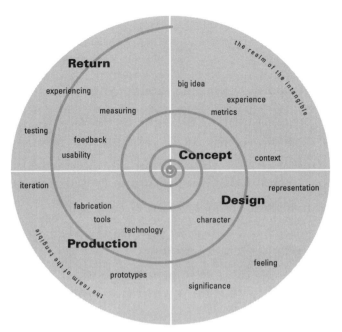

The realm of the intangible

Return
experiencing
measuring
big idea
experience
metrics
testing
feedback
usability
Concept
context
iteration
fabrication
tools
technology
representation
Design
character
Production
feeling
prototypes
significance

The realm of the tangible

Putting the prototype at the center of the development process gives teams permission to play around. They know that there will be opportunity to interact, discuss, test, and develop further. This organic approach reduces the push and pull of personal opinions, as the team can trust in the process to provide mid-course corrections. The very fact of displaying the work as an evolving spiral gives the team permission to explore, secure in the knowledge that they will be able to rein in and test the project against business goals.

The spiral model also lowers risks by building in time and resources for testing—for making mistakes and correcting them earlier. The spiral can be unwound into a timeline format when the process needs to be tied to project management. It also brings all the key people to the table. The process promotes learning for the entire group.

In short, developing through successive prototyping offers the following essential benefits:

• saves money and reduces risk by testing earlier and making mistakes faster

• provides more iterations and opportunities to find the Big Idea

• gives permission for teams to explore

• engages all key stakeholders

• promotes authenticity as there are fewer surprises

• connects cross-divisional and diverse teams

- represents different interests simultaneously

- produces prototypes that are harder to reject. They linger in the mind in a way that reports and words cannot.

- Prototypes are easier for management to evaluate.

Representing work using the prototyping method plants the idea in the minds of stakeholders that the prototype is meant to be shaped, like a piece of clay. When everyone has the same goal, the process goes faster.

Prototyping makes thinking and feeling interactive and collaborative. Good prototypes don't just communicate the intent of the idea: they convince. If you are making a product, build it out of foam. If you are offering a service, shoot a short video of the steps in the personal experience, what the customer will encounter. Shape your ideas with the prototype and let your ideas be shaped by the prototype.

The prototyping model provides a way to circulate an idea from the invisible world of imagination to the tangible world of business. Each cycle refreshes ideas, puts business in the context, and provides non-linear opportunities. The model is one of turning to the imagination and encouraging it to focus on expression through the product. The model is something that you can apply casually—getting an idea, doodling a sketch, and pitching it at the coffee machine—or as a formal undertaking, where the iterative process is managed over a long period of time.

There are zillions of ideas.
It's coming up with the ones that will actually **impact** that's hard.

Danny Hillis

The purpose of obtaining feedback is to hold focus on the human experience and share the results of imaginative work. What is the experience the product is intended to create? Focus on making your customers' lives better. If they can't see that your innovation is going to improve their hotel experience or their game playing or the state of their shoes, you might as well stop now. And what are the behaviors you are encouraging with your product? Remember, you are not designing things; you are designing human experience.

Clarifying
the Concept

Establishing a project's essential goals is just one part of the concept. In successive prototyping the concept is the collection of intangibles—the organizing principles of context and rationale, vision and mission, customer problems and opportunities, intended audience and desired behaviors, spirit and human experience, as well as the Big Idea—that defines your intention.

Though a concept often emerges spontaneously through the operation of the undermind, as well as through the usual techniques of doodling, conversation with oneself, brainstorming, and quiet contemplation, having the entire team buy into the concept is what achieves alignment and power. Clarifying the concept means asking and answering relevant questions:

The Context

What is the overall context of the venture? What research—customer surveys, market studies, consumer trends, disruptive technologies—can you bring to the table? What are the strengths, weaknesses, opportunities, and threats? Can you represent the context visually as a collection of forces acting on the present situation?

The Big Idea

What is the vision for the venture? What idea cuts through all the peripheral matter and expresses the core vision? What mission will focus the team's efforts? What are the customer benefits, the unique selling proposition, the organizing principle that will persist and propagate through the team and extend throughout the market?

The Metrics

How will you define success? What metrics—financial, social, and intangible—will determine how far you've progressed toward the goal?

The Imaginative Experience

What experiences do you want to create for your customers and stakeholders? What values will you express? Will the concept enhance some aspect of the customer's experience? Does the idea inspire?

When embarking on the concept, you'll often get only some of the elements at first. You might clarify the Big Idea but not the financial elements, or discern the customer experience without the context of research. But the draft idea is enough for you to go forward to the next step, of building it. Going through the process of representing it, playing with it, and letting others interact with it inevitably deepens the team's understanding. In the prototyping model the team should be as flexible with the formulation of the concept as they are with playing with the prototype. With each return the idea becomes firmer, more focused, its outlines clearer. Give the idea room to grow, adapt, and evolve to meet the aspirations you have for it.

Shaping the Design

Concepts are intangibles that circulate in the shared imagination. Design is the means of shaping concepts, giving them form, function, consistency, pattern, structure, and pizzazz. Like *imagination*, the word *design* means different things to different people: to a CFO design is the corporate logo applied to a hundred items, from T-shirts to computer start-up screens; to a merchandiser design is what guides the flow of consumer interest through a retail space; to a software manager design is the user interface, the branding, and workflow; and to a Web developer design is the blend of information architecture, look-and-feel, and underlying infrastructure.

From the Intangible to the Tangible

191

For the past decade design has been playing an increasingly important role in business. According to Mark Dziersk of the Industrial Designers of America, "When industries are competing at equal price and functionality, design is the only differential that matters."[12] Martha Stewart, the high priestess of home design, asserts, "Don't talk down to people about good design. Choosing it is not about how much money you make."[13] In the Imagination Economy good taste does not elude the masses. A legion of influences, including IKEA's affordable but stylish furniture, the VW Beetle and PT Cruiser, the iMac, the evolving look-and-feel of the Windows and Mac operating systems, a parade of chic consumer products, and the rising popularity in the mass market of designers such as Philippe Starck and Karim Rashid, have placed design at the core of business success.

In the prototyping process the role of design is to express the concept through the organizing principles of imagination:

The Organizing Principles

Representation

What does it look like? What are its shape and contours? How does it feel in your hands? What are its textures and aroma?

Connections

How does the design fit in its larger context? How does it function? What does it remind you of?

Feeling

What is the emotional tone of the design? Does it instruct? Evoke? Does it shout or is it understated?

Significance

What meaning does it inspire? What behavior does it suggest? What story does it tell?

Character

Great works of design are idiosyncratic. They embody elegance and personality, and possess a quality of wholeness that originates from a single intelligence. Great designs are just right, with nothing out of place, working at all scales from the micro to the macro to form a pleasing whole. At the center of design is *gesture*. The designers at ItalDesign, one of Italy's leading design consultancies, have tried to capture digitally the remarkably powerful and expressive gesture of the company's founder, Giorgetto Giugiaro.

The design process is a reflection of the brainstorming process: start with many rough ideas, play with them, get the feeling right, and pare them down to a few options. Get feedback, clarify the concepts, and develop the finer aspects of the design with each iteration. Along the way the design sensibility—the language and principles—becomes clearer.

Building
the Production

While design provides a language of representation and a plan for developing connections, feelings, and significance, production is about tangible fabrication. It is the physical thing—the piece of paper that bears the sketch that you can hold and pass around, the foam model you can chip away at, the spreadsheet you can e-mail, and the three versions of the role-playing skit of customers applying for a loan in a portable banking stall. Production takes the concept and design and makes them real, tangible, solid, and substantial.

Technology is now playing a significantly larger role in production. The pencil-and-paper sketches that used to cover the walls of design studios have been replaced with digital sketches. Foam and clay models are being superseded by interactive 3-D models. Although there will always be a place for physical models—nothing replaces the sensual experience of seeing, feeling, and holding an object—they can be expensive and time-consuming to build. Organizations such as Thomson, Philips, and virtually every automobile manufacturer are making design, engineering, and process decisions on virtual models. Cheaper, faster, and better production tools have made prototyping technology available to a wider set of audiences. What was once exclusive to the largest organizations—3-D modeling, CAD, animation, stereo lithography—is now accessible to small organizations and even individuals. But the basic guidelines of production apply to all organizations, large or small.

Use Appropriate Technology

With each iteration the technology changes. Start with tools that promote easy brainstorming and ideation, and progress to tools that provide higher degrees of fidelity.

Don't Throw Away

Select tools that enable your team to pass the results of one iteration on to the next. The real optimization in prototyping is about workflow and asset flow. Make sure you can exchange data easily, freely, and in every direction, with each person who is involved in the process.

Make Your Own Tools

Toronto designer Bruce Mau says, "Hybridize your tools in order to build unique things. Even simple tools that are your own can yield entirely new avenues of exploration. Remember, tools amplify our capacities, so even a small tool can make a big difference."[14]

Production deals with the hard concerns that concept and design often do not. Production worries about material cost, production optimization, fabrication problems, and storage, and reflects bottom-line thinking. The more the concept, design, and production can integrate through the prototyping gyrations, the smoother the whole process will be.

Feedback: Engaging in the Experience

With a set of virtual or tangible prototypes on hand, the fourth step in the prototyping cycle extends an invitation to stakeholders to experience the idea. For team members this means playing around with, talking about, tearing apart, and building up the prototype to move the project forward. For customers it means getting a sense of what works and what doesn't, what they like and what they don't. For business partners, buyers, and brokers, the prototype is a trial product, something substantial to respond to. And for management and investors, the prototype can instantly provide a sense of confidence and conviction in the product development.

The point is to give stakeholders a real experience. With some prototypes—say, of software design or financial services—it makes sense to establish context and provide the background concept and design intent. In other prototypes—children's toys, for example—it makes more sense to just put the prototypes in the middle of the room without any explanation and let the kids do what they would naturally do. In each case, though, getting feedback and understanding the user's experience drives the prototype to the next iteration. Listening, watching, and being sensitive to the social dynamic are crucial at this stage. The beauty of the feedback and experience stage is that there are no wrong answers or responses. If everyone is authentic in their reaction to the experience, feedback will naturally advance and elevate the prototype to the desired concept, design, and product.

Don't Just Show and Tell, Show and Ask

The point of the prototype at this stage is to start conversations and elicit ideas, impressions, and observations from the people involved.

Listen to What They Say—But Watch What They Do

It's important to pay attention to body language. Non-verbal communication is as telling as what people vocalize. Notice what people get interested in and what turns them off.

Usability Testing

Measure the experience against the metrics you've defined. If the goal is to enhance performance, measure the performance. If the goal is to get someone to consume, then measure that.

Feedback provides continual learning. What people should agree on are the essential goals and the process to reach those goals. The process will produce a series of mid-course corrections that keep it on track, returning to the spirit of the product. The spiral must not be unraveled into a timeline-based project management process.

From the
Intangible
to the Tangible

195

The Returns

The essential idea behind prototyping is to intensify the circulation of energy between intangible and tangible, between invisible and visible, between intention and manifestation. Artist Doug Hector thinks of projects as going through different seasons, each having an element of birth:

There is a season of dreaming, where the design never stops, and that unfolds to the season of implementation, where options are a distraction and dreaming is a digression. And what brings it all together is that everyone is responsible for the big picture, for the impact of their work. So you need multiplicity of intelligence. It's not just about tolerance. It's dignified intelligence.[15]

Versions of successive prototyping are evolving in every industry. Extreme programming is an iterative method of software programming that engages customers at every step of the prototype. Managers, customers, and developers become part of a collaborative team dedicated to customer satisfaction. According to founder J. Donovan Wells,

XP improves a software project in four essential ways: communication, simplicity, feedback and courage. XP programmers communicate with their customers and fellow programmers. They keep their design simple and clean. They get feedback by testing their software on day one. They deliver the system to the customers as early as possible and implement change as suggested. With this foundation XP programmers are able to courageously respond to change requirements and technology.[16]

In extreme programming, customers write up their software experiences, documenting their joys and woes. The software engineers become part of this conversation in order to understand customers' requirements. XP programmers continually seek to find optimal metaphors for data transactions. There are daily stand-up meetings to review progress, paired programming to facilitate ideas, continuous focus on simplification, emphasis on collective code ownership, unit testing, ongoing integration, and short iterative development. This practice has been adopted by major corporations, including Ford, DaimlerChrysler, and Credit Suisse, and has dramatically increased the Carnegie Mellon Capability Maturity Model rating from chaotic to managed and optimizing.

Maytag has used prototyping to reinvent its assembly lines. Moving from a traditional linear assembly process that was becoming less efficient and increasing employee boredom, Maytag experimented with prototype variations of assembly models that depended on small workgroups. Over a series of phases the groups eventually convened on a method where the worker is in the center of a small workspace and the parts are brought to her, like tools being handed to a surgeon in an operating theater. The *Economist* reports that a reworking of the company's Jackson, Tennessee, dishwasher factory "improved quality by 55%, cut work in progress by 60%, freed up 43,000 square feet and increased capacity by 50%. Such factories can now turn out any model at any hour of the production day, in response to feedback from the department stores that sell Maytag's products."[17]

The spirit of prototyping is applicable in service industries, financial services, creative development—in fact, any type of collaboration where people need to convert ideas into products, processes, or services. Prototyping ties together many of the elements needed to thrive in the Imagination Economy, producing a process that encourages ideas to flow through teams. What helps drive it is a simple and flexible representation of the outcome of the iterative process. The visual reference alone is often sufficient to instill change, flexibility, and responsiveness. Complex iterations feel lighter, the shared vision happens faster, and the "over the wall" mentality gets smaller.

Using an iterative development process introduces new management concerns. How do you know you've finished? Do you try for more variations, to bring a more fully developed and articulated product to market? Or do you aim for speed, to bring a product to market faster? What you choose to prototype and what you choose not to prototype, whom you prototype for, and what you measure are decisions that reflect the spirit, values, and vision of the organization.

Though the nature of prototyping can range from the emotional (to engage the spirit of the consumer) to the analytical (to determine technical requirements), the key to success is to be honest in your prototyping. Don't go through the motions. Invest yourself. Let the process determine where you end up. Focus on the human experience.

The Culture
of Failure

When Andy Grove, CEO of Intel, said, "Make mistakes faster," he was acknowledging the need to incorporate blunders and oversights into the business process. Many big business failures could have been averted through better prototyping and earlier failure. The $6-billion collapse of Iridium—the global cellphone connected by satellites— might not have happened if, among other things, the company had tested the user experience of carrying a six-pound phone.

The Palm Pilot, though not perfect in its first release, nonetheless captured its initial market by remaining true to the experience that you could look up a phone number and date faster on your Palm Pilot than in a paper datebook. This concept and design spec helped propel the Pilot's success where over fifty personal digital assistants, including the Apple Newton, had failed. It's just as important to know what experience you're striving to create as how you're going to achieve it.

If failure is inevitable in business, developing strategies to manage it is a smart thing to do. Failing early and failing often is one approach to failing faster, at less cost, and less publicly than the competition. Fail faster and smarter and you have more chances to learn and succeed. Making progress and making mistakes are kissing cousins. "If you're not making mistakes, you're not taking risks, and that means you're not going anywhere," asserts John W. Holt Jr., co-author of *Celebrate Your Mistakes*.[18]

At its root, risk is lack of information. Risk provides the excuse for business to generate more information, and the opportunity for business to develop the experiment that will generate the right information. Among the most widely accepted misconceptions in business today is that it's possible to create an organization where mistakes are rare rather than a necessary cost of doing business. The problem with this attitude is that it encourages mistakes to be swept under the carpet, blamed on someone else, or ignored entirely.

The **only** sure way to avoid mistakes is to have no new ideas.

Albert Einstein

Everyone wants to learn but nobody wants to be wrong.

Jack Feldman

IBM invests $4.3 billion a year in scientific research, compared with $800 million in product development—over five times as much on research and innovation that has no bottom-line ramifications. According to Director of Design Bob Steinburgler, IBM's really big idea is that

we organize ourselves differently. We have a research organization that does pure research. We have special projects teams in our business units that have nothing to do with day-to-day current products. Why does it work? Because *some* failure is tolerated. Failures at the research or concept level when you're experimenting or prototyping are very inexpensive compared to product failures. We do prototyping and then we do limited testing. Unlike Microsoft, which prototypes things and then lets the world test it, we have personal testing sessions. We learn a lot and sense whether there is a market for the product, and we see there is a break-even point."[19]

The fact is, these divisions have a steady stream of successes that have come about as a result of research, and these instill a certain amount of confidence in management.

Alan Horn, CEO of Castle Rock Entertainment, is constantly being presented with creative ideas: screenplays, first versions of movies, marketing plans. It's critical, he says, to have "a heartfelt, internalized respect for what people do."[20] When people come in to present an innovative idea,

I want to remember that they are completely vulnerable at that moment. My job is not to kill them but to find the bright, creative, special parts of their proposal and focus on those first, to ease their anxiety, make them feel less vulnerable. Then I have to find a graceful way into the parts of what they've brought that need improving.[21]

Dorothy Leonard and Walter Swap, in their book *When Sparks Fly*, introduce the notion of failing forward. When you test, they say, plan for the risks and learn from them so as not to repeat mistakes.[22] This approach of continuous learning is at the heart of the skilled organization. David Gardner of Harvard Business School defines a "learning organization" as "skilled at creating, acquiring, interpreting, transferring and retaining knowledge … through market research, experimentation, best practices and lessons learned, and then transferring that knowledge throughout the organization." But equally important is "purposefully modifying its behavior to what it has learned. The mechanism that the knowledge the company acquires is transferred to it is decision-making."[23]

So, success in a prototyping culture is like success in baseball: if you bat .300, you're in the Hall of Fame. But this means you'll miss seven out of ten times. Or, if you're Edison, you miss 1,800 times before you get a light bulb that actually works. We should know and expect that we're going to miss sometimes. But we must step up to the plate again tomorrow.

A Crash Course in Development: Unilever

Unilever is a $54-billion global organization that produces household brands—skin care, food, and other products. To meet its mandate of growing 10 percent each year (that's an additional $5.4 billion in revenue annually) the organization needs to grow its markets by increasing market share, either with existing products or by introducing new ones. As in many large companies, new-product introduction at Unilever involves engaging stakeholders from a number of divisions—marketing, research, and legal, among others. This slows down the creative process, requiring as much as ten months to bring a concept to prototype—clearly too slow to compete in the Imagination Economy.

Jim Rait, director of design in the Port Sunlight U.K. facility, realized that something extraordinary needed to be done to meet the company's growth demands. He states that "to implement this non-linearity, you need a dramatic collaborative event."[24] Rait developed a production process that reduced prototype development to two weeks. In intensive workshops he uses models called the Design Journey™ and Design Space™ that revolve around design as an agent of change. The key to the process is to get the right people in the room, have them develop a common vision, establish a common language, and develop prototype products based on the vision.

In the Design Journey a group of key stakeholders sits in a room and works to formulate the product vision—what exactly they are trying to accomplish with the new product. The Design Journey is depicted as the cross-section of a mountain, with the altitude of the path representing the amount of discomfort the group is experiencing. The group "begins with what they don't know," says Rait. "We ask them to leave their jobs at the door and come as human beings rather than just functional representatives. They bring all of themselves to the table."[25] As they build the vision, the tension mounts, as each person's point of view is put on the table. The tension reaches its peak usually just before the vision becomes clear to the entire group. But once it is clear, the path becomes smoother as the group moves from what they are building to how they will build it. In the Design Journey process the idea moves from charter to contract to capability, from awareness to vision, ideas, and action.

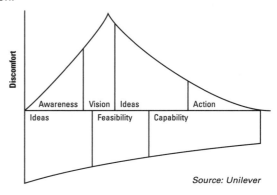

Source: Unilever

Design Space, a complementary conceptual model, is a visual way to remind each key stakeholder of the eight functional divisions that touch on new-product development: marketing, product design, purchasing, finance, operations, legal, and finance. According to Rait, "the key is to have the real decision makers in the room. With that, the project can move forward, allocating money and resources."[26] In the two-week process, organized as two three-day sessions, facilitators develop a common product vision in a kind of hierarchical pyramid with two faces: brand and design. Based on market research and product category, the teams define a product by its brand, clarifying the brand essence at the top of the pyramid, then the elements of personality, discriminators, reasons to believe, and consumer benefits at the bottom of the pyramid. They also define the design elements, with brand shape at the top of the pyramid and moving down through aesthetics, ergonomics, consistency, and packaging. This exercise is comprehensive, putting a face on the intangible.

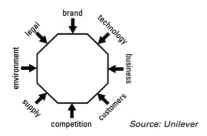

Source: Unilever

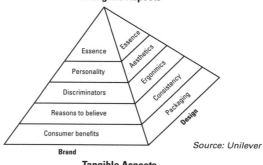

Intangible Aspects

Essence

Personality

Discriminators

Reasons to believe

Consumer benefits

Brand

Essence

Aesthetics

Ergonomics

Consistency

Packaging

Design

Source: Unilever

Tangible Aspects

The next stage is a classic exercise in prototyping. Designers sketch and then produce computer-graphics models, rendering the designs in conformance with the brand character and the design intentions. After three days the team produces a stereo-lithographed life-sized model of the product packaging. At the end of the two weeks the group is fully equipped to present a complete mock-up, with a comprehensive plan to bring the product to market. This dramatic process is revolutionizing Unilever's product development.

The next step, according to Rait, is to develop a digital infrastructure that will enable the process to be undertaken collaboratively by teams working in different geographical regions. It is conceivable that the process could be shortened even further as global design teams take advantage of time zones, digitally passing the designs from one office to the next, around the globe.

Thomson Electronics

Ted Woerner is director of design for Minneapolis-based Thomson Electronics. He has helped to develop a visualization center that uses a twenty-foot screen with seamlessly blended video projectors. The original concept for the center, devised by Mike Squillis, director of design development, was to blend bottom-line development with creative fulfillment. The visualization center was intended to enable the management team to approve life-sized electronic prototypes without the time and expense of producing physical prototypes. For designers, it provided the opportunity to change designs more quickly and visualize aspects of the design in context, viewing the television sets in living rooms and the point-of-purchase packaging in a retail environment.

According to Woerner, the visualization center accomplishes both jobs admirably.

The visualization center gives a lot more expression to our creative staff. There's an increased pride of ownership when a designer sees a creation on that big screen, beautifully rendered and animated in 3-D. That's a big emotional benefit for us. But the business doesn't sign off on emotional benefit; they sign off on bottom-line benefits. We sold it as a cost-reducing benefit.[27]

The center's capital costs were recouped in ten months by the reduction in the number of physical prototypes that were needed. And the time to market shrank significantly.

The center has a lot more uses than originally anticipated. Woerner states,

It's a big image-booster. When we bring customers and potential commercial partners to talk about our technology—not only about our products but the way we design our products—we make a very strong technology statement. [The visualization center] lets them know that we're a company that they should be doing business with. It shows them our leadership.[28]

In its first year the center was the site for more than two hundred meetings.

Large retail merchants, such as Kmart, Best Buy, and Circuit City, visit the center and can see the range of Thomson products in their retail environments. They see the product, its packaging, and the point-of-purchase support in a life-sized digital view of their own stores. The visualizations inspire the retailers to make decisions about product placement. This approach helps Thomson lock up the limited shelf space before their competitors can. According to Woerner,

If we can get our customers in a month or two before we could normally talk to them and sell our product, then we have a competitive advantage. And if we can give them visuals, so they are already thinking about what it's going to look like, whether they realize it or not, they are already planning what our product will look like on their shelves. That's a very strong and powerful idea.[29]

The visualization center helps Thomson repackage and leverage the value of its digital assets. It takes the design capital and uses it in different contexts—to help lock up shelf space at retail but also to provide images to marketing, to conduct market validation with customers, and even to train in product assembly. Switching the display from the two-foot experience of a workstation to the twenty-foot experience of the visualization center has a powerful impact on viewers. It revolutionizes the experience.

The visualization center also serves as a forum for the designers. At Open Forum Friday the designers have a chance to show their personal ideas to the rest of the design group. Woerner tries to keep the forum low-key, almost clandestine. He doesn't want people thinking, "'You guys have all this time that you can throw away an afternoon a week and brainstorm on stuff that 98 percent of the time isn't going to see the light of day?'" On the other hand, when the ideas do get developed, Woerner says,

They go, "We need those advanced concepts for a show that's coming up." Everyone is quick to lay claim to enjoying the benefits of creative efforts. Designers need a chance to stretch their creative legs. They produce about nine concepts for every one product that goes to production. To see the press that is generated by those advanced concepts—and we make an effort to recognize the designer—is pretty gratifying.[30]

The ripples from the visualization center extend even further. When Thomson's Patent and License Group—the most lucrative group in the company, generating $258 million in profit for every $300 million in revenue—found out about the visualization center and the Open Forum Fridays, they saw huge opportunities and have now become regular attendees. When new product ideas are presented, product managers have the first shot; they are given forty-five days to state whether or not they will choose any of the products. The ideas that don't get picked up are turned over to the Patent and License Group, who try to realize revenue from them. "It's a win-win situation," says Woerner. "If they develop a product that is licensed and it reaches a level of success, then the pressure is on the product group to risk some of these new products. It gives the designers a creative outlet and provides a huge energy throughout the system."[31]

The Evolving Spiral of Imagination

Prototyping can be a playful activity. It's a kind of visual storytelling that gives us an anchor in the world of reality around which to shape our ideas. The benefits go far beyond the simple avoidance of error and failure. Prototyping is a way for us to forge a path into the world we don't know we don't know, and in the process uncover knowledge, opportunities, and possibilities we were unaware of at the beginning. Prototyping offers the chance to dip into the real potential of an idea.

Too often, business will look at the cost and risk associated with investing and ask, "What's the worst that can happen if we don't do this?" In the Imagination Economy the prototyping process asks the question, "What's the best that can happen?"

BUILD
SOME-
THING

Master the art of presentation.
Not to tell, but to ask and listen.

Gray Holland's Drawing Class

"I tell everyone that they can learn to draw. The first day I take them through a couple of exercises to learn how to draw, and I say the rest of the term is just practice. The key demo is: I take a pencil and I draw very slowly and it kind of wobbles. It's just a dull line.

"That lack of energy is stored in that line forever. Students say, 'It's just a piece of lead scraped off on some textured paper.' I try to get them to the point where they realize this is energy. This is my energy that I put *into* it. Then I draw a couple of accelerated lines, and build up a gradated line.

"What are you going to respond to? What energizes you? This is a line—there's no design here—it's just a line. But the energy, literally, the physical energy, the emotional energy, *everything*, is stored in that line.

"That's why I can walk up to a Van Gogh painting and just be in rapture—captured, feeling that person's energy. When I saw Van Gogh's work in person, I felt I was sitting on the edge of a razor blade balanced between brilliance and insanity. And I felt it. I felt what it was to be him. The painting is dead: it's inanimate, it doesn't move, it has no kinetic energy. I believe that his energy, its intent, is trapped in that."

From an interview with Gray Holland.

Fail early.
Fail often.
Fail to learn.
Failure does not have to equal pain and punishment.

It's easier, and a lot safer, to enclose yourself in complex planning exercises. But investing a lot of energy in abstractions locks you into ideas that are not always the best ones. This is a formula for big failure. Letting go of the need to plan fully before testing ideas is a tough lesson for most corporations. The more you experiment, the more you learn. The more you learn, the more you bring to light.

How could this work in your organization?

Design is a mental habit of seeing things simultaneously in their narrowest details and in their broadest implications.

Trevanian

Visualize and demonstrate wherever possible. Simulate. Collaborate. Innovate.

We are not in the business of designing things, services, or processes. We are in the business of designing human behavior.

Melvin Kransberg's Three Laws of Technology:

Law 1: Technology is not good.

Law 2: Technology is not bad.

Law 3: Technology is not neutral.

Buxton's Corollary: Without informed design, it is more likely to be bad than good.

8

The Imagination Marketers

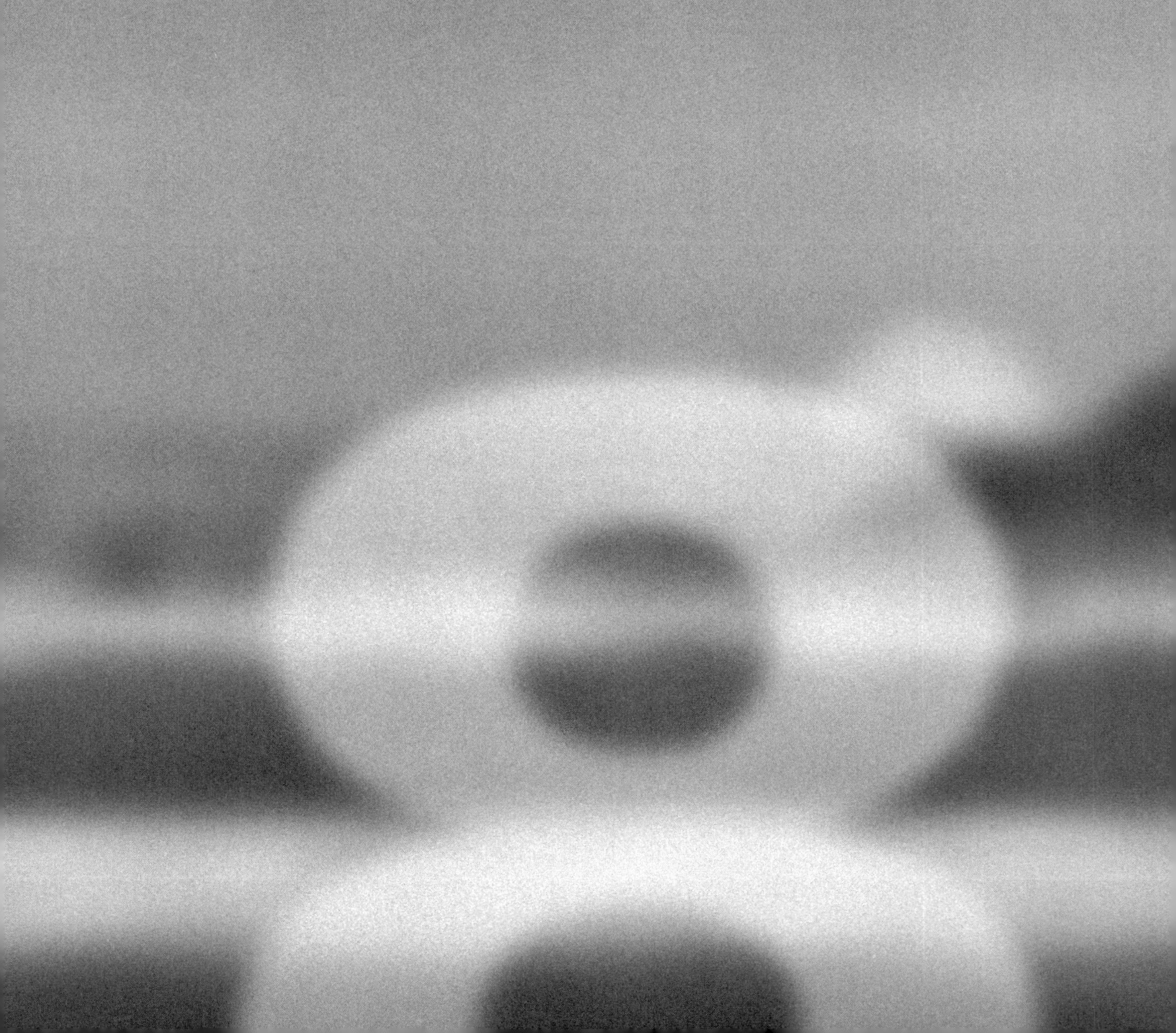

They are the ones
who have captured our imaginations
by making us
stop and take notice
of what they do.

The Man
Who Loved the Mountain

There was a man who loved the mountain. He spent much of his time interacting with nature, and because he loved the mountain, he learned to climb it. One day he and a friend were climbing a difficult ice-covered rock face that not too many people had climbed before. It was so difficult, he realized he needed better tools to make this kind of climb successfully. So he spent some time studying the problem and testing all the different tools there were, until he came up with an idea he thought would work better.

He found someone to help build the new tool, and even though it was a bit of a crazy idea, it was enormously successful. Then he and a friend started a business so they could make and sell these tools to other climbers who loved the mountain. Everyone loved it, and many people even said this new tool had forever changed the way people climb.

Well, the company grew bigger and bigger. They made other things and different tools. And because they loved the mountain, they made a new tool that was better than the first. It was kinder and gentler to the mountain, and more deeply honored the spirit of the climber and the climb. And the company continued to grow.

They started to make clothing and other equipment that were all about soulful, quiet sports. They created products that were born of need, like the first tool was. And they continued to love the mountain, and created a philosophy, a credo to live by. That credo was: to be committed to the core, the soul, the center of sport, and the environment and lifestyle that go with it. The company kept growing.

They grew to be a group of people committed to living in accordance with the spirit of freedom and of wandering that comes from a deep love of nature and a desire to be in her midst. They made many changes to their business, and even erected a new building that was true to their vision and protective of nature. They gave millions of dollars to charities that cared for the earth; they turned to organic raw materials and eliminated toxins. They recycled everything. And the company grew. It grew so big that *everyone* was wearing their clothes, even the president of the United States of America!

And then something happened. The man who loved the mountain stopped to listen to his heart. He wondered if they should keep growing, and why. He thought about the $1 billion they could make. But his heart said no.

So they all got together to talk about and remember what was important. They decided they would make the company smaller. And they did. They cut out 40 percent of their products, and decided they would only grow big enough to keep the company alive for a century.

They started using half the space in their product catalogs to ask people to save old forests and care for rivers. They continued giving lots of money and help to those who help the earth. They started to research new ways of doing things that would be even kinder to the environment than their current practices. And they kept sharing their message with the world so that more people would understand what was important to them.

And the company grew, and they loved the mountain.

The Power of Storytelling

There are many thoughts about storytelling, and many different kinds of stories to tell. Psychologist Joseph Campbell popularized the role of storytelling in the 1980s, though he had been studying it for decades before that. Campbell was a great student of world religions, and he combined the notions of religious mysticism with myth and legend and the teachings of Carl Jung on archetype and the collective unconscious. Campbell and George Lucas were friends, and Campbell's work had a great influence on the *Star Wars* trilogy.

Author and storyteller Steve Denning works with the corporate world in an effort to bring the power of storytelling to knowledge management. He defines the *springboard story* as one that allows us to make a forward leap in understanding. As indigenous cultures know, storytelling is a way to teach and learn over long periods of time. It's a kind of road map that passes on the accumulated wisdom about our history and helps us understand unseen parts of the journey.

Stories also tell us what we may need to know about where we are headed, through examples of crisis and change. Stories are a powerful tool for learning because they always impart something of ourselves and our experiences that we might not otherwise have uncovered.

Storytelling is becoming an increasingly important part of knowledge management as corporations are faced with sharing growing amounts of complex knowledge and information with growing numbers of people. In a crowded, busy, noisy world, stories rich with metaphor and meaning are easily remembered. They are an accessible way of understanding different mindsets and cultures, different ways of being.

Ultimately, if we look closely at our stories, they speak to us about what we consider to be most important. In the Imagination Economy the stories we latch onto are the ones that speak to us about the ideas that matter most. The successful storytellers are the ones speaking to us through their businesses.

Jones Soda Company

Everything about the Jones Soda Company is just like one of its newly launched beverage lines—WhoopAss Energy. There isn't a single aspect of Jones that doesn't shout confidently, "I'm young, I'm hip, and I'm happening."

This not so little company got its start in 1987 when founder and president Peter van Stolk successfully acquired distribution rights for Just Pik't Juices in Western Canada. Van Stolk's strategy was to "run with the little guy," a slogan that is alive and well with Jones today. Rather than go the conventional route, Jones chose to distribute through smaller independents and seemingly unlikely venues, via branded coolers placed in truly unexpected locations such as skate, surf, and snowboarding shops, piercing and tattoo parlors, and fashion and music stores. Focused on the 12- to 24-year-olds—a market segment that spends $10 billion annually on beverages—Jones zoomed in on extreme sports, sponsoring a number of key players like Tony Hawk and Willy Santos.

This master of brand creation experienced its fourteenth consecutive quarter of sales growth at the end of 2001. Its final sales revenue, tallying $20 million for the year ending December 2000, translated into shareholder equity that more than doubled the previous year's.

Jones Soda claims its line is one of the most innovative beverages ever to hit retail shelves—a claim that's totally justified. Everything about Jones is unique, from its packaging and labeling right down to its choice of flavors, channels of distribution, and intensely interactive Web site. The flavors include Green Apple, Crushed Melon, Fufu Berry, Blue Bubble Gum, and, of course, Happy. The menu for its line of WhoopAss Energy drinks is just as quirky, and even its healthy line of Jones Juice offers that classic flavor, Dave.

As if this branding weren't enough to positively captivate its target audience by so fluently speaking their language, Jones goes the full half-pipe and offers customization. Customers send in photographs of themselves, or their dogs, or their friends—whatever they happen to want to express—and Jones puts them on the bottle labels. The continually changing labels also include original art. Under-the-cap quotes are sent in by the real people who drink, and love, Jones Soda. An extensive Web site network supports this culture with a gallery of customer photos and artwork, quotations, stories that individuals can create on-line, along with a slew of constantly unfolding action, activities, contests, and links. And if you simply must have your own brand (perfect for gift giving), send in your photo for the front, your quote for the back, and $50

($35 + shipping), and Jones will send you your very own case of twelve.

This is a company that has and shows the energy of its customers. Jones Soda has successfully tackled an intensely complex brand proposition: it has captured the imagination and loyalty of the entire powerful youth market by unequivocally celebrating the power of one.

Nexia Biotechnologies

If you thought the only Spiderman suit you could ever own was a cheap polyester knock-off Halloween costume, guess again. With expertise in molecular and cellular biology, embryology, dairy science, and animal husbandry, Montreal-based Nexia Biotechnologies is one of the world's largest producers of authentic recombinant spider silk, and a leading North American animal transgenic company. Transgenic science is not exactly new, having been in place for a number of years producing everything from new strains of canola to monoclonal antibodies and immunoglobulin fusion molecules. So Nexia had no trouble raising over $40 million in funding through their IPO plus an additional $25 million from prominent investors. Connecting the anatomical similarity between the spider silk gland and the mammary gland of the goat has led Nexia to innovate a family of spider silk proteins that have resulted in the registered trademark BioSteel® Extreme Performance Fibers. Spider silk boasts a unique combination: it has enormous tensile strength and elasticity while being ultra-lightweight, which makes it ideally suited for numerous uses, not the least of which is ballistic protection armor. But as spiders are impossible to farm, this highly desirable fiber was unavailable—until Nexia came along. By successfully putting the spider gene into mammary gland cells of goats that have been genetically altered to breed and lactate early, Nexia can mass-produce top-drawer spider silk in the most cost- and time-effective manner possible to date. It has also formed a strategic alliance with the Institute of Plant Genetics and Crop Plant Research in Germany—a company that has successfully produced recombinant spider silk in transgenic plants.

Nexia's BioSteel fibers are expected to come in useful where consumers and industry demand fibers with a high degree of toughness, strength, flexibility, suppleness, and lightness. This could include specialty ropes and nets, sporting goods and apparel, and performance composites, as well as numerous medical applications. Wound closure systems, including vascular wound repair devices, hemostatic dressings, patches, and glues, sutures, and ligament prosthetic devices are among the possibilities that should theoretically lead to faster patient healing and fewer complications. Nexia is also working with the U.S. Army and the Canadian Armed Forces to develop performance fibers for soft-body armor applications.

In the Imagination Economy, spiders and goats aren't such unlikely bedfellows.

If at first the idea is not **absurd**, then there is no hope for it.

Albert Einstein

Electrolux

In the average kitchen, plates, cups, glasses, and cutlery make a long journey in a typical day—from the cabinet to the table to the sink to the dishwasher and back to the cabinet again. In a concept design for a new model of dishwasher, Electrolux and Design Continuum of Milan have rethought and simplified this journey.

In this design, dishes are grouped by meal in dishwasher-safe baskets and stored in cabinets within the washer itself. All the breakfast dishes are grouped together. In the morning the breakfast basket is removed and placed on the table. At the end of the meal the basket is loaded and placed in the dishwasher's wash compartment. By grouping dishes by meal and storing them within the washer itself, the consumer saves time, gains storage space, and maximizes kitchen efficiency.

This feature was developed by exhaustive market research that spread over six European countries and involved over ten thousand participants. The idea that dishwashers could be an exciting technology was novel but inspiring. "Consumers want more features, more technology, more excitement. And they're willing to pay for it," according to Jonathan Young, senior industrial designer at Electrolux in Stockholm.[1]

Other useful features include a quick wash for items such as mixing bowls or measuring cups that need to be used several times when cooking a meal, a built-in trash compactor, and extra storage space in the dishwasher. It has removable racks, and the exterior is not at all typical, with an art deco appearance that is both decorative and functional. The idea was a stretch goal to encourage Electrolux designers to think in new directions and incorporate some of the features into the next year's models.

Koziol

In 1982 two brothers, Stephan and Bernhard Koziol Jr., took over the management of their family plastics company and focused the product line on young, contemporary trend items. In 1992 they formulated the company vision of Ideas for Friends, and started designing, manufacturing, and marketing a happy and playful brand of sensually and sensibly designed products that balance playfulness, shape, and function.

Most Koziol products are happy little critters for the home or office. Made from ecologically safe, recyclable plastics in bright, translucent colors, the core idea is to transform ordinary household items such as dishwashing brushes, butter dishes, staplers, corkscrews, and tape dispensers into "ideas for friends." In this way the Koziols convert familiar items into new items, low-interest products into unique gifts, and create a new product category in the process.

Koziol products have real character. Lola the plastic spoon is long and slender, with a large head for scooping up noodles with a smile. Coco, the brightly colored two-footed knife, stands on its own legs, has a strong handle and a long serrated nose, and has no sharp edges—making it safe for cake-cutting kids. Elise the watering can has a long slender nose and makes the daily chores seem like fun.

Koziol embraces many of the principles of the Imagination Economy. Its designs circle around the human experience. Its vision flows through its products, its organizational structure, its Web site, and its international distribution.

The organization is structured in autonomous creative teams, made up of designers and marketing experts who make their own decisions, guided by the goals of high quality and efficient operation. This non-hierarchical workgroup approach allows teams to set their own trends and make products that are the "special something that complements a positive lifestyle."[2] Koziol's design philosophy starting point is "the same for every product. We ask lots of questions, we listen long and hard, and we take a good look. Enthusiasm, professionalism and a sense of humor are integral parts of this process."[3]

Koziol also cross-fertilizes ideas by looking to talented young and up-and-coming designers. It actively seeks a visionary character in its products by opening its designs to competition, inviting designers to submit ideas for cash prizes as well as training internships. The internships give young designers the opportunity to work with marketing and product design as well as bring their ideas to market. Any person who submits a design also has the opportunity to license it should Koziol want to bring it to market.

Koziol's fun and innovative designs have won many Best of Show awards but have also spawned a wide collection of copycat products. Plagiarism is hard to fight through legal channels, so Koziol protects its brand with the support of Aktion Plagiarius. An arm of the Association of German Industrial Designers, it focuses public attention on the highly charged issue of pirated brand-name products by awarding prizes every year at the Ambiente trade fair to companies that create product knock-offs. The award: a black garden gnome with a long golden nose.

RONA Incorporated

RONA is Canada's leading retailer and distributor in the hardware, home improvement, and gardening products market, with annual sales of $3 billion and a staff of sixteen thousand. The company got its start in Quebec in 1939, when a group of small merchants came together to create a buying group to give themselves a greater competitive edge. That alliance grew and evolved into the current network of 540 stores, most of which are dealer/owner/shareholder-operated. RONA's founding entrepreneurial spirit is alive and well, reflected in its unique ability to operate successfully while presenting many different retail faces, ranging from the neighborhood hardware store and mid-size lumber yard to the big-box format. RONA has continued to build successfully on that spirit by creating a network of alliances with over $10 billion in buying power.

RONA has made a commitment to the communities that support it. In addition to a number of charities that are assisted corporately, independent merchants promote social, cultural, and humanitarian causes in their communities with time as well as products and money. In 1998 RONA created a foundation to help advance struggling and disadvantaged youth. It also created an environmentally sound recovery program for used paint products.

RONA has continued to innovate in the areas of strategic partnerships, distribution, and e-commerce as well as retail development and store concept and design. In 2001 RONA launched a full-scale test: a new big-box concept store, designed to redefine the standard of retailing in the home renovation market. This stunning 130,000-square-foot innovation differentiates itself by focusing on providing "Information, Inspiration and Imagination." RONA has succeeded in doing not only that but also in catering to a highly diverse clientele, including women who plan projects and hire contractors, all forms of do-it-yourselfers, handymen, and more traditional builders and contractors. Despite the complexity of its customer base RONA delivers an experience beyond expectations—easy to navigate, full of inspiring idea-stimulators, and fun.

RONA has commissioned research to help it target those who have the most influence in home purchasing decisions. "Women control or influence more than 75 percent of household purchasing decisions," says Claude Bernier, executive vice-president of RONA Inc. "In the home improvement industry that represents more than $18 billion. We understood the importance of making our stores appealing to a very diverse clientele, and our willingness to change reflects that."[4] The research clearly indicates that women don't want to be treated differently than men, but they do want to be seen as individuals.

Bernier says the key to delivering the right experience, and the right mix of experiences, is to understand not only that there are differences between customer groups, but that individuals want varying experiences as well. As a result RONA was able to create a series of diverse experiences that appeal to the growing female-driven business as well as to the more traditional customer. The unique Paint Boutique offers paint chips that are substantially larger than the industry standard; colors are organized into harmonious palettes; and there's a sitting area supported by visualization tools and qualified professionals to help customers with their choices. To keep this area tranquil, the paint- and color-mixing lab is separated by a glass partition. And what would have greater appeal to the busy contractor than not having to get out of his truck and stand in line? For him RONA created a 25,000-square-foot indoor drive-through lumberyard: drive in, pick it out, have it loaded up, and away you go. The entire experience is so successfully customer-focused because RONA took the time to understand who its customers are and to incorporate their feedback through the development process.

RONA's new concept store offers everything you'd expect (usually with a new spin on it) and a lot that you wouldn't. Of course there are workshops and demos as well as Web-linked computer stations throughout the store. "Ambiance Boutiques" offer accent pieces for the home. There's an old-fashioned hardware store harking back to RONA's roots and to its customers' earliest memories of hardware. And there is the cut shop, for those who are fumbly with lumber.

Bernier knows that his customers don't buy a deck, they build a safe haven from the busy world; they don't buy paint, they buy a home-creation dream. "Hardware stores used to be a place you went to get one specific item. Everyone would run in and out as fast as possible," says Bernier.

> Now it has become an outing. Some of our customers will spend hours browsing and shopping. To succeed in fulfilling our customers' needs, we must engage them emotionally and respond to them intuitively. If we're going to deliver the dream, we need to understand the essence of the desired experience. That begins by creating captivating real or virtual environments and developing products and services that excite and inspire our customers' lives. This is not just a place to buy two-by-fours.[5]

The point is, it's a human experience. It's no coincidence that RONA's marketing statement is: "Build on your imagination."

SETI@home

The fact that tens of millions of computers are connected to the Internet at any single moment and that most are sitting idly or performing computationally light tasks has become an enormous opportunity for those involved in peer-to-peer computing. P2P, as it is known, first came to public attention with the rise of Napster, the on-line music-sharing service that disassembled and restructured the entire music industry. The majority of the Internet is connected with client-server architecture in which servers act as central sources of data and programs. Clients don't act independently, but send instructions to servers and wait for responses each time they interact with the Net. By contrast, P2P clients communicate directly with each other, enabling individual computers to share data and computational resources. P2P is the ultimate decentralization. It can be used to create communities based on common interests and to tackle massive computational problems that otherwise the community would not have the resources to solve.

SETI@home is an organization dedicated to searching for extraterrestrial life by processing the faint radio signals from sky surveys and examining them for patterns. The idea is that an extraterrestrial civilization of equal or greater advancement than ours would expose its presence by the radio noise it emits through its broadcasts. If the civilization were within a few dozen light years of the earth, the SETI radio telescope would detect it. But finding the weak patterns within the noise is like finding a pin in a mountain of hay.

The SETI@home organization invites users to download a screen saver that retrieves a portion of the full radio signal database, performs an analysis, and sends back the results. The screen saver displays the progress of the calculations in a beautiful visualization. Since its launch in May 1999 over 3.3 million users have donated almost 800,000 years of computation time. Though SETI@home has not yet found the presence of extraterrestrial life, the number of users continues to grow as the interest in the story and the sense of possibility grows.

Grameen Bank

Micro-financing is the business of granting loans ranging in size from $25 to $500 to people too poor to qualify via the banking industry's traditional metrics. Professor Muhammad Yunus initiated the concept in 1976 in Bangladesh, along with some of his colleagues who saw the possibilities in millions of small loans. What evolved was the Grameen Bank, an organization that has turned into the largest rural finance institution in India and led to numerous spinoffs in other countries. It has proven an effective and popular measure in the ongoing struggle against poverty, enabling those without access to lending institutions to borrow at reasonable rates and start small businesses. Not only is there a direct benefit to individual lives, but this lending activity also has a powerful impact on the overall economic success of entire communities and villages.

Early on, as the network of borrowers expanded, Grameen began exploring other possibilities to accelerate the progress toward a poverty-free world. It became involved in leasing unused fishing ponds and irrigation pumps. These activities spawned the Grameen Fisheries Foundation, the Grameen Krishi Foundation, and the Grameen Trust. Eventually, Grameen ventured into the textile industry and even the Internet world, creating new divisions and organizations.

The positive impact of micro-financing reaches well beyond the obvious. There are countless stories of those who, with loans as small as $150, have made the journey from poverty to successful entrepreneurship, often creating new jobs for others who previously lived in poverty. It's easy to see how the return on this kind of investment has true momentum.

The government of India owns a 10 percent interest in the Grameen Bank; its borrowers own the balance. Since its inception the Grameen Bank has helped more than 2.3 million borrowers in 38,951 villages and trained more than 4,000 individuals from around the world. There has been more than $1 billion lent, with a repayment rate of over 95 percent. There are approximately 223 programs in at least 58 other countries that are built on the Grameen financial system.

Solar Water Disinfection: SODIS

Water is the basis for life. Yet one-third of the rural population in developing countries—about 700 million people—have no access to safe drinking water. The countries most affected are often poor in resources—but rich in sunlight. Traditionally, thinking about solutions to the water problem always centered on improving access to clean water. With a change of focus to improving the quality of existing water, SODIS came into existence.

Professor Aftim Acra at the American University of Beirut was the first to research solar water disinfection. Eventually, a network project evolved, and in 1991 the Swiss Federal Institute for Environmental Science and Technology (EAWAG) began in-depth laboratory and field tests assessing the potential of SODIS (solar water disinfection). In March 2000, EAWAG/SANDEC won the US$50,000 first prize out of sixty submissions in the SIMAVI World Waterfund international competition for fresh ideas on improving water supply or water sanitization. The criteria for submission included the potential for wide application and a preference for self-financing maintenance.

It works like this: transparent bottles are filled with water and placed horizontally on a flat surface for about five hours. The illness-causing micro-organisms in the polluted water are killed off by the effect of the ultraviolet light in solar radiation. Painting the bottom half of the bottle black or placing it on black-painted corrugated iron or plastic sheets enhances the solar water disinfection. Solar thermal water treatment makes use of the fact that black absorbs light.

Extensive field testing has been conducted in Bolivia, Burkina Faso, China, Colombia, Indonesia, Thailand, India, and Togo as well as numerous other countries. The results are a water supply of better quality than clean rainwater. SODIS also seems to be effective in reducing the level of arsenic in collected water samples.

Improving access to clean water has typically been a complex and expensive process. But solar water disinfection is practically cost-free. A study conducted by the World Health Organization estimates the cost per family for this self-directed process to be approximately $5 per year. This simple technology requires sunlight, which costs nothing, the conversion of throwaway plastic soft-drink bottles from trash into valuable tools, and a black surface or paint. Water collected in a bottle, left on the roof in sunlight during the day, and allowed to cool overnight supplies enough clean, safe water for each day. The greatest challenge seems to be education, since people are accustomed to complex and expensive processes to deal with the access-to-water problem;

accepting SODIS as a successful solution requires a dramatic change of mindset. Suddenly, what once seemed an enormous and costly project—ensuring access to clean water—can be undertaken by those who need it for themselves.

Give a man a fish, and you give him a meal. Teach a man to fish, and you give him a living.

Chinese proverb

Electronic Arts and Anim-X

Since Pong took the world by storm in 1973, video games have evolved into ever more realistic high-fidelity experiences, spawning a $20-billion global industry. Though the subject matter of the thousands of games is different, how you play them is much the same: you slip a CD-ROM into a computer or game box, turn it on, and actively pursue the game, either solo or with other people on-line. And when you're done, you turn it off.

Now, Majestic, an Internet-based interactive game developed by Anim-X and published by Electronic Arts, is changing the playing field. Inspired by *The X-Files'* conspiracy themes and the mind-bending movie *The Game*, Majestic brings players into the center of an unfolding story of international espionage and conspiracy to uncover the operations of a secret government. Majestic players become the heroines of their own adventure.

But here's the twist. With Majestic, the game contacts you. Its characters e-mail you, send you instant messages, and direct you to Web sites that may or may not be part of the Majestic network. Characters contact you as if they were people you knew, asking questions about the problems you've solved. Every so often they will try to intimidate you, warning you to stay away from certain clues and provoking a response from the shadow government (if you sign up for the phone option). You arrive at work and a semi-legible fax is waiting in your in-basket. When you get home, there are voice-mail messages and you're not sure if they are from computers or other players. To solve certain puzzles you need to phone and e-mail other Majestic players. According to EA's Ralph Guggenheim, "Majestic is a game that plays you."[6]

Majestic stretches the limits of game playing by blurring the line between fantasy and reality. Its real-time system of telephone, e-mail, chat, fax, and pager can contact you any time, advancing the plot as if you were actually involved in a real-world conspiracy. The system tailors the experience from mild to fully engaging.

Interestingly, the game has received a very wide range of reviews, from those who love it and rank it among their favorites to those who think it's a gimmick. However, everyone recognizes that it is innovative. Majestic has created a new genre of game playing.

Majestic embraces many of the elements of the Imagination Economy. It will change gaming by placing the emphasis on the player as the main character. It's a form of virtual reality where you don't have to put on stereo goggles or data gloves. Majestic works by engaging the imagination, a lesson that other game companies will soon pick up on.

The innovation of Majestic is not just on the screen but behind it. Majestic's success lies in how it has partnered with Web developers, including HVC technologies for wireless paging; Spinner.com, the Internet's largest music service; Akamai Technologies to optimize Web site performance; RealNetworks for delivering media; SPACE.com for space-related subjects; and UPI International News for news and images from every part of the globe.

Consumer Creativity: Apple

The world of retail has made the shift from selling products to selling experiences. In FAO Schwarz stores you can enter the worlds of Star Wars, Barbie, and Lego. At Niketown over half the floor space is dedicated to exhibits, memorabilia, and multimedia presentations celebrating the spirit of sport. The flagship store for REI (Recreational Equipment, Inc.), a chain with over sixty out-lets in Seattle, has a 65-foot climbing mountain, a 470-foot hiking trail, a rain room to test waterproof gear, and thirty tents to set up and disassemble.

The trend has now extended to computer equipment: at Apple retail the goal is to sell creativity. With clean lines, white walls, frosted glass partitions, bold graphics, and blond wood, each Apple store radiates an atmosphere of understated panache, like an upscale design consultancy. The stores entice visitors not only to touch the computers but to do something with them—make movies, create on-line photo albums, burn custom CDs or DVDs. Every computer is equipped with a fast Internet connection. The stores' theme is interconnectivity, demonstrating how to join Mac applications with digital cameras, Personal Digital Assistants, and MP3 players.

What is most striking about the stores is the room to breathe and walk around. The walls are like empty canvases, encouraging the visitor to look upward and outward, and providing plenty of inner elbow room for ideas to germinate. The aisles are wide and uncluttered, enabling you to wander without bumping into others. The workstations are comfortable and intimate, inviting visitors to stay and expand their thinking. It is a dazzling mix of fun and learning.

The stores are organized around different types of experiences sought by different types of consumers, with sections devoted to home use, kids, teenagers, pros, movies, and photography. A theater offers ongoing entertainment, product demos, and guest lectures. And a genius bar, framed with posters of Apple ads' geniuses—Einstein, Earhart, and Picasso—is the place to have questions answered by experts.

Apple knows its customers and strives to celebrate each individual voice resonating as part of the greater community. We are social creatures and instinctively want to belong to groups. However, we also want to feel we have a visible place within that group, that we don't disappear into a sea of homogeneity. Clarity, communication, and the celebration of individual ideas connects Apple with its consumers.

There are countless ways of achieving greatness, but any road to achieving one's maximum potential must be built on a bedrock of respect for the individual, a commitment to excellence, and a rejection of mediocrity.

Buck Rodgers

Phattycakes

Tired of having to dress according to someone else's rules, Halifax entrepreneur Kristi McKinnon created Phattycakes to boldly go where no one had gone before. The idea first came to her at age fifteen, born of her frustration with the lack of real choice in plus-size ready-to-wear. She had no option but to shop in stores that obeyed the rules of plus-size dressing—offering single-colored plain options that might appeal to someone twenty-five years older than herself. One of the events that tipped the scales was shopping for a dress for the prom—something she claims would have ended in disaster if she hadn't had someone who could sew for her.

When Kristi took a government-run entrepreneur's course, she was told she had a real spark. That was enough to give her the push in self-confidence she needed. But her first dip into the market wasn't with plus-size clothing. She created an assortment of average-size clothing and took a booth in a consumer trade show. To her surprise, people her size approached the booth looking for clothing they could really live in. That's when McKinnon realized she wasn't being true to herself, prioritizing what she thought would be more lucrative over what she believed was the right thing to do. "If you don't create a niche for yourself, you'll just be doing what everyone else is doing," says McKinnon.[8] That niche was something McKinnon understood intimately: she decided she would be the one to offer the choice that was missing for plus-size young women.

McKinnon says she's "out to break all the rules."[9] And though the business started in response to her frustration and a sense of intuition, the market is ready for her to go full force. She's already received awards for her work, and has been surprised by the enormous press attention. She has appeared on national television and radio—a testament to the power of an idea grounded in authenticity. By cutting through old beliefs and connecting to her own core, McKinnon was able to create something that captured the imaginations of those trapped in outmoded paradigms, as she had been. She dared to speak out about something that was "unspeakable" and, by doing so, created a line of clothing that allows those who are typically closeted away by our society to celebrate their own individualism.

"I'm not recruiting people to be fat," she says. "That's hard at times."[10] Rather, McKinnon's take is real: what she wears is not going to change her size. So, given the choice, she would rather be able to dress in a way that reflects who she is and lets her be in sync with her age group. But the best part for McKinnon has been the response to all the press. She's been swamped by e-mails from across the country from young women just like her who want to buy her clothes.

The Other Side of the Mountain

The man who loved the mountain is Yvon Chouinard, creator of the famous pitons that started it all and eventually led to the company known as Patagonia. The privately held Ventura, California–based company employs a thousand people, has annual sales of $233 million, and boasts a growth rate of about 9 percent.

Patagonia was born out of a true love for nature and quiet sports, the experience of communing with the earth. Its products have always been inspired by necessity, designed to follow function, and created with the greatest respect for the core of the sport and the sportsperson. Driven by this passion, and true to it, Patagonia's reputation grew as a manufacturer and supplier of innovative quality equipment and clothing. Its products and business grew exponentially, until the fateful day when, approaching sales of $1 billion, Chouinard decided enough was enough.

The company returned to its roots, reduced its product line from 900 to 650, and realigned its vision. Patagonia uses 50 percent of its catalog and 25 percent of its ads to rally support for the earth's sustainability. It has donated over $17 million in cash and millions more in product. It is one of the few companies that truly lives its vision, remaining faithful to its passion and allowing the inner voice to lead the way. The Patagonia story is one vibrant with imagination and rich in inspiration.

Returning
to
Imagination

9

The world of possibility
       is always there.
  All you have to do
      is decide to open the door,
          and walk in.

Some
Big Questions

Investing in imagination is a considerable proposition. It involves real effort and a willingness to change. To a degree, it requires a leap of faith. It will undoubtedly meet with opposition, perhaps even real difficulty. It might be unpleasant and uncomfortable. Others will perhaps think you have lost your mind. And maybe they're not far from the truth, as we know that part of tapping into the river of imagination is returning to our beginner's mind.

So Why Bother?

We already know that tapping into the power of imagination is the starting point of innovation. It is the place where the big ideas come from—everything from discovery and invention to the design of the system that protects those inventions. We know that shared imagination drives work teams and projects, inspires unusual collaborations, and creates culture.

So What?

Consider the qualities of something that is truly imaginative. How would you define them? They might include:

- *Beautiful*, as in aesthetics: beauty is a way of expressing and experiencing goodness.

- *Inspiring*, as in awakening: inspiration leads us to invention.

- *Infectious*, as in contagious: infections have their own momentum.

- *Powerful*, as in moving: being moved connects us deeply with emotion.

- *Meaningful*, as in significant: meaning helps us understand purpose.

- *Engaging*, as in captivating: entertainment holds our attention.

- *Stimulating*, as in interesting: a stimulated mind churns to seek new connections.

- *Expansive*, as in broad: there is a sense of going beyond our conscious awareness and returning to it.

- *Appealing*, as in attractive: appeal allows the experience of pleasure.

- *Inquisitive*, as in curious: the mind probes for questions.

- *Arresting*, as in holistic: when we are arrested, everything else stops.

- *Awesome*, as in transcendent: awe awakens the spirit.

- *New*, as in fresh: doing something new invites creativity.

- *Connected*, as in relevant: context gives our sense of meaning a point of reference.

- *Sensuous*, as in feeling: emotional awakening arouses passion.

What is common to all these aspects of imagination? What connects them to us? What is it about these qualities of imagination that are of value to us? Why should we revere them, seek them out, use them as touchstones?

Although everyone interviewed for this book had a different reason for investing in imagination, what is common is a desire to express a personal philosophy and connect with a higher principle. Some of those reasons are:

- belief in a higher purpose

- to make a positive contribution

- to leave the world a better place

- to create a positive experience for someone

- to seek pleasure and enjoyment

- to understand myself, others, and life more deeply

- because it feels good

- so I can do better

Whatever the reason, whatever the personal motivation, the one idea common to all is aspiration.

Aspiration Gives Us Something to Strive For

Aspiration is the desire to achieve something that is perceived to be better, higher, or bigger. In the business world we might describe this as "pushing the envelope." Personally, it could mean attaining a place of greater knowledge (to aspire to know more) or of greater standing (to be better than you are) or of idealism (to thrive beyond your basic needs). In each case it involves attainment, be it of information, experience, or enlightenment.

To aspire means to have a strong desire to achieve something high or great, to seek, to attain, to accomplish. Aspiration gives us a personal vision, a sense of purpose and meaning, a reason or motivation to participate, partake, impart, understand, and contribute. To aspire is to stretch for an ideal, to reach, to hope, to dream. Curiously, aspiration also means "to breathe." So what supports aspiration? How do we propel ourselves along the path to those ideals?

Aspiration requires growth.

It is **never** too late to be what you **might** have **been**.

George Eliot

Growth Is Its Own Reward

If we do not recognize growth as a significantly valuable return, then there is no point in investing in imagination. Growth is innate. It is a natural part of the cycle of life. In fact, it is what connects us to the cycle of life. The observation of nature, all forms and aspects of life, the earth itself, and even our universe as we know it, shows us the continuous, cyclical involvement in some form of evolution.

Growth can be a logical or an instinctive progression. It can also seem random and illogical. Growth can occur slowly or dive forward in giant leaps and bounds. Growth requires both nourishment and space. Elements that encroach on these have an impact on the way we grow, the direction and speed at which we grow, and our relationship to the people and elements surrounding us. Imagination is a source of nourishment for growth and evolution. Growth changes us. So how do we grow? How do we continue to open and evolve?

Growth requires learning.

Consistency is contrary to nature, contrary to life. The only completely consistent people are **dead**.

Aldous Huxley

Learning Drives Change

The *Encyclopaedia Britannica* describes *learning* generally as "the alteration of behavior as a result of individual experience. When an organism can perceive and change its behavior, it is said to learn." There are many schools of thought about learning, ranging from the behaviorist and associative to Gestalt integration and numerous cognitive, linguistic, and processing models. However, with each of these theories, there is a sense of incompleteness in that they do not seem to account for all the possible aspects of learning.

It is easy to see the relationship between the activities of imagination and the process of learning. Imagination represents (has an idea), makes connections (creates associations), and synthesizes (joins elements to create a sense of understanding or relevant context). But imagination does something more: it seeks meaning. Aside from specific processes, when we consider the essence of learning, of understanding meaning, we can see that it requires the perception of some core truth. This may be through observation, discovery, invention, or reasoning, but as we grow, we do connect in some way to truth.

Do big truths hit us over the head like a giant gong or do they reveal themselves slowly? Is it possible simultaneously to hold everything we understand and believe to be true in our conscious awareness? Do we relearn the same truths or are they always different? When we act on a truth, how does it feel? When we perceive truths, how does this contribute to our understanding?

There is an expanded opportunity for learning when we coach, mentor, and train others. These activities require that we understand what we are teaching at a deeper level in order to be able to communicate the content effectively. In this way we continue our own learning, and so the cycle is repeated each time we share our knowledge with others.

There's something genetically inherent in a tree that prevents it from growing beyond a maximum height. Organizations that try to grow beyond the current disposition of their genetics may get into trouble. The analogy is highly imperfect, because business organizations can always continue to grow; I don't know how you would seek to define their limit. You just have to understand that your people and the ideas that are driving your organizational activities don't get out of sync, and that activities stay true to the form of your key ideas. This is where teaching, coaching, and mentoring all serve an important purpose.[1]

Kerry Stirton

What Is Truth?

Far be it from anyone to attempt a complete answer to this question. In fact, for many this is THE question—the one that calls for a lifetime of wondering, consideration, evaluation, contemplation, and reflection. It is perhaps the one question for which we may not even hope to find an answer. Whatever the truth really is, be it a single core essence or many different ones, we do understand some elements of truth that guide us in our quest for meaning.

Whoever undertakes to set himself up as a judge of Truth and Knowledge is shipwrecked by the laughter of the gods.

Albert Einstein

Truth can be defined as "fidelity" or "constancy." It is synonymous with genuineness and sincerity. Truth also concerns itself with facts, connects itself to the real state of affairs, be they grounded in fundamental or transcendental reality. The apprehension of truth presupposes a judgment proposition whereby something of the outer world is measured against the inner world. There is a complex synthesis involved in perceiving or observing truth that engages our ability for logic and reason with our capacity to feel.

Truth seeks to make a transcendent idea conform with known facts in an effort to avoid error, misrepresentation, or falsehood. So a ***big truth*** would require all aspects of your perception in order for you to be able to understand and assign meaning to it. In other words, you're not likely to get to a higher level of truth unless you engage increasingly broader aspects of yourself and your resources for learning. Perception of truth requires vision and insight by the whole person, and not merely by the mind. The more of yourself you bring to a situation, the bigger the truth you'll experience. (This may be why concrete metrics alone do not allow the imagination to flourish.) And sometimes truth cannot be understood without a measure of faith.

Imagination leads to aspiration.

Aspiration calls for growth.

Growth requires learning.

Learning seeks the perception of truth.

Truth ignites the imagination.

Exploring the Playful Aspects of Imagination

Being imaginative is not about *becoming* anything. It is about tapping into something, doing something, revisiting something. By letting go of the restrictions of the serious and efficient corporate world, we give ourselves the opportunity to play. Play is embarking on a journey that we make up as we go along—one without a predetermined course. Play isn't simply the work of childhood; it is the ability to be in tune with intuition.

A study conducted on a group of students at the School of the Art Institute of Chicago clearly demonstrated the power of play. Getzels and Csikszentmihalyi observed that students who considered more objects, and more unusual ones, who played with them more, and who delayed settling on a final composition for as long as possible, changing their minds during the process, produced more original pictures with higher aesthetic value, as judged by the instructors. In a follow-up study seven years later, the most successful artists were those who used the playful approach.

If we don't have the opportunity for legitimate exits from the structured world, we become stuck, stiff, and mechanical. You'll never hear the word *automaton* shouted from a sandbox.

It is important to have intellectual benchmarks to drive you—a point of view, information, and knowledge. These raise the level of intellect and thus the level of creativity. But if we never take the time to free ourselves from the encumbrances that can accompany all this— the stresses that go alongside hard work and continuous pressure—the mind is never relaxed enough to apply its information and knowledge to develop the intellect. Play is the magic powder of the mind.

We need the permission we enjoyed in childhood to let ourselves be truly imaginative. Otherwise, information and knowledge, though they may help with content, become barriers rather than stepping stones. We live in a time when intellect is confused with information. Many equate accumulating information with improving intellect. But information is useless without application, and it is necessary to sort through the information to determine what matters in relationship to our lives. Sift the wheat from the chaff.

The freedom to bounce out, to be childlike with appropriate and valuable information, to roll it about, let it slip and bubble, leads to wisdom. "Playful" is not the same as "unproductive," and "childlike" does not mean "childish." Play gives us permission to test things and try them out without fear of failure. It is a chance to zoom about without the weight of quantifiable deliverables. All too often business confuses the need to measure with the need to control. Lighten up! Trust in the play process to bring forth new invention. Play lifts our spirits and engages us deeply. Besides, it's fun.

It's rare that you're in a playground and you don't see invention. There's always invention. A teeter-totter is never a teeter-totter. It may be evil invention, it may be strange invention, but it's always invention.[2]

Norm Simon

Exploring the Profound
Aspects of Imagination

One of the qualities of those who invest in imagination is that they seem not to be reacting to the stressful immediate pressures that drive today's economy. Their brand of innovation is true imagination—tapping into the source, finding other ways of knowing, and bringing something back that blasts through the busyness and noise of the world and stands alone in its truthfulness. These are the pioneers who make manifest the expansive sense of possibility that redefines the meaning of success. They have a way of always letting thought percolate in the undermind, so that it is ever bubbling up with new ideas. True innovators, creators, and inventors, their vision bears the hallmark of truth, their passion is unavoidably contagious, and their actions downright inspirational.

The Long Now Foundation

When Danny Hillis, chairman and chief technology officer of Applied Minds, Inc., heard a story about oak beams, it brought him to a new way of seeing. Hillis, a Disney fellow and the man who pioneered the concept of parallel computers that is now the basis for most supercomputers, is an inventor, scientist, author, and engineer. He holds over forty U.S. patents covering parallel computers, disk arrays, forgery prevention methods, and various electronic and mechanical devices.

As the story goes, during the renovation of New College, Oxford, originally built in the fourteenth century, the forty-foot solid oak ceiling beams in the common room were found to be rotting. Since that kind of lumber is hard to come by, the contractors were faced with something of a dilemma. The people heading up the renovation knew that Oxford University owned some forest, so they sought out the appropriate forester. Upon inquiring whether or not the forest contained any big oak trees, they were told, "Yeah. We have the oak trees that were planted to replace the beams in New College."[3]

Inspired by this long-view thinking, Hillis reflected on the idea that we live in a very confined period, where something that happened five years ago is considered old news. Says Hillis: "When I was a child living in the sixties, the future was 2001. I watched the movie and imagined what it would be like, and in the late eighties the future was still in 2001. I realized that the future was shrinking one year per year for my entire life. And it's here now."[4]

Hillis understood that everything is moving so quickly that we can't envisage life fifty or a hundred years ahead. The downside of this speeding-up of time is that we cannot imagine anything that will take more than a couple of years to tackle, so we don't take those things on. As a result, long-view problems like world hunger become intractable, because they call for long-term action.

This insight guided Hillis to the realization that he wanted to work on a project that would last beyond his own lifetime. As an engineer and someone who enjoys design, he decided to build a clock. "A long-lasting, slow clock that would tick once a year and gong once a century and the cuckoo would come out once every millennium."[5] He started working on this 10,000-year clock, and his friend, Steward Brand, started the Long Now Foundation to focus collective creative energy on the next 10,000 years and to promote "slower/better" thinking in a world of faster/cheaper.

At the heart of the clock is a device that might be described as an exquisitely beautiful organic modern sculpture. It is designed to track the positions of the sun and moon, correcting for the wobbling of the Earth's orbit. The only number on the clock is the year, displayed in five digits, and there is an astrolabe showing the positions of the stars.

In addition to Hillis's 10,000-year clock, the Long Now Foundation has initiated the All Species Inventory project with a mandate to record and genetically sample every species of life on earth within the span of our generation, and the Rosetta Project, inspired by the Rosetta stone, to create a meaningful archive of a thousand languages for linguistics research and the recovery of lost languages. When completed, the clock will be placed on a mountaintop in Nevada surrounded by national parks filled with 5,000-year-old Bristle Tongue pine trees.

Representation: The Role of Beauty

To create and observe beauty is to participate in the appreciation of aesthetics. Because of its easy access, beauty offers a quick route to understanding. It opens our awareness to deeper truths, as with the elegance of a mathematical equation or scientific formula. The beauty of Monet's water lilies may well impart the truth of the scent, sound, and feeling of those flowers on a pond, but it does so through the visual doorway of beauty. The expression of beauty and the ability to perceive it can lead to other ways of knowing. Beauty offers the opportunity to see newness by connecting to something we hold to be true. The Latin root of *beauty* means "goodness" and, as such, returns us to the core of beauty's intent. The potential for its expression is essentially limitless.

Truth is **beauty**, beauty **truth**. That is **all** ye know on earth and **all** ye need to know.

John Keats

Wabi-sabi is the Japanese art of finding beauty and profundity in imperfection and the natural order of things. One of its underlying principles is the importance of authenticity—beauty as it is truly meant to be, not forced or contrived. Wabi-sabi reveres simplicity, sparseness, humbleness, and nonconformity. With its grounding in nature, Wabi-sabi appreciates that nothing is permanent, perfect, or complete. Instead, it sees beauty in the process and cycle of change and becoming. It sees perfection in imperfection, wisdom in not knowing, essence in the hidden or diminished.

The ability to recognize beauty is the ability to appreciate true essence. When we can discern the essence of a thing or an idea, we can begin to internalize its meaning and connect it with other ideas and experiences within us. We can understand the value and goodness in simply "being" and in becoming. This frees us from the intense pressure of goal orientation and gives us permission to take a different view, appreciating the process itself. In fact, to contemplate beauty in this way helps us to understand that the real value lies in the process.

What is your vision?

What do you see? What is the picture you hold in your mind's eye?

What do others see in you?

What do others see in the work you choose to do?

What things can you see differently by changing your mindset?

The Body Shop, Canada

When The Body Shop went about setting up its head office in Toronto, the directors thought about the best possible approach. They bought a building and warehouse for conversion and wanted the space to reflect their corporate culture. They applied their cultural values to everything from the materials used in construction to the layout itself, the creation of a daycare center, and the preservation of gardens behind the building that had been wetlands before.

With little knowledge of buildings and the process ahead of them, they decided to try something different. They went out to the community and asked thirty diverse professionals—lawyers, social workers, landscape architects, engineers, environmentalists, and artists—if they would come to view the new building and listen to The Body Shop team talk about the corporate culture they wished to sustain. After that introduction they would all gather at a hotel for twenty-four hours to come up with the perfect design for The Body Shop building—for free. They all leapt at the chance, scarcely believing their good fortune in being asked to participate in such an innovative process. As well, the chance to collaborate with professionals from so many walks of life without having to jump through the ego-driven boundary hoops of "mine/yours/stay away" was too good to pass up.

The group was divided into three teams, each with a staff member. Then, following the architectural design process known as a *charette* (where teams work quickly and roughly on a design project for a restricted period of time, after which the designs are collected rapidly onto a moving cart), each team went off and did a design, and in the end they all worked as a unified group with their architect to pull together the best of the three designs. Says The Body Shop president Margot Franssen: "It was so easy, I can't tell you. We had a design in twenty-four hours! And it came from the best minds in the city and it was this unbelievably wonderful creativity that was happening—everybody loved it."[6]

Part of the building houses a daycare center that can care for twenty-eight children—even though there was only one child from The Body Shop staff who would attend. Franssen's theory is that women don't have children because they don't have enough help taking care of them, not because they don't want to. And she was right: within eighteen months the daycare was full to the max with The Body Shop employees' children.

The Body Shop's respect for the ecosystem led to a design that ensured anything that left the building would be cleaner than when it came in. For example, the waste water is cleaned before being sent back out into the environment. Brilliant? Not according to the provincial government. Franssen describes the experience:

We were fined for tampering with the water system by the Ontario government. They said, "You're not supposed to touch your water before it goes into the sewer." And we said, "Well, we cleaned it," and they said, "Well, it doesn't matter. On our books we don't have anything to deal with that, so you're tampering with the water and we're going to fine you." I finally went to the premier and said, "This is nuts."[7]

Thankfully, the premier came to his senses and realized the contribution The Body Shop was making. Needless to say, the fines were removed.

"There's a gap between what you can do and the reality of the law," says Franssen. "The law can be so far behind where creative people are. You have to always jump that gap and fight for your cause. And creative people get tired because they are always fighting battles that you shouldn't have to fight."[8]

A human being is a part of the whole called by us universe, a part limited in time and space. He experiences himself, his thoughts and feeling as something separated from the rest, a kind of optical delusion of his consciousness. This delusion is a kind of prison for us, restricting us to our personal desires and to affection for a few persons nearest to us. Our task must be to free ourselves from this prison by widening our circle of compassion to enhance all living creatures and the whole of nature in its beauty.

Albert Einstein

Connection: The Role of Relationships

Gary Hawton, president and CEO of Meritas Mutual Funds, believes that everything we do, every decision we make, each one of our actions, has an effect on the world beyond what we can see. So much of our world is unseen or hidden, and often what we perceive to be reality is in fact an incomplete illusion.

Consider a basic transaction: a purchase. When we make a purchase decision, we typically evaluate things like value for money, quality of the goods, perhaps availability of supply, usability, and so on. Our perception and evaluation of the exchange centers on our personal experience of it. But consider the chain of events that could flow from that single transaction. The money that you spend translates into income for the vendor. With this income the vendor pays his suppliers, his employees, his landlord, himself, and presumably invests some as well and eventually realizes a profit. All the recipients paid by the vendor then, in turn, spend their portion of it in similar ways. Presumably, you could trace your expenditure back to everyone and everything involved in the creation, research, development, manufacturing, distribution, and (to some degree) consumption of the product in question.

Irrelevant? Not according to the work of social psychologist Dr. Stanley Milgram. He discovered the small-world effect, which led to the popular Six Degrees of Separation theory that shows all people are separated by only five acquaintances. Similarly, the butterfly effect in chaos theory refers to the notion that because of the impact of seemingly random occurrences, a butterfly flapping its wings in the Amazon Basin can cause hurricanes on the other side of the globe a year later. In other words, our actions have implications that reach far beyond what is immediately before us through visual representation. Gary Hawton says, "Spin your world around. When you get home from work today and look into the eyes of your six-year-old daughter, imagine that if you were living on the other side of the world, she might be just coming home from work too."[9]

Farming provides familiar metaphors for growth and interconnectedness. Farming is an activity that requires patience; results are attained over long periods of time, through the participation of many people, as well as nature. The idea that we reap what we sow is most frequently understood at the individual or personal level. But consider this metaphor in the context of community: the growth from the seeds that are sown by one may be reaped by another. In light of the small-world or butterfly effect, this doesn't seem like such a stretch. Unlike the butterfly, though, which is unaware of its impact on the weather, our cognitive ability affords us the opportunity to imagine possible outcomes before we act.

How do you define yourself?

What is your personal frame of reference?

Whose company do you keep?

What flows out of everything you do?

How does your output affect your environment, your customers, your employees, and your company profit?

What do you invest in?

What value do you attach to your work?

Charlie Trotter's Culinary Education Foundation

Those who know Charlie Trotter describe him as a passionate, energetic man of vision. The vision of Charlie Trotter's restaurant is to make an aesthetic, cultural, and social contribution. To that end, Chef Trotter's recipes have been described as simply unparalleled. Likened to a jazz musician's, Trotter's style is spontaneous, complex, rich, intuitive, and fresh.

This well-loved chef, author, and television host started cooking professionally in 1982. Charlie Trotter's restaurant in Chicago is the recipient of awards, recognition, and accolades too numerous to mention, including the prestigious James Beard Foundation "Outstanding Restaurant" and "Outstanding Chef." In addition to its main dining rooms Trotter's offers seating at the kitchen table (literally) or a more private booking in the studio kitchen of Trotter's PBS cooking show.

In an effort to inspire youth, Trotter's hosts weekly restaurant dinners for high school students. They arrive in busloads to tour, dine, and learn about diverse foods, organic farming, and etiquette first-hand. Charlie Trotter's Culinary Education Foundation is a non-profit organization created to inspire interest in education and cooking, and to offer scholarship opportunities for those seeking a career in culinary arts. Scholarships are awarded each spring. The foundation is supported by the volunteer efforts of Trotter and his friends and associates, who occasionally host fundraising dinners. They have raised more than $250,000 to date.

Emotion: The Role of Passion

In the business world, emotions are frequently perceived as highly complex, inaccessible, unproductive, and even destructive. There is little room for emotion except in specific contexts because, like imagination, emotions are impossible to quantify and difficult to contain. But emotions themselves are not unproductive or destructive. On the contrary, emotion is our conduit to all the other aspects of imagination. We have the experience of feeling "good" or "bad" about something; we trust a hunch, catch a hint, follow a gut feeling. It is not the emotions themselves but the way we choose to accept or deny, express or not express them that can cause difficulty. But emotions can be intense and overwhelming—and in environments where self-control is a prerequisite, emotions can even be perceived as a threat.

What you can do, or dream you can, begin it. Boldness has genius, power, and magic in it.

Johann Wolfgang von Goethe

Even so, we all know that it simply is not possible to think our way through everything. We do not *think* about being happy, we simply are. We do not *consider* being upset, we experience it. Who would want to abandon the opportunity to feel intense passion? What would the *Pietà* look like if Michelangelo had thought his way through it? How could a

Experience teaches us in a millennium what **passion** teaches us in an hour.

Ralph Iron

man spend three years of his life crafting one sculpture if he wasn't ignited by passion? Can invention come from apathy?

Trust your emotions to help you "see" the invisible, to connect you with your undermind and inner voice. We do not live our lives strictly in the realm of the concrete—we have deep resources that help guide us in our process of understanding and meaning. Emotions are the things that invite us to make profound connections that lead us to the doorway of the "Aha!" experience. Throughout our process of growth, from the perception of beauty to the making of connections and the search for understanding, emotion navigates us toward a deeper place of wisdom and meaning, and ultimately to a greater sense of truth.

Returning
to
Imagination

243

What wakes and inspires you?

What are you passionate about?

Are you living a passionate life?

What emotions do you evoke in others?

How do you feel about your work?

How do you feel about your life?

Do you move others by inspiring them?

It is the consistent choice of the path with heart which makes the warrior different from the average man. He knows that a path has heart when he is one with it, when he experiences a great peace and pleasure traversing its length. Any path is only a path, and there is no affront, to oneself or to others, in dropping it if that is what your heart tells you … Look at every path closely and deliberately. Try it as many times as you think necessary. Then ask yourself and yourself alone one question: Does this path have a heart? If the path does, it is good. If not, it is of no use.

Carlos Castenada

Deka Research and Development

Dean Kamen is the founder and president of Deka Research and Development, a company focused on the development of fundamental technologies. Kamen is a true inventor and entrepreneur. Among his inventions are the first wearable infusion pump (adopted for use in chemotherapy, neonatology, and endocrinology), the first insulin pump for diabetics, the HomeChoice™ dialysis machine, and the Independence 3000 iBOT™ Transporter.

The idea for the iBOT came when Kamen saw a man in a wheelchair struggling to get over a curb. From this experience Kamen observed that while wheelchairs offer mobility, they do not offer independence. And so the Independence iBOT Mobility System was born. The core idea is actually quite simple: to give disabled people maximum autonomy. However, the applied engineering that brought the idea into reality is far more complex.

The iBOT deals with the problem of balance via built-in gyroscopes. These prevent it from tipping over or pitching sideways when negotiating rough terrain. It has six wheels and moves along like a wheelchair, at chair level. However, one of the spectacular aspects of the iBOT is that its base extends so that the chair frame can raise the driver to eye-level height. When it does this, it balances itself on two wheels, and the driver continues to sit with hands free. The iBOT, developed for Johnson & Johnson, is currently undergoing extensive testing and awaiting FDA approval.

While the iBOT might appear to be a wheelchair at first glance, it is far from it. In addition to its ability to rise vertically to eye level and balance on two wheels, it can cross extremely rough terrain and go up and down stairs. Rather than confining its user to a chair with limited range of movement, it promises real independence and the kind of freedom that comes with bipedality to those currently dependent on wheelchairs for mobility. It means they can go for a walk on the beach to watch the sunset, reach the cereal box on the top shelf at the grocery store, climb up and down stairs, maneuver through difficult spaces, and give the people they love a full-body hug—standing at eye level.

During a talk he gave at a recent TED conference, Kamen, winner of the National Medal of Technology, explained part of his personal philosophy. In light of his achievements it was no surprise when he stated, "I won't take a project on unless I know I can positively impact the lives of other people."[10] Those who have tested the iBOT so far say with absolute certainty that he has done just that.

In keeping with that philosophy, and combined with his passion for science and technology, Kamen started FIRST (For Inspiration and Recognition of Science and Technology) in 1989 to interest and inspire students in mathematics, science, and technology, and has since recruited many leaders of Fortune 500 companies, education, and government in this campaign. FIRST is a co-operative experience involving collaboration between students, companies, teachers, and government. Its first robotics competition included twenty-eight teams and was held in a space that was only fourteen feet square; today there are more than five hundred teams participating nationally. The FIRST Lego League robotics competition aimed at younger students has grown to fifteen thousand participants in the U.S. and more than five thousand internationally.

Interpretation: Meaning and the Role of Truth

What does it mean to be authentic? In the most simplistic terms it means to be *real*. Doing something of value is synonymous with acting on your beliefs. If these are tied to your aspirations, what you hold to be true and possible, then you cannot help but act out of passion. You don't have to be conducting world-changing research in order to be doing something of value. Each person has a different vision, voice, and purpose, even in the context of collective work. For some, work is tied to a higher purpose; for others it is grounded in a more earthy one. But for all, living authentically means living in alignment with your beliefs and values.

But how can you tell when someone or something is authentic? If it is authentic, it has staying power, and if it has staying power, it goes deep. There is danger in trotting around the globe collecting great aesthetic experiences without understanding their meaning. Lifestyle branding gurus who create images that mirror an idea without connecting it to a core truth may generate some excitement, but they won't last long.

Partly, truth gives us freedom. Freedom gives us power over our own lives—power to choose how we want to live, what we want to do, what is important to us. Consider the company that sells its product on the promise that it will change your life—give you eternal youth, beauty, or unlimited wealth. Or the company that talks about caring for people and the earth, and then strips the rain forest for financial profit, taking out an entire village in the process. These are the kinds of inauthentic corporate messages that deny people real choice, real freedom.

What happens when technology seeks to change the world? Institutions seek to narrow the options of people. And once those options are narrowed, we supply people with the illusion that they have control over those options. It seems to me that when we talk about humanity and maintaining the notions of humanity in the work that we do, we need to understand that there are those technological moments [that give us freedom] and there are those that are all about illusion and the narrowing of options for people, and then betting on how those options come out in the mass market. The solution is knowing the difference.

John Hawkenberry

I don't want to achieve immortality through my work. I want to achieve immortality through not dying.

Woody Allen

To what do **you** aspire?

What do **y o u** stand for?

What is **your** purpose?

Are **you** living an authentic life?

Are your outward expressions
in alignment with **your** inner values?

What will **your** legacy be?

Are you being true
to what **you** believe in?

Are your company's values
in sync with **your** own?

of imagination is the power of *choice.*

So, what are you doing with your imagination?

The greatest differentiator in the manifestation

Words to Dream by

1. At the core of every transaction is the human experience. Have heart.

2. Authenticity matters. Be true to yourself.

3. Misfits make more interesting bedfellows. Dare to be different.

4. Seek beauty. Discover other ways of knowing.

5. There's a world of infinity in details and so much to know. Go slow.

6. Know that there is no norm. Embrace diversity.

7. We make manifest what we believe. Understand your values.

8. Nothing makes sense all alone. Appreciate the connectedness of all people and all things.

9. Have hope. Build a bridge to the future.

10. Have faith. Believe in that which you cannot see.

11. We imagine our own reality.

Dream

BIG

Stay awhile.

Don't Forget to Come Back

Notes

Chapter 1: Enter the Imagination Economy

1. www.design.philips.com/vision/index. Philips Design's Web site.
2. Thomas Stewart, "Barely Managing," *Ecompany Now*, 28 March 2001.
3. Amy Cortese, "Masters of Innovation," *BusinessWeek*, 23 March 2001.
4. Polly La Barre and Alan M. Webber, "Fast Talk: The Innovation Conversation," *Fast Company* (July 2001).
5. Ibid.
6. Seth Godin, *Unleashing the Idea Virus* (New York: Hyperion, and www.ideavirus.com, 2001), v.
7. U.S. Progressive Policy Institute Web site, www.ppionline.org/ppi.ka.cfm?knlgAreaID=107.
8. Interview with Carolyn Gallagher, 7 June 2001.
9. Interview with Margot Franssen, 30 May 2001.
10. Interview with Seth Weaver Kahan, 24 May 2001.

Chapter 2: The Pressures on Imagination

1. Interview with David Martin, 15 August 2001.
2. Ibid.
3. John Howkins, *The Creative Economy: How People Make Money from Ideas* (London: Penguin Books, 2001), 116.
4. Nancy Hass, "The House That Bloomberg Built," *Fast Company* (November 1995).
5. Gary Hamel, "Strategy as Revolution," *Harvard Business Review* (July/August 1996).
6. Jerry Useem, "Dead Thinkers' Society," *Business2.0* (November 2001).
7. Danny Hillis, keynote address at Siggraph 2001, Los Angeles, 12–17 August 2001.
8. Clayton M. Christensen, *The Innovator's Dilemma* (New York: Harvard Business School Press, 1997), 7.
9. Daniel Pink, Free Agent Nation Web site, www.freeagentnation.com.
10. Richard Saul Wurman, *Information Anxiety* (New York: Doubleday, 1989), 32.
11. Rolf Jensen, *The Dream Society: How the Coming Shift from Information to Imagination Will Transform Your Business* (New York: McGraw-Hill, 1999), 52.

12. Douglas J. Cardinal, from notes prepared for a symposium on creativity held in Ottawa, 2000, cited in *Renaissance II: Canadian Creativity and Innovation in the New Millennium*, ed. Richard I. Doyle (Ottawa: National Research Council of Canada, 2001), 42.

Chapter 3: Exploring the Worlds of Imagination

1. Interview with John Kennedy, 25 April 2001.
2. Arthur Koestler, *The Act of Creation* (London: Arkana, 1990).
3. Interview with Alan Kay, 8 May 2001.
4. Ibid.
5. Linda Tischler, ed., "The Innovation Conversation," Fast Company Web site, www.fastcompany.com/ftalk/sanfran.
6. Douglas J. Cardinal, from notes prepared for a symposium on creativity held in Ottawa, 2000, cited in *Renaissance II: Canadian Creativity and Innovation in the New Millennium*, ed. Richard I. Doyle (Ottawa: National Research Council of Canada, 2001), 40.
7. Interview with Maureen O'Donnell, 7 May 2001.
8. Steven Pinker, *How the Mind Works* (New York: W.W. Norton, 1997).
9. Joseph B. Pine, James H. Gilmore, and Joseph B. Pine II, *The Experience Economy* (Boston: Harvard Business School Press, 1999).
10. Nathan Shedroff, *Experience Design 1* (Indianapolis: New Riders, 2001), 42.
11. Thomas Moore, *Care of the Soul* (New York: HarperCollins, 1992), xiii.
12. Guy Claxton, *Hare Mind, Tortoise Mind: Why Intelligence Increases When You Think Less* (London: Fourth Estate, 1997).
13. Ibid.
14. *Webster's Third New International Dictionary of the English Language*, 1986.
15. Ibid.

Chapter 4: Measuring the Intangible

1. John Howkins, *The Creative Economy: How People Make Money from Ideas* (London: Penguin Books, 2001).

2. Alan M. Webber, "Trust in the Future," *Fast Company* (September 2000): 211.
3. In a letter to Isaac McPherson, 1813, as posted by the University of Virginia at etext.virginia.edu.
4. Howkins, *The Creative Economy*, 35.
5. Kevin T. Amiss and Martin H. Abbott, "Method of exercising a cat," U.S. Patent US5443036; posted by Delphion Inc. at www.delphion.com/details.
6. John Schwartz, "Compressed Data: Don't Mind That Lawsuit, It's Just a Joke," *New York Times*, 29 January 2001.
7. Interview with Alan Kay, 8 May 2001.
8. www.despair.com/info
9. Peter Martin, www.ft.com, 8 November 2001.
10. Howkins, *The Creative Economy*, 187.
11. Ibid., 116.
12. Ibid., 182.
13. Ibid., 116.
14. Richard Dawkins, *The Selfish Gene* (Oxford: Oxford University Press, 1990).
15. Meritas Mutual Funds, "How We Invest," www.meritas.ca/index2.
16. Interview with Gary Hawton, 12 November 2001.

Chapter 5: Fostering Imagination

1. Interview with Moses Znaimer, 29 May 2001; also CityTV publicity poster and postcard.
2. Ibid.
3. Dr. Judah Folkman, guest speaker, Gairdner Foundation Public Lecture, Toronto, 26 October 2001.
4. Interview with Warren Pratt, 23 May 2001.
5. Ibid.
6. Ibid.
7. Richard Saul Wurman, *Information Anxiety 2* (Indianapolis: Que, 2001), 97.
8. Interview with William Thorsell, 7 May 2001.
9. Ibid.
10. Interview with Richard Saul Wurman, 17 September 2001.
11. Ibid.
12. Diane L. Coutu, "A Reading List for Bill Gates—and a Conversation with Literary Critic Harold Bloom," *Harvard Business Review* (May 2001): 64.
13. Michael J. Gelb, *How to Think Like Leonardo da Vinci: Seven Steps to Genius Everyday* (New

York: Bantam Doubleday Dell, 1998).

14. Interview with Joyce Wycoff, 11 May 2001.

15. Bruce Mau, "An Incomplete Manifesto for Growth," www.brucemau.com.

16. Douglas J. Cardinal, from notes prepared for a symposium on creativity held in Ottawa, 2000, cited in *Renaissance II: Canadian Creativity and Innovation in the New Millennium*, ed. Richard I. Doyle (Ottawa: National Research Council of Canada, 2001), 43.

17. Guy Claxton, *Hare Mind, Tortoise Mind: Why Intelligence Increases When You Think Less* (London: Fourth Estate, 1997), 58.

Chapter 6: Shared Imagination, Inspired Vision, and Open Ideas

1. Interview with Norm Simon, 21 May 2001.

2. Interview with Piero Carcerano, 5 April 2001.

3. Malcolm Gladwell, *The Tipping Point: How Little Things Can Make a Big Difference* (New York: Little, Brown, 2000).

4. Interview with Bran Ferren, 3 June 2001.

5. James C. Collins and Jerry I. Porras, *Built to Last: Successful Habits of Visionary Companies* (New York: HarperCollins, 1994).

6. Interview with Doug Walker, 23 May 2001.

7. Ibid.

8. Linda Tischler, ed., "The Innovation Conversation," *Fast Company* Web site, www.fast company.com /ftalk/sanfran.

9. Interview with Doug Keeley, 11 June 2001.

10. Ibid.

11. Ibid.

12. Ibid.

13. Ibid.

14. Interview with Sabaa Quoa, 7 June 2001.

15. Ibid.

16. Ibid.

17. Ibid.

18. Interview with Margot Franssen, 30 May 2001.

19. Ibid.

20. Ibid.

21. Ibid.

22. Interview with David Wexler, 17 May 2001.

23. Ibid.

24. Linda Tischler, ed., "The Innovation Conversation," *Fast Company* Web site, www.fast company. com/ftalk/sanfran.

25. Interview with Carolyn Gallagher, 7 June 2001.

26. Alan G. Robinson and Sam Stern, *Corporate Creativity: How Innovation and Improvement Actually Happen* (San Francisco: Berrett-Koehler, 1997), 105.

27. David Bohm, *On Dialogue*, ed. Lee Nichol (New York: Routledge, 1996), 17.

28. Interview with Carolyn Gallagher, 7 June 2001.

29. Ibid.

30. Interview with Kerry Stirton, 30 May 2001.

Chapter 7: From the Intangible to the Tangible

1. Bill Gross, in a speech given at TED X, Monterey, California, 24 February 2000.

2. Ibid.

3. Ibid.

4. Ibid.

5. Steve Kaneko, in a speech given at IDSA Conference, New York, 8 November 2001.

6. Jerry Hirshberg, *The Creative Priority: Driving Innovative Business in the Real World* (New York: HarperCollins, 1998), 16.

7. Michael Schrage, *Serious Play: How the World's Best Companies Simulate to Innovate* (Cambridge, Mass.: Harvard Business School Press, 2000).

8. Ibid, 2.

9. Ibid.

10. Linda Tischler, ed., "The Innovation Conversation," *Fast Company* Web site, www.fast company.com/ftalk/sanfran.

11. Bill Buxton, in a speech given at IdeaCITY Conference, Toronto, 9 June 2000.

12. Frank Gibney Jr. and Belinda Luscombe, "The Redesigning of America," *Time*, 20 March 2000.

13. Melody Roberts, Smart Design, in a speech given at IDSA Conference, New York, 8 November 2001.

14. Bruce Mau, "An Incomplete Manifesto for Growth," www.brucemau.com.

15. Interview with Doug Hector, 26 June 2001.

16. www.extremeprogramming.org

17. Special Report on Mass Customization, *The Economist*, 14 July 2001.

18. John W. Holt Jr., Jon Stamell, and Melissa Field, *Celebrate Your Mistakes And 77 Other Risk-Taking, Out-of-the-Box Ideas from Our Best Companies* (New York: McGraw Hill, 1996).

19. Bob Steinburgler, in a speech given at IDSA Conference, New York, 8 November 2001.

20. Dorothy Leonard and Walter Swap, *When Sparks Fly* (Boston: Harvard Business School Press, 1999).

21. Ibid.

22. Ibid.

23. Mark Johnson, in a speech given at IDSA Conference, New York, 8 November 2001.

24. Interview with Jim Rait, 20 June 2001.

25. Ibid.

26. Interview with Jim Rait, 14 September 2001.

27. Interview with Ted Woerner, 14 August 2001.

28. Ibid.

29. Ibid.

30. Ibid.

31. Ibid.

Chapter 8: The Imagination Marketers

1. Michelle Howry, "Dishing the Dirt," *I.D. Magazine* (October 2001): 75.

2. Ibid.

3. Koziol promotional invitation, on www.koziol.de.

4. Interview with Claude Bernier, 9 January 2002.

5. Ibid.

6. "Majestic," part of episode 3-01, *NextTV*, producer Lina Cino, CityTV, Toronto.

7. Apple Computer Inc., promotional literature, 1999.

8. Interview with Kristi McKinnon, 23 May 2001.

9. Ibid.

10. Ibid.

Chapter 9: Returning to Imagination

1. Interview with Kerry Stirton, 30 May 2001.

2. Interview with Norm Simon, 23 May 2001.

3. Danny Hillis, in the keynote presentation at Siggraph 2001, Los Angeles, 15 August 2001.

4. Ibid.

5. Ibid.

6. Interview with Margot Franssen, 30 May 2001.

7. Ibid.

8. Ibid.

9. Interview with Gary Hawton, 12 November 2001.

10. Dean Kaman, in a talk given at TED X Presentation, Monterey, California, 21 February 2000.

Return on Imagination

254

Index